Foodies and Food Tourism

**Donald Getz, Richard N.S. Robinson,
Tommy D. Andersson and Sanja Vujicic**

(G) **Goodfellow Publishers Ltd**

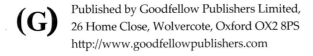

Published by Goodfellow Publishers Limited,
26 Home Close, Wolvercote, Oxford OX2 8PS
http://www.goodfellowpublishers.com

British Library Cataloguing in Publication Data: a catalogue record for this title is available from the British Library.

Library of Congress Catalog Card Number: on file.

ISBN: 978-1-910158-00-5

Design and typesetting by P.K. McBride, www.macbride.org.uk

Cover design by Cylinder

Printed and bound in Great Britain by Marston Book Services Limited, Oxfordshire

Contents

List of figures

List of tables

Preface

The authors are all foodies who love travel, not to mention doing research and writing about our passions. The stimulus for this book arises directly from our research, first in Australia as a kind of test of theory and methods (see the pertinent publications by Robinson and Getz), and then from a major consultancy we undertook for tourism and agriculture clients in Sweden. We rely heavily on data and analysis from those projects.

Although food tourism is a minor topic in academic institutions, food and tourism are very important in the real worlds of hospitality, destination marketing, and tourism development. Students in hospitality and tourism in particular should therefore be knowledgeable about food lovers and food tourism trends.

Pedagogically, this book can be used in teaching in several ways:

- As a required text for a food-tourism course (targets: tourism and hospitality degree programmes)
- As a supplementary text within tourism and hospitality, and within event management degree programmes, because food events are so important
- As an optional book for research students preparing to do a thesis or dissertation
- As an adjunct resource for cultural, sociological and anthropological studies programs with coverage of food heritage, consumption, practices and identity.

There are many potential users of this book in industry and policy:

- Destination management and marketing organizations
- Restaurant, catering, hotel, and resort sectors
- Economic development offices
- Event development agencies
- Agricultural and food industry companies

Foodies and Food Tourism adds considerable value to the growing number of titles pertaining to food and food tourism by focussing on the demand-side, and is unique by way of employing the authors' research findings. As well, theory development on food tourism has been weak and this book advances a number of lines of theory development.

Some highlights:

- Viewing food tourism first and foremost from the food-lover's perspective
- Demand-side approach to planning, developing and marketing
- Theory and praxis combined
- Global outlook
- A textbook for student and a resource book for practitioners

About the authors

Donald Getz, PhD, is Professor Emeritus at the The University of Calgary, Canada, and Visiting Professor at several other universities. He has authored a number of books on event management and tourism, wine tourism, family and small businesses. Currently he advises agencies and institutions in a consulting capacity.

Richard N.S. Robinson (PhD), who teaches and researches at the University of Queensland, UQ Business School, is a former chef with 18 years' experience in the prestige club, heritage facility and hotel sectors. His research focuses on tourism/hospitality industry workforce issues and food tourism. He has coordinated and worked on research teams for funded national and international projects in these areas. His work has been published in leading academic journals, edited books, international conference proceedings, practitioner periodicals and numerous consultancy and government reports.

Tommy D. Andersson, PhD, Professor Emeritus at School of Business, Economics and Law at University of Gothenburg received his PhD at University of Gothenburg in Managerial Economics in 1979. He has served as professor in Accounting at Bodo Graduate School, Director of tourism research at Mid Sweden University and as professor in Tourism Management at University of Gothenburg. He has also been president of the European Chapter of CHRIE and program director of a master program in Tourism and Hospitality Management at University of Gothenburg.His main research interest and publications are in the area of Event Management, Experience Economics, Restaurant Management, Economic Impact Analysis and Culture Economics.

Sanja Vujicic, PhD, runs an experience consultancy. She has more than ten years of academic research and advisory experience within the field of market communication, tourism experience design and destination marketing. Before founding Experience Consulting she held an academic and an Assisting Director position at the Centre for Tourism, School of Business, Economics and Law, University of Gothenburg, where she also received her PhD in Business Administration. Sanja has among other things worked as a freelance photographer on national and international basis, and was responsible for planning and producing photographs for destinations.

Acknowledgements

We are grateful to the following contributors for helping make this a better book. Important sections have been authored by:

Dr. Alessio Cavicchi, University of Macerata, Italy

David Gration, University of the Sunshine Coast, Australia

Dr. Roger Haden, Manager, Educational Leadership, Le Cordon Bleu Australia

Dr. Atsuko Hashimoto, Brock University, Canada

Dr. Liz Sharples, Sheffield-Hallam University, England

Dr. David J. Telfer, Brock University, Canada

As well, we wish to thank the following contributors:

Dr. Bing Pan, Head of Research and Assistant Professor, the Office of Tourism Analysis, College of Charleston.

Claes Bjerkne, senior adviser Bjerkne & Co, former chairman of Visita (the Swedish Hospitality Industry association, and former CEO of Göteborg & Co)

Ditte Furstrand Nytofte, project manager international marketing, Wonderful Copenhagen

Clause Meyer, Associate Professor at CPH University Department of Food Science, cofounder of Noma, owner of the Meyer Group

Mats Nordström, chef at restaurant Vasa Allé, Gothenburg

Bengt Linde, restaurateur and chairman of the board at the Gothenburg Restaurant Association

1 Introduction

Learning objectives

Readers are expected to learn the following from this chapter:

- Definitions of: food, foodie, food tourist, cuisine, gastronomy
- The scope and meaning of a foodie lifestyle
- Why food tourism is growing globally, and its importance to cities and destinations
- How foodies and food tourism fits into tourism, hospitality and food studies
- Sub categories of food tourism by type of food, cooking styles, cuisines, etc.
- How food and beverages are linked.

Purpose and overview of the book

Food tourism has attracted significant scholarly attention over the past decade, and given that the proclivity of travellers for food experiences is projected to increase, this trend is likely to continue (*Culinary Tourism*, 2011). Indeed, all travellers and tourists must eat, therefore food is an important destination attribute. It is estimated that upwards of 25% of tourism expenditure is attributable to food products (Correia et al. 2008). More than this there is recognition of the importance of food and beverages in influencing how visitors perceive a destination (Wolf, 2006) and in generating satisfactory travel experiences.

As a cultural artefact, food provides a medium for the expression of local culture. As such food (and beverages) are fundamental to destination imaging and indeed food purchase by tourists stimulates the local economy at all levels (Hjalager and Richards, 2002). Timothy and Ron (2013), in the editorial to a special issue of *Journal of Heritage Tourism*, had this to say about the importance of food:

> *In short, foodways and cuisine are a more important part of the tourism system than simply food and food services; they are imbued with cultural meaning, experience and permanence. Cuisine is, without doubt, one of the most salient and defining markers of cultural heritage and tourism.*

Food is definitely an attraction, and has matured into a highly sought-after niche market in its own right (Okumus et al, 2007). Many destinations are now promoting themselves as centres of gastronomy and employing food and beverages as attractions. Examples come from all over the world, such as Cornwall, England. Dr. Liz Sharples has contributed this profile.

The UK, Cornwall Food and Drink

Dr. Liz Sharples, Sheffield-Hallam University

The county of Cornwall is located at the end of a peninsula which forms the south-westerly point of the British land mass. The spectacular Cornish coastline extends for nearly 300 miles.

With a total population of only 532,300 (Cornwall Council, 2014) this county is one of the less inhabited regions of the UK. However, in the summer and peak holiday months, the population swells dramatically as Cornwall welcomes visitors from the UK and overseas. It is one of the UK's most popular holiday destinations, attracting approximately 5 million tourist visits each year. In 2011 the county experienced 4,245,000 trips from domestic tourists alone, generating an income of £1,122 million (Visit England, 2014).

Visitors are attracted to Cornwall for a number of reasons including its magnificent landscape, mild climate, unique history and culture, well established art scene and access to adventure sports such as surfing, hiking and rock climbing.

Recently it has also become a significant 'pull' for foodies as the county has a food scene which arguably rivals any other area in the UK. The county is now home to a wealth of award-winning food producers and a number of celebrity chefs have established gourmet restaurants here, including Rick Stein at Padstow (Rick Stein, 2014) and Jamie Oliver at Watergate Bay (Jamie Oliver, 2014). Restaurant menus in the county reflect the abundance of excellent Cornish produce including freshly caught seafood, and this region is well known for a number of traditional delicacies including Cornish pasties and clotted cream.

The key marketing organisation which has helped to put Cornwall on the gastronomic map is Cornwall Food and Drink, based in Truro, (Cornwall Food and Drink, 2014) which has a mission to harness the expertise of food businesses in the area to promote Cornish food and drink, both inside and outside the county. Businesses who wish to be involved with the organisation can join as members, for a moderate membership fee, and then benefit from a range of professionally run marketing campaigns, events and activities.

One recent marketing initiative by Cornwall Food and Drink has been the publication of *The Great Cornish Food Book*. This book, which has been commissioned, written, published and produced in the county, brings together a colourful collection of food related stories, recipes, culinary tips and profiles of local food heroes. It is a mouth-watering celebration of all that is great about Cornish food. Available for sale in over seventy local bookshops, hotels, restaurants, cafes, food shops and key visitor attractions, the book is designed to serve as an attractive guide to visitors who may wish to seek out good gastronomic opportunities during their stay. However the book also serves as an attractive souvenir, reminding visitors of their stay and promoting the county and its culinary excellence to a wider audience.

References

Cornwall Council (2014) at http://www.cornwall.gov.uk/council-and-democracy/data-and-research/data-by-topic/population/?page=22137, last visited on 1/3/2014

Cornwall Food and Drink (2014) at http://www.cornwallfoodanddrink.co.uk/, last visited on 16/4/2014

Jamie Oliver (2014) at http://www.fifteencornwall.co.uk/), last visited on 12/4/2014

Rick Stein (2014) at http://www.rickstein/Rick-Stein.html, last visited 16/4/2014

Visit England (2014) Local Authority and County Analysis 2006 - 2011 at http://www.visitengland.org/insight-statistics/major-tourism-surveys/overnightvisitors/Index/Regional_Results_2011.aspx, last visited 1/3/2014

The UNWTO *Global Report on Food Tourism* (2012) is a good indicator of how food tourism has proliferated and gained in importance. They said:

> *For many of the world's billions of tourists, returning to familiar destinations to enjoy tried and tested recipes or travelling further afield in search of new and special cuisine, gastronomy has become a central part of the tourism experience. Against this background, food tourism has gained increasing attention over the past years. Tourists are attracted to local produce and many destinations are centring their product development and marketing accordingly. With food so deeply connected to its origin, this focus allows destinations to market themselves as truly unique and appealing to those travellers who look to feel part of their destination through its flavours.*

Here are short excerpts from its sections on Korea and Spain (UNWTO *Global Report on Food Tourism*, 2012, p. 36):

> *The linkages between food and local, regional and national development and its impact in the tourism and travel industry are growing, and nations are now becoming more aware of its importance. Since 1999, the task of turning traditional food into a tourism product for domestic and foreign tourists in Korea has been pursued with vigor. The Korea Tourism Organization has developed gastronomic tours in Korea in collaboration with celebrities such as top chefs or gastronomists, as well as famous Korean entertainers.*

Among the reasons for visiting Spain, oenogastronomy is one of the fastest-growing motivations over the past years. Out of these 56.7 million international tourists, more than 5 million said that the enjoyment of Spanish food and wine constituted one of their main reasons for choosing Spain as a tourism destination. These visits generated receipts of over 5 billion euros and the visitors rated their satisfaction at 8.3 out of 10. For its part, the food and agriculture sector in Spain represents 7.6% of GDP and employs more than 400,000 people.

A study by Deloitte and the Tourism Industry Association of Canada (2012, p. 9) made the following observations about food tourism in North America:

Approximately 35% of Canadian travellers surveyed indicated that they would travel primarily for a culinary purpose (e.g. to attend a food and wine festival), and over 50% consider food and beverage offerings in narrowing down their destination choice. South of the border, the Travel Industry Association of America recently reported that 60% of American leisure travellers indicate that they are interested in taking a trip to engage in culinary activities within the next 12 months.

The academic study of food tourism is also global in scope, including Asia. Kivela and Crotts (2005, 2006, 2009) have focussed on Hong Kong and concluded that its gastronomy is a major contributor to creating high-quality visitor experiences and that in turn directly influences return behaviour. Regarding Singapore, where promoting cuisine is a theme of growing importance, Henderson (2004) identified the critical connection between food and tourism. In that country, policies were shaped by a number of distinctive features. And Tussyadiah (2005) observed that in Japan culinary tourism had been a major factor in the development of more than one region.

An organization of note is the World Food Travel Association (formerly the International Culinary Tourism Association) which has grown in response to the upsurge in interest and the increasing economic importance of food tourism. This description is from its website (www.worldfoodtravel.org):

The World Food Travel Association changed its name from International Culinary Tourism Association in 2012 to meet the needs of our changing industry. Over the years, the Association identified strong industry needs in food tourism education and research; food tourism product development; and food tourism promotion. The Association has been a leader in developing products and services to meet the needs of our industry, media and consumers. The Association has also been instrumental in forging strategic partnerships with related organizations, and by driving though leadership at regional and international food tourism industry events.

Our Mission

The World Food Travel Association (WFTA) promotes food, drink & culinary cultures through travel. We serve as the central hub connecting key industry segments and partners with business to business (B2B) and business to consumer (B2C) relationships. We facilitate food and beverage discovery world-wide, including the creation, production and marketing of products from farm to fork. We accomplish our work through destination marketing organizations, industry trade associations, the media, universities and consumer food communities.

To attract 'foodies' – people with a passion for food who will travel specifically because of their special interest – requires a much better understanding of their involvement with food, trip motivation, and travel preferences and patterns. This line of niche-market research has to be theory-based to provide a general understanding of food tourism, then supplemented with specific market intelligence pertinent to each destination.

In this book we take a demand-side approach to food tourism, in contrast to the many other books and papers which have taken a primarily supply-side, and sometimes a disciplinary approach to the study of food and tourism. Supply-side approaches look at how it is being, or should be, developed and marketed. Disciplinary approaches start with a particular perspective, especially cultural studies, anthropology or geography, and assess the phenomenon of food tourism according to their theories and methodologies.

Scant research exists on the foodie as a contemporary niche market within leisure and tourism, and we rectify that gap by providing results from our own extensive surveys, and those that have been published by various industry groups and other academics. This is contextualized by relevant theoretical perspectives, including social worlds, ego-involvement, travel careers and destination image. Implications for food-tourism development and marketing are discussed, complete with case studies of cities and destinations that understand the target markets and have succeeded in making food tourism a mainstay of their attractiveness. We also include profiles of products and marketing approaches, and some interviews with experts and practitioners.

Terminology

■ Food, foodie and food tourism

'Food' is anything nutritious that people eat. In some countries it is legally defined, and in many places it is heavily regulated. While it is generally recognized that all humans have a fundamental right to be free of hunger, famine is a periodic curse in some areas while others enjoy food in abundance. With a growing human population and the threats coming from climate change, the future of food supplies and food safety are global issues that concern everyone.

What exactly people eat, and how they prepare their food, involves cultural and social studies, and for those with sufficient money and time, food, cooking and dining become part of one's lifestyle, giving rise to the terms 'food lover' and 'foodie'. The authors realize that food tourism is a luxury, but it is an important one that people gladly embrace when they gain sufficient discretionary income to support their interests. It does raise important ethical issues about equity and the distribution of the world's resources; it generates debates about power and privilege; and sometimes gives rise to resentment and antagonism. Yet it is a fact of life, a global phenomenon, and it deserves our attention.

Food: anything nutritious that people eat

Food tourism: travel for the specific purpose of enjoying food experiences

Foodie: a food lover; one whose personal and social identity encompasses food quality, cooking, sharing meals and food experiences; foodies incorporate all aspects of food into their lifestyle, which often leads them to travel for new and authentic food experiences.

There are several dimensions to being a foodie which are explored thoroughly in this book:

■ Behaviour, including shopping, cooking and eating, and especially travel for food experiences

■ Self-identity: what people feel about food or food tourism that defines who they are, including their values and attitudes

■ Social identity: how people relate to each other and form or reinforce their identity by being a foodie or food tourist in social settings; this includes sharing food experiences with others and belonging to food-lover groups

Tourists have to eat, but they do not have to take any interest in what they are eating, and the food is not necessarily an attraction. Food is often a 'hygiene' factor in the literal sense (causing many illnesses) and in the sense that bad food experiences can ruin a trip (Pendergast, 2006). While food and tourism are inseparable, many tourists avoid eating anything unusual (they are neophobes), many are ambivalent about their food experiences (it's not a big deal for them), while others go literally anywhere for a memorable and novel food experience (they are neophiles).

Confusion about other important terms has been noted by many, including Karim and Chi (2010, p. 532) who said "Tourism activity related to food has been labelled such as food tourism, culinary tourism, or gastronomy tourism. These terms have the same meaning: people travel to a specific destination for the purpose of finding foods".

We employ 'food tourism' in this book - to keep it simple and broad, and to avoid any bias or stereotype associated with other terms. The other two terms most frequently used to describe food tourism that have come into vogue are 'culinary tourism' and 'gastronomy tourism'.

■ What being a foodie is NOT!

It goes without saying that people have to eat, and that wanting to eat food that tastes good is a common human trait. If that is all there was to being a food lover we would not be making such a big deal about it in the realms of tourism, hospitality and culture. Being a foodie is definitely not about gluttony, or over-indulging in food and beverages. It is possible to say "I love eating and therefore I am a food lover", but that is not the same as being a glutton, which implies excessiveness and greed.

Our research shows clearly that quality is a paramount concern of the foodie: quality of produce, cooking, and food-related experiences. Some would associate those attributes with luxury, and it does take money to indulge oneself this way on a foreign trip, but we also have to acknowledge that one can be a foodie and stay at home! Food quality is therefore much more important than eating or drinking a lot. This is not to say that foodies never over-indulge! It happens.

Finally, some people believe that being a foodie is a reflection of healthy-living values, or that foodies *must* engage in only healthy eating. This is a problematic area, because our research shows that health concerns are important to foodies, but not paramount. It is reasonable to conclude that many foodies are health conscious, but it is not a defining characteristic. If one was to insist that being a food requires healthy eating, then several serious issues arise: what is 'healthy' is often open to medical debate, and seems to keep changing; there are definitely cultural norms that affect one's interpretation of healthy; and being healthy in general does not preclude indulgences at various times.

■ Foodie lifestyles

It has been generally accepted that we live in the era of the 'experience economy' as articulated and popularized by Pine and Gilmore (1999). In this economy people value experiences more than objects and mere consumables, so that foodies and food tourists are willing and often eager to pay for rewarding and novel experiences. Consumption in this economy holds symbolic value, and consistent patterns of symbolic consumption generate and help define discernable lifestyles.

Lifestyle: A way of life or style of living that reflects the attitudes and values of a person or group (thefreedictionary.com)

The term 'lifestyle' is popular, but rather vague. There are a number of possible connotations, including the view that your lifestyle sets you apart from others, that a healthy or moral lifestyle is highly desirable, or that some people have enviable lifestyles (e.g., lifestyles of the rich and famous). A 'bohemian' or 'counter-culture' lifestyle comes close to the concepts of sub-culture and social worlds, as discussed later.

This is how an American marketing firm describes the foodie lifestyle: (http:// www.hartman-group.com/hartbeat/understanding-the-foodie-consumer)

As we've described, consumers embracing foodie lifestyles love to smell and taste fine foods and actively seek out new food experiences. For foodies, in fact, it's all about the experience whether at home, in stores or eating out. Dining out is a favorite foodie behavior: foodies love the theater of restaurants, watching chefs in action and sitting at chef's tables...These bon vivants are just as likely to embark on a culinary vacation to Napa Valley, Tuscany or Provence as they are to seek gustator aspects of discovering new meals, wines and recipes locally...

Foodies are information junkies. They are inveterate enthusiasts of food-oriented magazines, television shows and scour the Web in pursuit of recipes and knowledge about various ingredients. Foodies are typically immersed in the collection and use of a broad range of cookbooks.

A precondition is that 'lifestyle' is voluntary and reflects one's personal and social identity, so if you do not have enough to eat it is pointless to talk about a foodie lifestyle. As well, there are aspects of lifestyle that are socially and culturally influenced, and in this vein it is clear that the term 'foodie' is historically very recent in origin and reflects a number of profound trends that we later identify as arising from several propelling forces. These forces can change, and so can notions of what is socially acceptable or desirable.

In this way, lifestyles incorporate and reflect fashion and 'political correctness'. It is therefore possible to foresee a not-too-distant future, (this is scenario making, not prediction) shaped by constraining rather than propelling forces, in which being a 'foodie' and 'food tourist' hold negative connotations linked to unsustainable practices, and therefore the words and associated lifestyles might fade away. It is quite possible that living a 'greenie lifestyle' will take over in terms of popularity, or by necessity.

■ Gastronomy and cuisine

Unfortunately, gastronomy, and the related terms gourmet or gourmand, are frequently value-laden in usage, as they imply a lavish or elitist perspective on food preparation and dining. Dictionary definitions from Merriam-Webster (online) emphasize the connection to 'fine' or 'good food' which is certainly open to interpretation, and regard the 'gourmand' as given to excessive eating:

Gastronomy: the art or activity of cooking and eating fine food

Gourmet: a person who enjoys and knows a lot about good food and wine

Gourmand: a person who loves to eat and drink: a person who eats and drinks too much

Culture and style enter the picture when we speak of cuisine and culinary tourism.

Cuisine: a style of cooking (as in French cuisine); food that is cooked in a particular way (e.g., spicy food)

Culinary: of or relating to the kitchen or cookery

According to Wikipedia, 'cuisine' means:

> "'cooking; culinary art; kitchen'; ultimately from Latin coquere, 'to cook': a specific set of cooking traditions and practices, often associated with a specific culture. It is often named after the region or place where its underlining culture is present."

Various definitions of 'culinary tourism' have emerged, so let's look at several:

Culinary or food tourism is defined by the World Food Travel Association (WFTA) as:

> the pursuit of unique and memorable eating and drinking experiences (Wolf, 2006)

Smith and Xiao (2008: 289) defined it this way:

> "Culinary tourism is any tourism experience in which one learns about, appreciates, or consumes branded local culinary resources. In other words, culinary tourism is an intentional and reflective encounter with any culture, including one's own through culinary resources. Culinary tourism encompasses travel specifically motivated by culinary interests as well as travel in which culinary experiences occur but are not the primary motivation for the trip."

The World Food Travel Association definition, from the book *Have Fork Will Travel* (Wolf, 2006), implies that culinary tourism is motivated by a desire for unique dining experiences, whereas Smith and Xiao's approach also encompasses food experiences while travelling for other purposes. These are both definitions made from an industry perspective, reflecting what destinations and the food business want; they do not necessarily define food tourism as a foodie would.

Gastronomy, since the early 18th century, has dominated the study of the relationship between culture and food. It focuses on the various cultural components of food. The French scribes Brillat-Savarin, with *The Physiology of Taste* (2000), and Grimod de La Reynière with *Almanach des Gourmands* (1803-1812) were pivotal in establishing gastronomy is an interdisciplinary topic that included the study of discovering, tasting, experiencing, researching, understanding and writing about foods.

The following definition provides an insight into some of the nuances that have since emerged.

> *Most dictionaries define gastronomy as "the art and science of good eating," or "the art and science of fine eating." The etymology of the word is generally attributed to the title of a poem by French attorney Joseph Berchoux, "Gastronomie" (1801). Early descriptive writings often assume gluttony. One versed in gastronomy is said to be a gastronome, while a gastronomist is one who unites theory with practice and thus becomes a gourmand (gourmet).*

(Source: Gale Encyclopedia of Food and Culture, 2004)

Although the term gastronomy continues to resonate strongly in the context of some of Europe and Asia's classic cuisines (Kivela and Crotts, 2009), the term mitigates against the democratization and accessibility of food, especially in a tourism context since food does not necessarily have to be consumed and understood only in Michelin star restaurants. Moreover, as Santich's (1996) gastronomy definition implies, the activity must be intellectualised: "reflective eating, which, however, expands to reflective cooking and food preparation as well, maintaining the association with excellence and/or fancy food and drink" (1996, p. 115). No doubt many individuals engage with their food at the esoteric and epicurean, rather than the corporeal, level, but we do not consider the intellectualising of food as a necessary prerequisite, or defining dimension, of food involvement.

■ Sub-categories of food tourism

While we are concerned with food in general, there are people with special food interests that can motivate travel. For example, the term 'olive tourism' has been used by Alonso and Northcote (2010) who advocated collaboration between olive farmers, tourism organizers and government to support in the sustainable development of olive growing and tourism.

Croce and Perri (2010) give case studies of 'best practice' experiences including a winery tour, dairy farm, brewery, olive mill, and distillery, plus examples connected to rice, bread, cured meat, balsamic vinegar, foie gras, salmon, pasta, snails, salt, fruit, chocolate and cocoa, and tea. Boniface (2003) discussed honey, meat, fish, cheese, apples and cider. With regard to various foods and drinks as tourist attractions she concluded (p. 151): "They reveal how much custom, belief, ritual and tradition – folklore and myth even – can be held and conveyed in a food in its process of production and method of preparation." Basically, anything that is eaten or drunk can be packaged as an experience at the site of production, manufacture, or distribution.

A scan of the internet reveals numerous specializations in cooking styles, food preferences and associations between produce and specific places. Although olives are grown in many warm climates, including California and Australia, they are especially associated with Mediterranean countries, and this brings terroir and place identity into the discussion (see the following definition). One could also segment foodies according to what, or how they want to eat, which is reflected in numerous websites and blogs devoted to, for example, Italian and various ethnic/racial/geographically-delimited cuisines, fast/slow food, cooking on gas or BBQ, fusion, organic, local produce, gluten-free, low-fat, Halal, Kosher, etc.

BBQ as a style of cooking can be done anywhere, but it has a particular connotation in the southern USA. Hence, several states have designated BBQ trails (e.g. North Carolina's at www.ncbbqsociety.com/bbqmap/trail_map.html). Chocolate lovers may want to make a pilgrimage to Belgium: (www.visitbelgium.com/?page=chocolate-lovers).

The truth is, many places around the world can promote a particular dish, style of cooking or unique produce as a tourist attraction. Authenticity is assured by the combination of place and product, unless of course the very same experience can be had in many other places! But places can rely on quality food services and destination restaurants, even if they have no unique terroir.

■ Terroir

Literally, in French, *terroir* means soil. In the wine world it has come to mean "the combination of factors, including soil, climate, and environment, that gives a wine its distinctive character" (www.thefreedictionary.com). Foodies associate terroir with local and fresh, authenticity, provenance, and distinctive taste. This is reflected in books such as Trubek's (2009) *The Taste of Place: A Cultural Journey into Terroir*, and Jacobsen's (2010) *American Terroir: Savoring the Flavors of Our Woods, Waters, and Fields*.

Trubek's examination compares French and American understandings of the concept, noting that cultural tradition and knowledge is the essence of French terroir while Americans rely on scientific explanations; in North American there is a serious risk of terroir becoming a marketing or branding gimmick.

Bertella (2011) stressed the need for a knowledge-based approach to developing food tourism, specifically related to terroir, or the specific needs of places. His results indicated "...five types of knowledge as particularly relevant in food tourism: local food knowledge, scientific food knowledge, tourism knowledge, local managerial and political knowledge, and global managerial and political knowledge." Croce and Perri (2010) discuss at length the concept of terroir and the notion of transforming a terroir into a tourism destination. They stress sustainability in this process, in a triple-bottom-line approach.

■   Beverages and tourism

It is obvious that eating and drinking go together, and many people consider certain beverages to be food. Pettigrew and Charters (2006) determined that wine is much more associated with food than is beer. Wine and food tourism in particular go together, and wine is often associated with fine dining, but the two can exist without each other. The importance of beverage-oriented tourism has been identified (e.g., Plummer et al, 2005) including the existence of aficionados of wine, beer, tea, coffee, and whisky who search out producers and manufacturers.

Wine tourism

Since there is overlap between wine and food in relation to lifestyles and tourism it is useful to review here some of the wine tourism literature, with emphasis on the wine lover (we cannot call these people 'winies' or 'winos' for obvious reasons!). Wine tourism has received a great deal of attention from scholars and marketers, and *Global Wine Tourism* (Carlsen and Charters, 2006) provides a good overview of research on this special interest. *Explore Wine Tourism* by Getz (2000) examines wine tourism development at the levels of winery and destination. In the early days of research on wine tourism it was dominated by supply-side topics, much in the same way that food tourism is developing – with demand-side work coming on stream much later.

In 2000, as covered in *Explore Wine Tourism*, scholars had a rather sketchy picture of the connections between wine and food, and how a love of either or both led to tourism. Here are some of the most relevant facts and opinions contained in that book, which collectively reflect research and industry development through the 1990s. These snippets do demonstrate that the phenomenon was understood, albeit without much empirical evidence, and that the food and wine connection was already well established.

■   The appeal of wine tourism embodies a complete sensory experience, involving taste, smell, touch, sight and sound. In addition, Getz argued that wine tourism should be culturally authentic, romantic, fun and educational (p.2).

■   'Wine country' had entered the popular lexicon, and its appeal was well documented. Peters (1997) said wine country was synonymous with "civilized enjoyment; food, wine and conversation often come together in harmonious ways." Macionis and Cambourne (1998) suggested that wine tourism provides tourists the opportunity to experience, history, food, territory and culture. Hall and Macionis (1998) defined wine tourism as being based primarily on the motivation of tasting and/or experiencing the attributes of a wine producing region.

- Consumption of wine had been shifting from quantity to better quality, and wine consumers tended to be older, better educated and with higher incomes – the same profile as that of the international pleasure traveller.

- Wine had become associated with healthy, modern living, with fine dining and romance, and with attractive places to visit.

- Australia was a world leader in developing wine and food tourism in the 1990s. In the Australian Rural Tourism Strategy (Commonwealth Department of Tourism, 1994), a number of trends were identified: more special-interest tourism with a growing interest in specialty foods and beverages; a search for authenticity including rural areas associated with wholesome lifestyles and sustainability; health consciousness; and growth in what was termed REAL travel (rewarding, enriching, adventuresome, and a learning experience).

- Most empirical research on wine tourism was based on surveys at wineries, which yielded only a partial understanding.

- Subsequent research on wine tourists has demonstrated that the personality trait called 'sensation seeking' impacts on wine tourists attitudes and behaviour (Galloway, Mitchell, Getz, Crouch, & Ong, 2008), leading to a stronger interest in tactile, new, and learning experiences. This is similar to foodies and novelty-seeking.

Previous research on wine lovers and the connection to wine tourism has been influential in our approach to studying foodies and food tourism. Several papers demonstrated the fact that wine lovers are natural wine tourists (Brown and Getz, 2005) and that good food experiences were a major part of valued wine tourist experiences (Getz and Brown, 2006). Our research (Robinson & Getz, 2014) suggests a natural association is made between famous wine regions and preferred food tourism destinations. The theoretical construct called *ego-involvement*, much valued in leisure studies, was employed to compare serious wine lovers with others, and to help segment them according to personal characteristics and wine tourism preferences and behaviour (Brown, Havitz and Getz, 2007). Echoes of that research are heard in later, analytic sections of this book.

Although overlapping, with similar demand-side profiles, it would be a mistake to lump foodies and wine lovers together without due consideration of the geographic context (obviously wine producing regions are somewhat unique) and the nature of the experiences on offer. Foodies have the entire world as a potential food basket.

Other beverages

Beer tourism is somewhat limited by the fact that beer is brewed all over the world, and is often considered to be a commodity much like soft drinks. For the beer aficionado, however, there are special places associated with production of the best, most unique, or favourite brews. These places include Belgium, and especially its monastery brews. At the website beertourism.com the connection between beer and food is prominent:

Discover the wonderful world of Belgian beer and the people who create it at BeerTourism.com. Explore our surprisingly-diverse little country, from the North Sea coast to the Ardennes, from Antwerp to Ostend. Enjoy the finest beer cuisine and learn how to match a menu with the right beers.

Another famous region for beer tourism is Yorkshire, England where the ale trail takes visitors on a tour of pubs, many featuring local food produce, or of breweries. (http://www.yorkshire.com/what-to-do/delicious/delicious-ale-trail, accessed Nov. 21, 2013).

Beer tourism has been studied in Canada (Plummer et al, 2005; 2006) and in Germany (Pechlaner et al, 2009).

Coffee tourism is well established in a number of countries including Costa Rica, Columbia, Ecuador, Brazil, Indonesia and the Big Island of Hawaii. According to the blog CoffeeKrave, Seattle and Italy are also coffee destinations because of their coffee cultures (http://www.coffeekrave.com/the-top-coffee-tourism-destinations/, accessed Nov. 14, 2013).

In the book *Coffee Culture, Destinations and Tourism* (Jolliffe, 2010) the phenomenon is explored in detail, including a focus on cafe districts as well as coffee-producing regions. Kleidas and Jolliffe (2010) examined coffee tourism using the words of coffee tourists themselves. These beverage lovers seek authenticity and variety in their experiences, and they value the environments where coffee is grown. This interest in terroir (which the authors describe as literally meaning land, but embodying a sense of place, and also referring to the interactions of soils, topography and climate that shape taste) is much the same as for wine and other agricultural produce. Kleidas and Jolliffe also noted a strong interest in knowledge acquisition and a growing concern for environmental sustainability.

Tea tourism will take the beverage lover to completely different parts of the globe, notably, China, India, Sri Lanka, Japan, and Indonesia. See also *Tea and Tourism: Tourists, Traditions and Transformations* (Jolliffe, 2007) which provides the essential overview, and includes articles such as that by Huang and Hall who suggested using a tea festival to enhance a sustainable, gastronomically-related tourism identity for locals.

Here is an example of tea tourism through the offer of a tour company:

World Tea Tours is the original pioneer of tea adventure travel. Led by world renowned, professional tea authorities, the custom-crafted tours are a combination of abundant, hands-on, invaluable tea experiences mixed with real involvement with the native cultures of tea producing and consuming regions. Each unique tour offers unparalleled, educational experiences for the tea business professional and avid tea lover alike. (www.worldteatours.com)

Whisky tourism is confined to a very few places, although isolated distilleries in a number of countries do attract visitors. Most 'whisky' lovers know that this spelling comes from Scotland, whereas 'whiskey' with an 'e' is the Irish and American version. Styles of whiskey attract their own followers, just like wine and beer. For Scotch lovers, following the Malt Whisky Trail (http://www.maltwhiskytrail.com/) is rather like a pilgrimage, and the unique terroir of the Highlands and Islands is definitely a selling feature. Many 'pilgrims' will begin or end their journey in Edinburgh. Researchers Martin and McBoyle (2006) examined management issues related to Scotland's Malt Whisky Trail, concentrating on its nature as a public–private tourism marketing partnership.

Summary

In this introductory chapter we have provided an overview of foodies and food tourism, and have defined key terminology. Food tourism is a recent global phenomenon of considerable importance to cities and destinations, and its prospects for continued growth are strong. But to be competitive, marketers must understand the foodie and the experiences they will travel for - this requires demand-side research and planning.

Foodies can be examined in different ways, related to their behaviour, self, and social identities, and these are themes developed throughout the book, particularly through research findings. Being a foodie is much more than eating, and it relates to one's entire lifestyle. Research has clearly revealed the key dimensions of being a foodie: a concern for quality of produce and meals, love of cooking, sharing meals and other food-related experiences; and of course many are motivated to travel by these factors.

There are many possible sub-categories when looking at food tourism, including a specific interest in beverages, styles of cooking, or food types. All of these can be attractions, especially when the foodie can experience the authentic culture of others through their food and drinks.

Study questions

1 Define these key terms: food, foodie, cuisine, gastronomy

2 In what ways can we explore what it means to be a foodie?

3 What is a foodie lifestyle?

4 Are all foodies alike?

5 Explain food tourism from both a supply and demand perspective

6 What is terroir and why is it important in both wine and food tourism?

7 What are some of the sub-categories of food tourism? Can you suggest others and find attractions or destinations for them?

Additional readings

Carlsen, J., and Charters, S. (Eds.) (2006). *Global Wine Tourism: Research, Management and Marketing*. Wallingford, England: CABI.

Croce, E., Perri, G. (2010). *Food And Wine Tourism: Integrating Food, Travel and Territory*. Wallingford, England: CABI.

Hall, C.M., and Gossling, S. (Eds.) (2013). *Sustainable Culinary Systems: Local Foods, Innovation, Tourism and Hospitality*. Oxford: Routledge.

Wolf, E. (Ed.) (2014). *Have Fork Will Travel*. Portland OR: The World Food Travel Association.

2 Perspectives on Foodies and Food Tourism

Learning objectives

Readers are expected to learn the following from this chapter:

- A systematic approach to understanding and creating knowledge about foodies and food tourism: the elements of, and interconnections between the experience, antecedents, outcomes, dynamic processes, and planning and management
- How foodies and food tourism are studied in food studies, tourism, hospitality, the social sciences and humanities, and economics and business
- Constraining and propelling forces that explain the food tourism phenomenon
- Trends in food tourism

Understanding and creating knowledge about foodies and food tourism

Figure 2.1 illustrates how the core phenomenon of this sub-field consists of food-tourism experiences and the meanings attached to them by tourists and other stakeholders. The two basic questions are: "What aspects of food (i.e. food-related experiences) attract people to travel?" and "What aspects of food experiences satisfy or disappoint travellers?" The meanings people attach to their experiences are of great interest to psychologists, sociologists and cultural anthropologists. To some foodies a given experience can be purely hedonistic (i.e. pleasurable, fun) or identity building (as in "I am a true food lover, with expert knowledge"). To others, an experience can be about social belonging and group identity, say as a member of a social network.

Knowledge is also required about the antecedents (the demand side, including social-world and cultural influences), planning and marketing (who develops and markets food tourism, and why), outcomes (both intended and unintended, at personal, group and societal/environmental levels), spatial and temporal patterns of food tourism, and the other dynamic processes of policy and knowledge creation that influence the system.

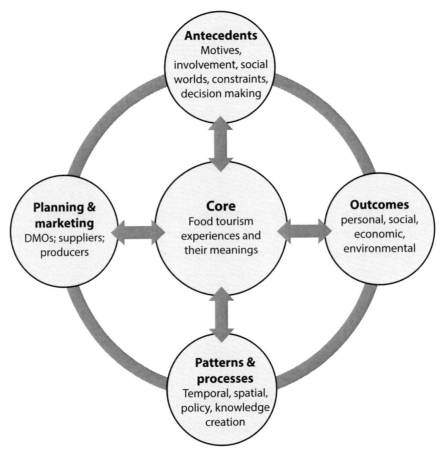

Figure 2.1: Understanding and creating knowledge in food tourism

■ A guide to using the framework

Understanding the foodie and food-tourism experience is the major purpose of this book, so there is pertinent material throughout. Searches of the Contents and Index can focus on key terms that are connected to each of these elements of the framework:

- **Core**, the key terms to search: 'foodie', 'experience', 'identity', 'meaning', 'authenticity', 'serious leisure', 'communitas', 'social bonding', 'neophilia' and 'novelty seeking', 'hygiene factor'

- **Antecedents**: in addition to the Core terms above, see: 'involvement', 'motivation', 'seeking and escaping', 'lifestyle', 'social worlds', 'psychology', 'decision-making', 'image', 'propelling forces', 'trends', 'satisfaction', 'information search', 'word of mouth'

- **Planning and marketing**: 'planning', 'strategy', 'clusters', 'stakeholders', 'marketing', 'communications', 'media', 'brand(ing)', 'image', 'reputation', 'media and media management', 'co-creation', 'engagement', 'service dominant logic', 'hallmark event', 'iconic event', 'segmentation', 'psychographics'

- **Outcomes**: see 'goals', 'benefits', 'impacts', 'willingness to pay', 'spending', 'yield', 'sustainability'

- **Spatial and temporal patterns**: 'geography', 'history', 'forces and trends', 'clusters', 'local', 'terroir', 'provenance', 'foodways', 'foodscape', 'experiencescape', 'attractiveness';

- **Policy**: covered under 'policy', 'development', 'planning', 'sustainability', 'strategy', 'DMO', 'destination'

- **Knowledge creation**: see all the 'research' sections, research notes, the Appendix, and the summary in the conclusions

Studying food tourism

In Figure 2.2 we have positioned food tourism at the nexus of three fields of study: food, hospitality, and tourism. Each of these has unique perspectives to offer on foodies and food tourism. While food-studies people might see food tourism as an interesting phenomenon with some impact on agriculture or culture, tourism suppliers, restaurateurs, and destinations clearly see it as a special-interest segment to be developed for profit and competitive advantage.

■ Food studies

Because food is essential to all humans, it is at once a source of worry (will we run out? is GM food a threat or saviour?), of joy (just ask the foodies!), and pride (whose cuisine is the best in the world?). Food is an integral part of culture, in part owing to the fact that producing food through agriculture, fishing, hunting or gathering goes a long way to shape communities and nations. According to Delamont (1994) food is one of the most important sources of cultural distinction among communities and regions, owing to the forces of globalisation. In a rich, consumer society, food (or what people eat) is a hotly debated topic in the context of health, while in poorer and less naturally endowed parts of the world over-consumption and waste is looked upon as an ethical issue, even as neo-colonialism.

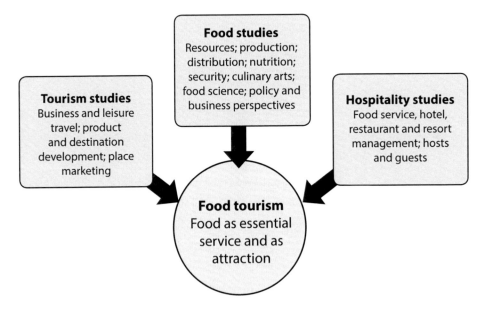

Figure 2.2: Food, hospitality and tourism studies

Food studies begin with sources, so its ties to agriculture, fisheries and natural resources are essential. So too are all the inputs to producing food, the business of food supply chains, and the livelihoods of farming/fishing communities. Policy is also a major theme, as food everywhere is on the political agenda and increasingly the subject of regulations and strategic planning by nations. When we consider the consumption of food, it begins with a combination of what's available (as influenced by natural resources and food economics), preferences (which are influenced by culture, including religion) nutrition (how concerned are people about healthy eating?) and even fads and fashion. How food is prepared requires food science, and culinary arts – the combination of which shapes the curricula of cooking and restaurant management. Both sociologists and anthropologists look at the bigger picture of the roles played by food and its consumption in society and culture. For example, in the sociology of food a concern is for inequitable access to food, while in a cultural anthropological context a topic of interest is 'foodways', or how geography and culture interact to shape cuisine.

If we start this discussion from the perspective of agriculture and fisheries, then we need to consider the full supply chain and how tourism changes demand. First, some tourists go straight to the source to 'pick your own' places and to farm stays. Second, foodies are fond of the 'fresh and local' mantra, so markets are extremely popular with them - especially if there is an opportunity to learn about, and to buy authentic local produce. Third, the supply-chain connects producers to the food-service industry, although any number of intermediaries might complicate the process, such as transport, wholesalers, and retailers of food. Tourism can increase demand, and change what is produced, particularly when chefs start to build their menus and reputations around regional cuisine and consequently favour close-in producers. Finally, the supply chain can extend abroad as tourists take food and beverages home with them, and more importantly begin to purchase foods from the places they have visited. The food brand of those supplier regions or countries can then be enhanced, leading to increases in certain exports.

Hall and Gossling (2013), in their book *Sustainable Culinary Systems*, discuss the many challenges associated with modern, industrialised food production and different positions on what sustainable means in this context. Their overview identified the components of a culinary system, within each of which sustainability issues arise:

- Inputs to the production of food (e.g., resources consumed or altered)
- The agriculture and fishery sectors
- Food processing and packaging
- Distribution (e.g. shipping, storing, wholesaling and retailing)
- Equipment required (e.g. for storage and transport)
- Hospitality and food-service businesses
- Households (personal and family shopping, kitchens, cooking, disposal)
- Disposal and recycling at a larger scale (e.g. city waste and recycling systems)
- Outputs including waste and emissions

We can conclude that food tourism planning should take into account the entire system, seeking both to minimise and ameliorate the negative impacts, and to strengthen the positives. Foodies are increasingly educated about food systems and want to be certain their food is safe and healthy, and many foodies take a particular interest in the concepts of local and sustainable food supply.

This topic is mainstream enough to have a Wikipedia article, with this definition:

> *Local food or the local food movement is a "collaborative effort to build more locally based, self-reliant food economies - one in which sustainable food production, processing, distribution, and consumption is integrated to enhance the economic, environmental and social health of a particular place".*

Advocates of local food might stress the reduction in energy consumption, or the contribution to a local economy. Others emphasize food freshness and quality. The term 'locavore' has been used, but it should be clear that this option of local food is definitely not available to everyone. The following statement from a group of locavores mentions the concept of 100-mile production which has been picked up as a kind of slogan for local food:

> *We are a group of concerned culinary adventurers who are making an effort to eat only foods grown or harvested within a 100 mile radius of San Francisco for an entire month. We recognize that the choices we make about what foods we choose to eat are important politically, environmentally, economically, and healthfully" (see: www. Locavores.com)*

This localism movement has also gained expression in the harvesting of traditional and non-commercial ingredients. Developed societies have become increasingly removed from the source of production of food, or even natural foods, given the highly processed nature of many supermarket shelf items. The 'foraging', or 'wild culture' movements are something of a backlash to these phenomena, and these movements have found greatest expression in a generation of restaurants globally, that trade under these philosophies. While restaurants and chefs championing molecular gastronomy, such as Heston Blumenthal and Adria Ferran, dominated the food scene for a decade, Noma is now top of the world restaurant list with its celebrated, and much imitated, wildculture style.

Research note on food studies and foodies

Sidali, K., Kastenholz, E., & Bianchi, R. (2013). Food tourism, niche markets and products in rural tourism: combining the intimacy model and the experience economy as a rural development strategy. *Journal of Sustainable Tourism*, DOI: 10.1080/09669582.2013.836210.

These researchers examined the local food concept and concluded that it variously encompasses narratives on a reconnection with nature, resistance to globalisation, creation of personal identity, freshness and taste, support for local producers and other environmental concerns. They contrast these concerns with mainstream consumers who are purportedly disinterested in food provenance. Clear connections to ethical and fair-trade practices are evident.

Food-specific activism is on the rise. Witness this mission statement from a citizen watchdog group:

> *Food & Water Watch works to ensure the food, water and fish we consume is safe, accessible and sustainable. So we can all enjoy and trust in what we eat and drink, we help people take charge of where their food comes from, keep clean, affordable, public tap water flowing freely to our homes, protect the environmental quality of oceans, force government to do its job protecting citizens, and educate about the importance of keeping shared resources under public control. (www. foodandwaterwatch.org)*

This leads naturally to a discussion of food security. According to the Food and Agriculture Organization (FAO) of the United Nations (1996), food security is a condition that "exists when all people, at all times, have physical and economic access to sufficient, safe and nutritious food to meet their dietary needs and food preferences for an active and healthy life". Currently this is not a universal condition, and with worries about the impacts of global climate change and industrial food production rising, it might only become harder to achieve.

Ethically, one has to ask if being a foodie or food tourist jeopardizes other people's food security? The answer is not simple or clear, because those in the greatest need are not situated in the richest nations that are blessed with both food surpluses and the economic means to enjoy food consumption and related travel. Individual reflection and action is needed on this question, for no global answer is available.

When it comes to food advocacy, consider the Terra Madre Network (from: www.terramadre.info):

> *The Terra Madre network, which integrates new members every day, is made up of all those who wish to act to preserve, encourage, and support sustainable food production methods. These methods are based on attention to territory and those distinctive qualities that have permitted the land to retain its fertility over centuries of use. This vision is in direct opposition to pursuing a globalized marketplace, with the on-going, systematic goal of increasing profit and productivity...Day after day, the Terra Madre family grows, strengthens, organizes, and defends local cultures and products, and makes real the Slow Food concept of Good, Clean, and Fair quality. Good refers to the quality of food products and of their taste; Clean, to a production process that respects the natural environment ; and Fair, in which there is dignity and appropriate economic return for the people who produce, including respect from those who consume.*

Another relevant, global movement is that of Slow Food (from: www.slowfood. com):

> *Slow Food envisions a world in which all people can access and enjoy food that is good for them, good for those who grow it and good for the planet. We oppose the standardization of taste and culture, and the unrestrained power of food industry multinationals and industrial agriculture. Our approach is based on a concept of food quality that is defined by three interconnected principles: good, clean and fair.*

> *GOOD: a fresh and flavorsome seasonal diet that satisfies the senses and is part of the local culture.*

> *CLEAN: food production and consumption that does not harm the environment, animal welfare or human health.*

> *FAIR: accessible prices for consumers and fair conditions and pay for producers.*

Slow Food believes food is tied to many other aspects of life, including culture, politics, agriculture and the environment. Through our food choices we can collectively influence how food is cultivated, produced and distributed, and as a result bring about great change. Informed and selective consumers become co-producers by demanding food that is good, clean and fair.

■ Hospitality studies

Hospitality and food are inseparable. Commercially, food is a key part of traditional hotel, resort, catering and restaurant management training, including that of chefs and food services in general. Most hospitality students learn something of food science and the culinary arts, but only some specialize in these areas. In most educational and training institutions, hospitality is taught within the commercial context, the aim being to prepare students for careers in industry or perhaps as entrepreneurs.

However, there is an alternative approach. Lashley and Morrison (2000) in the edited book *In Search of Hospitality* focus on the social context of hospitality in which food and meals figure prominently in host and guest interactions. This includes the rituals associated with hospitality given to friends or strangers - including tourists - but there are particular implications for foodies when considering the importance of food and meals in facilitating social exchanges of all kinds. Status displays can be part of the foodie lifestyle (featuring the display of knowledge, story-telling about wonderful food-tourism experiences, or the provision of expensive food and beverages), but perhaps more importantly are the opportunities afforded through cooking and eating for social bonding and identity building. For foodies, the shared meal can be full of symbolic meaning. What the host serves can reflect wealth, attitudes towards the environment and health, or particular interests in cuisine derived from ethnicity, religion, study or travel.

It has been realized that hospitality services are a major player in the experience economy, and that merely providing food is not in itself sufficient to attract and satisfy food lovers. The entire food experience must be designed, including food on the plate, service, ambience and entertainment (Barrows, 2008 in *The Sage Handbook of Hospitality Management*). Chefs and food-service businesses are being required - and gaining competitive advantages – from providing more healthy and regionally authentic options.

Research note on hospitality and foodies

Andersson, T. D., & Mossberg, L. (2004). The dining experience: do restaurants satisfy customer needs? *Food Service Technology*, **4**(4), 171-177.

This is an exploratory paper where the main idea is to develop an analysis of dining as a multidimensional experience. In order to assess the relative importance of various aspects of restaurant services, customers were asked to estimate their willingness to pay for six aspects of the dining experience: food, service, fine cuisine, restaurant interior, good company and other customers. Customers were asked to evaluate an ideal restaurant experience as well as their latest restaurant experience. Thus the actual evaluation could be compared with an ideal value to explore where restaurants have opportunities to enhance customers' restaurant experiences. Results clearly indicate that social needs are important for customers at evening restaurants whereas physiological needs dominate for customers at lunch restaurants.

■ Tourism studies

Throughout history people, whole nations even, have migrated because of food, leading to conflicts that many believe will re-emerge with terrible consequences if global climate change wreaks its predicted havoc on production. However, tourism studies largely focuses on freely-motivated travel for reasons of business or pleasure, and therefore tourism scholars are interested in how food generates travel, and how satisfaction with food experiences (or unhealthy, unsafe delivery) influences the reputation of places.

Tourism has many points of departure, and with regard to food we can begin with rural, farm or agri-tourism. Barbieri and Mahoney (2009), referring to farm diversification strategy, suggested that agri-tourism refers to tourism based on agricultural production, while rural tourism simply means travelling in rural areas. Page and Getz (1997), in *The Business of Rural Tourism*, considered it to be a very broad concept based on distinct characteristics of non-urban and remote environments, such as poor accessibility, lack of infrastructure and high seasonality of tourist demand.

Rural tourism includes farm tourism and connects with food production in a number of other ways. The imputed benefits of agri- or farm tourism have frequently been stated:

- Helping farmers financially through new sources of tourist income
- Preserving farm communities and rural lifestyles
- Landscape preservation (assuming viable farms)
- Fostering green and sustainable practices (connected to the branding of local produce)

In an increasingly globalized system with higher costs to consumers, yet often weak commodity prices which threaten traditional farming patterns and practices, agri-tourism has been suggested as a solution. This approach is based on the branding of local agricultural products, sharing culinary knowledge and heritage, and assuring customers of the quality and safety of local food production (Che, 2006; Du Rand and Heath, 2009; Knowd, 2006).

Ollenburg and Buckley (2007) stated that agri-tourism provides opportunities for farm operators and their families to continue farming and maintaining their rural lifestyle. Local communities also gain benefits from enhanced environmental awareness and the conservation of local customs, for example, relating to food production and preparation (Carlsen & Edwards, 2008; Everett & Aitchison, 2008; Gössling et al., 2011). Observers have also argued that the application of organic agriculture in agri-tourism and combinations of eco- and agri-tourism not only contribute to the development of rural areas but also foster environmentally sustainable development (Krešić & Sučić, 2010; Zumbado-Morales, 2010).

Food tourism is also an important theme in urban tourism, encompassing a number of specific topics: food events as attractions (with links to convention and exhibition centres); restaurant and beverage streets or districts; the importance of food alternatives catering to a wide variety of tourist preferences and needs, and the possibility of branding cities for foodies. Our examples and case studies reveal much about how a number of cities develop and promote food tourism.

Research note on food tourism

Everett, S. (2012). Production Places or Consumption Spaces? The Place-making Agency of Food Tourism in Ireland and Scotland. *Tourism Geographies*, **14** (4), 535-554.

Everett (2012, p 41) has echoed many others in saying that the reputation of Scottish food had been poor, but the Taste of Scotland campaign had helped revitalize the country's offer and made food tourism a realistic proposition. "Now championed by the 'Eat Scotland' campaign, it is enjoying a heightened reputation for quality food experiences. Significantly, when the International Culinary Tourism Association (2010) unveiled its first major report, it cited Scotland as one of the planet's most 'unique, memorable and interesting places' for food and drink. Certainly, food promotion is regarded as crucial to reach a target of £12.5 billion from tourism by 2017 (The Scottish Government 2010)."

■   Social Sciences and Humanities

In the applied fields of tourism and hospitality management, or from any economic development perspective, food tourism is business. But to many scholars it attracts attention for more theoretical or philosophical reasons, giving rise to a number of interesting discourses. We start with cultural anthropology, as the cultural dimensions of food and food tourism have attracted scholarly attention for a very long time.

Cultural anthropology

This is the study of human origins and evolution, language and culture. Anthropologists study the nature and functions of societies, and make systematic comparison of cultures, including the cultural influences on food and its preparation and consumption. They also study social organisation with a focus on symbolic representations of culture, and are well known for conducting ethnographic research, including participant observation and auto-ethnographic accounts of experience.

Boniface (2003:14-16) evaluated 'food and drink tourism' through a cultural lens, concluding that major influences on this phenomenon include consumer reaction to increasing standardization, an interest in other cultures, the pursuit of rewarding experiences and pleasant sensations, desire for immediate gratification, and certain associations between food/drink and ritual, celebration, comfort, escape, and status. Concern for food safety has led to an emphasis on quality, while urbanization and the disconnect of everyday life from agriculture and other food production lead to the desire for discovery of old farm roots and rural culture. Increased consumer knowledge of, and interest in, food and drink fits well into a search for cultural authenticity. As well, Boniface observed that artisanal foods, and traditional methods and landscapes are now considered to be valued heritage.

Food and cuisine help define culture, and give rise to cultural differences in related areas such as the degree to which people enjoy cooking versus dining out, or the relative importance of shopping for fresh and local produce. In a globalizing world, however, cuisines are constantly changing and interacting, so that the preservation of traditions has become important to many people, while many food lovers seek out experiences that they believe to be culturally authentic.

Foodways or food culture: the ways in which humans use food, from its production through consumption

Because agricultural produce and practices (and related cuisine) help define culture and establish strong traditions, folklorists and cultural anthropologists have long studied the food-culture connection. It is natural that some of them would also study the tourism connection, which comes about when people want to discover and sample other cuisines, and conversely, when people want to share their culinary heritage. Anthropologist Lucy Long (2003) posits that cultural authenticity is a central issue in culinary tourism. Her work is founded in the anthropology of tourism, folklore and food studies. She is interested in 'chronotypes', that is, unique space-time convergences in which authentic culinary experiences can be obtained when travellers come together with food.

In a contrary opinion, Molz (2007: 77) says "culinary tourism is not necessarily about knowing or experiencing another culture but about performing a sense of adventure, adaptability, and openness to any other culture. Food and eating are mobilized as material symbols of the global in travellers' performances of cosmopolitanism through which travellers simultaneously transgress and reinforce their own culture's norms." This theme remains controversial, for several reasons. People might express a politically correct attitude towards other cultures, but still be neophobic about different foods. If they are willing to try new foods while travelling, people might not in fact be aware of what is 'authentic' and might easily be misled.

Frochot (2003) indicated that using a local food image reflecting traditions and rural authenticity is an essential way to promote destinations. Hughes (1995) argued that from cultural studies and political-economy perspectives, authenticity provides opportunities for developing local tourism in intensively competitive global market. Authenticity has become an important topic of discussion in heritage tourism in general. Tussyadiah (2005) indicated that Japanese tourists search for authenticity in the places they go, seeking good traditional food and local cuisine. In this way authenticity plays an important role in heritage tourism development (Hjalager & Corigliano, 2000). Sims (2009) argued that local foods which are conceptualized as 'authentic' products have potential to enhance visitors' experiences by connecting them to a region's culture and heritage.

Many authors believe that food and food tourism enhances the development of local identity (Everett & Aitchison, 2008; Fox, 2007; Macleod, 2009). This has been suggested especially for festivals and other events (Brown & Chappel, 2008). Hashimoto and Telfer (2006) claimed the combination of culinary traditions from different ethnic groups in Canada helps foster local identity.

Montanari (2006) is a culinary historian whose book *Food Is Culture* claims that everything having to do with food represents a cultural act, full of symbolism. He argued that food, once a practical necessity, evolved into an indicator of social standing and religious and political identity. Greg Richards (in *Tourism and Gastronomy*, 2002, p. 31) adds that gastronomy evolves within a changing environment and should not be fossilized. Sustainable gastronomic tourism is not just about preserving the past - it is grounds for creative tourism.

Gastronomy

Gastronomy can be defined as the study of food and culture, but as Santich (2004) points out is far more complex. While gastronomy, and those that practice it, are usually visualised as self-indulgent, excessive, obsessive and passionate, broader definitions of gastronomy acknowledge food and drink in terms of their social and cultural, rather than individual, functions and properties. Indeed, gastronomy's complexity has given rise to its popularity as a field of study. Food and drink was traditionally considered as a banal topic, one that described a bodily function, and hence unworthy of the devotions of academic institutions. However, gastronomy's cultural and social complexities and nuances have made it an attractive field of study in recent years and the following case study, expertly provided by Dr Roger Haden, Manager, Educational Leadership, Le Cordon Bleu Australia, highlights the internationalisation of the field of gastronomy, both in terms of enrolling students but also in the development of programs globally. This augurs well for the development of food tourism. In particular, Haden emphasises the flexible learning for pleasure dimensions on offer, and this links well with our discussions in Chapter 3 regarding foodies and food involvement. Education and food tourism are inextricably linked, as this chapter captures, and Haden's case study reveals a key dimension as yet not well considered.

Thinking foodies: a case study of a growth market

By: Dr Roger Haden, Manager, Educational Leadership, Le Cordon Bleu Australia

This case study draws on statistics related to two masters programs, The Le Cordon Bleu Graduate Program in Gastronomy (MAG), delivered by the University of Adelaide (active enrolments between 2001-2009) and The Le Cordon Bleu Master of Gastronomic Tourism (MGT), delivered as a part-time online (only) course of study since May 2012 by Southern Cross University. Both programs reflect the current educational trend toward so-called lifestyle degrees, defined as degrees that are delivered with flexible options that 'suit people's lifestyles,' but in this context specifically referring to food, wine and gastronomy related higher degrees, which have been developed in curricula in Western countries for well over a decade. The presence of these degrees reflects a deliberate choice on the part of students to engage in learning for pleasure.

The MAG was the first of its kind in the world (2002), a full-time masters program in gastronomy that could be completed on-campus or online, part-time or full-time. It attracted students from all over the world. In 2014 MAG had 217 alumni listed on its network, from the following countries: Australia (84), the US (53), Canada (10), New Zealand (8), UK, (7), India (7), Taiwan (7), Thailand (5), Singapore (4), Philippines (4), Malaysia (3), South Korea (3), Hong Kong, China, Japan, Malta and Israel (2 each) plus Norway, Germany, Ireland, Kenya, Greece, Ecuador, Jordan, Mexico, Peru and Indonesia. Median age for students was 35, with an 88% predominance of women. 70% had undergraduate degrees in a broad range of disciplines (gastronomy being viewed as a multidisciplinary area of scholarship) and 30% specialist experience in one or more food/drink related subjects (3-5 years professional or specialist experience). The MAG grew in popularity, but particularly as an online option. While on-campus student cohorts varied only slightly between 6 and an optimum level of about 12 (with some student attrition, changes from online to on-campus study, and vice versa), online applications grew steadily from 2003-9, the last year enrolments were taken. That year online applications totalled more than over 70. The program was shut down by the university in 2009 due to contractual issues with its partner, Le Cordon Bleu. Enrolled students were able to continue and all eligible to graduate had done so by 2012.

The Master of Gastronomic Tourism (MGT), launched in May 2012 by joint venture partners Le Cordon Bleu and Southern Cross University (New South Wales) was designed to capture interest in gastronomy but with a tighter focus on food and wine tourism and therefore, a growing industry with employment prospects. It was only made available online, reflecting research on student preferences. Numbers were initially projected at 35. 45 students enrolled in 2012. In 2013, 48 students enrolled, trending positively. At the time of writing (May 2014) over 110 students are enrolled in the program.

The flexibility of the online delivery mode should be considered a major influencing factor in the success of both programs discussed, particularly among mature age students wishing to fit study with work or other life activities. In light of this, direct marketing as such, for the MAG, was arguably less a factor influencing the steady increase in numbers (on-campus numbers remained relatively low), while advertising and scholarship places (The Food Media Club and The James Beard Foundation, for example) helped promote the program and were easily filled.

Elsewhere, Boston Metropolitan University began its Master of Liberal Arts in Gastronomy in 1991 (a collaborative effort between culinary authorities, Julia Child and Jacques Pepin) and is now the longest running program of its kind in the world. The much more recently developed University of Gastronomic Sciences, in Pollenzo, Italy, attracted attention with its focus on 'slow food,' sustainable agriculture and culinary heritage. Today it offers four themed master programs in Food Culture and Communications, focussing specialisations on Human Ecology, Identity, Luxury Products and Media.

The broader reasons for the trend to explore food and food culture more fully are beyond the scope of this case study but three key factors are instructive.

First, food and drink were for centuries conventionally regarded as beneath serious academic interest, whereby knowledge related to food and drink was either understood as being of a purely practical type (horticulture, husbandry, cookery, butchery, etc.) or else disregarded as beneath the interest of serious scholarship, due to the putative link between having 'an interest in food' and self-indulgence or worse, gluttony and so therefore sinfulness. Ironically, morality, the politics of class and everyday socialisation (food choices/taste, table manners, etiquette) all played a role in determining the 'appropriateness' of scholarly interests vis a vis 'food'.

Second, not surprisingly from within the academy, what the Americans call Food Studies (and roughly equating with the discipline of gastronomy) emerged as a multidisciplinary approach, the confluence of that broader post-structuralist critique of conventional disciplinary knowledge that had blazed a trail in academia during the 70 and 80s and which, among other things, opened up the universities to the study of 'culture' (defined as the everyday) and including all practices related to food. Studying food culture also, as it happened, touched on everything –from philosophy, ethics and religion to health, science, technology, literature, art, politics, social life – and so Food Studies/ Gastronomy evolved from the start as a multidisciplinary perspective.

Third, the link between education and lifestyle has been strengthening disproportionately to the propensity of prospective students to seek out full-time degree study on campus at the same institution. 'Life style degrees' in this context allow students to enjoy work life balance, study while being employed, or the experience of choosing between campuses, online/on-campus or overseas experiences with partner institutions. Just as food, eating and cooking has become a defining feature of contemporary Western lifestyles, so have food studies and gastronomy also benefited from this interest.

Sociology

Sociology is the study of human interactions, or social life, including patterns of relationships within groups, organizations and whole societies – how they emerge and function. Sociologists can shed light on the nature and meanings of being a foodie and food-tourism experiences, the social factors influencing food-related decisions, the nature and design of foodscapes, fashion and trends in food, and even resident perceptions and attitudes towards food tourism.

Within this disciplinary perspective, our major interest lies in how foodies define themselves socially (i.e. by reference to others, including friends and family), how they interact and form groups, and the meanings given to food tourism within various sub cultures and social worlds. Sociologists might also study food-tourism behaviour in various social settings (e.g. restaurants versus festivals) and at various stages in a trip (e.g. on the flight, in the hotel, while touring or self-catering, and during a conference). The generic meal experience has been studied in depth (see the discussion in hospitality) but other aspects of food tourism have not.

We are particularly interested in the concept of 'social worlds', as defined by the sociologist Unruh, discussed in Chapter 3. Not all food lovers get involved with others who share their interests, but they can at least connect to each other through online communities of interest.

Philosophy

Philosophy embodies critical thought on the nature of experience, the meaning of life and belief systems, aesthetics and ethics. Values fit into this perspective, as do discourses about the nature and meaning of concepts like creativity, taste, embodiment or perceived beauty.

There has been a great deal of philosophical debate surrounding the food movement and food tourism, embodying mostly ethical (and sometimes religious or political) positions on issues such as the negatives associated with consumerism, the desirability of preserving cultural traditions, the sustainability of industrial food systems, food safety and health, and elitism versus democratization within foodie culture. In terms of methodology, little has been done in the area of phenomenological research on foodies or food-tourist experiences.

Psychology

Psychology seeks to explain human personality and behaviour, including the study of perception, memory, feeling, knowing and thinking. Related to food, we need to consider personal needs, motives, and preferences, and how people experience food and travel. There are many implications for marketing and communications, such as how image is formed and messages received by target audiences.

Cognitive psychology is most relevant, focusing as it does on mental processes. For example, in marketing there is a need to gain the consumer's *attention* and make them aware of food-tourism experiences on offer. How the foodie *perceives* a possible experience, as in authentic versus inauthentic, is a matter for psychological investigation. Aspects of *observation* and *memory* pertain to how memorable a food-related experience will be. *Problem solving* is frequently required of the intrepid food tourist, and this connects with information searching and the desire to learn. *Creativity* enters the picture when foodies are physically and mentally engaged with cooking and presenting food.

All the literature on motivation to travel, both push and pull factors (or seeking and escaping) rests in psychology and social-psychological theory, as do foodie identity and ego-involvement theory. The nature of the food-tourism experience is largely a psychological construct involving cognition, emotion and behaviour, however most of our pertinent theory has been filtered through leisure studies. Finally, personality is related, as in the traits which separate novelty seekers (or neophiles) from conservative neophobes who resist new food experiences.

We discuss psychological concepts throughout the book. Consulting the Contents and Index, the following terms are important: identity; (ego) involvement; motivation; benefits; experience (including leisure and memorable experience; personality.

There is not yet a specific literature on food-tourism psychology, so we are largely confined to applying theory filtered through leisure and travel studies in general. The following research note is one of the few concerning food tourism that employs psychological theory.

Research notes: psychology of food tourism

Ryu, K. & Jang, S. (2006). Intention to experience local cuisine in a travel destination: The modified theory of reasoned action. *Journal of Hospitality and Tourism Research*, **30**, 507-516.

This article proposes a modified theory of reasoned action model in which past behavior was added to the original theory of reasoned action model. Using the proposed model, this study investigated the interdependence between attitudinal and normative components and also examined the model's ability to predict tourist behavioral intentions to try local cuisine in a hypothetical situation. A structural equation analysis showed that the model had strong predictive ability for tourist intentions to experience local cuisine. Attitude and past behavior were significant predictors of tourist behavioral intentions. In addition, the interdependence between attitudinal and normative components was partly supported. Implications of the findings are discussed as well.

Psychographic profiling and segmentation has been employed to explore foodies and food tourists. Methodologically, this approach can combine dimensions of values, personality, attitudes, self-concept, motivation and lifestyle, all with a view to determining the propensity of segments, and their reasons, to make decisions about someone or something like food experiences and travel (Demby, 1989). Elements of ego-involvement scaling are psychographic in nature, particularly those related to identity.

The International Culinary Tourism Association developed 13 'PsychoCulinary profiles' (Chawla et al, 2014:73) from a survey of over 11,000 international respondents. Five major segments were identified, ranging from "the dedicated foodies who love local, organic and authentic fare at one extreme, to the novice foodie who is new to the experience at the other extreme, and with an eclectic segment in between who seems to like a bit of everything." Note how these segments reflect the basic notion of involvement. It is also informative that only 8.1% of respondents considered themselves to be gourmets.

A study of Canadian adults who had travelled for leisure in the past 12 months profiled them on the basis of motivation, preferences and activities. It was conducted by Ipsos Marketing and reported by Chawla et al. (2014: 74-7). Factor clustering generated eight unique segments which focus on food consumption patterns within the overall travel experience, and this led to a concept for combining food experiences with urban, adventure, nightlife and culture interests. Short-break, urban food tourism is extremely popular and the Ipsos Marketing concept suggests a pairing of urban shopping and sightseeing with trendy restaurants, food festivals, and meeting artisan food makers. For culture lovers, the suggested food pairings are cooking classes, market tours, and ethnic neighbourhood tours involving food. Adventurists might find suitable pairings with far-stay experiences, vineyard hikes, or mountaintop dining. Those seeking nightlife should be inclined towards eating in bistros and progressive diners or touring gastropubs.

Chawla et al. (2014: 76-7) commented on the Ipsos Marketing concept by saying that "In this manner culinary tourists are not treated as a small niche segment, but as a diversified community, linked by a shared passion for food, yet touched in different ways depending on their traveler segment profile...Instead of marketing food as a standalone activity, one approach is to 'pair' it with other experiences."

Leisure studies

This has been very influential in applying various discipline-based theories and methods to the study of play, recreation, sport, events and travel experiences. Much of leisure studies is rooted in social-psychology theory and methodology. The concepts of greatest interest to us in this book are leisure experience, serious leisure, specialization, and ego-involvement as applied to leisure pursuits.

According to social psychologists and leisure researchers Mannell and Kleiber (1997) we have to examine leisure experiences not just by observing behaviour (as in cooking, playing, competing in sport, partying, or travel) but through the interplay of internal psychological dispositions (e.g. perceptions, feelings, emotions, beliefs, attitudes, needs, personality characteristics) and situational influences that are part of an individual's social environment (e.g. other people, group norms, human artefacts and media).

To fully study leisure and travel experiences, researchers have looked at what people are doing (i.e. the behavioural or 'conative' dimension, such as cooking, dining out, or travel) moods, emotions and feelings (i.e. the 'affective' or evaluative components, such as expressions of fun, memorable and rewarding experiences), and thoughts and images (i.e. the 'cognitive' component, including learning, problem solving and aesthetic appreciation).

To most people, leisure is seen as a mixture of pleasurable experiences that are generally characterised by feelings of fun, enjoyment and relaxation. As a result of the application of social psychological theory, leisure and event researchers are now more heavily focussed on studying the feelings, attitudes and motivations of people's leisure and travel behaviour, rather than concentrating purely on activities or participation rates. In other words, the variety, frequency and quality of the 'experience' has become more important to study as a measure of overall life satisfaction rather than the actual type of leisure or event that a person participates in (Smith and Godbey, 1991).

It might be tempting to just ask of foodies and food tourists, 'are you having fun'? This simple question has merit, as people generally know when and why they are having fun as opposed to suffering, working, or being obliged to do something. Indeed, there is an entire school of thought about leisure that empha-sizes hedonism and the pursuit of pleasure as fundamental human motives for behaviour of all kinds, including actions that can be interpreted as anti-social or self-destructive (Rojek, 1995). But we have other social-psychologically based leisure theories that can help with an understanding of foodies and food tourism.

When foodies are enjoying the moment, immersed or engaged to the fullest, they might say things like 'I get lost in my cooking, its so enjoyable', or 'this is the best restaurant meal ever', or 'I am totally into shopping at this farmers' market!" They might be expressing what theorists have called 'peak experience', defined by Maslow (1962) as "moments of highest happiness and fulfilment", or Csikszentmihalyi's concept of 'flow' (i.e. "the best moments of people's lives" which occur "…when a person's body or mind is stretched to its limits in a vol-untary effort to accomplish something difficult and worthwhile" (1990:3). When a food tourist loses track of time because the experience is so engaging and enjoy-able, that is a peak experience and one that will be remembered always. These experiences are not created by professionals or automatically a part of attending an event, they are of necessity co-created. We discuss this concept of co-creation more fully in Chapter 7.

Stebbins used the term 'serious leisure' to describe people in society whose work and leisure merge together because of the need to engage in "…the steady pursuit of an amateur, hobbyist, or career volunteer activity that captivates its participants with its complexity and many challenges" (1992, p. 53). Serious leisure is seen as the systematic pursuit, for deep satisfaction that participants find to be substantial and interesting; many devote a major part of their lives to acquiring and expressing the special skills, knowledge and experiences of their serious leisure activity (Stebbins, 2000b). For many people it brings them great pleasure and satisfaction, as well as providing, "personal expression, self-identity enhancement, and self-fulfilment" (Stebbins, 1992, p. 253).

Being an amateur chef is certainly a defining characteristic of many foodies, but is food tourism a hobby? Many foodies pursue cooking as a hobby, and col-lecting food-related things like menus, cookware, recipes, or even collecting 'res-taurants we have eaten in' are hobby-like. We earlier described it in the context of lifestyle, and lifestyles can in part be defined by hobbies, volunteering, and travel. Being a foodie presents opportunities for volunteering at events or getting active in societies devoted to food quality and security. Travel can also be hobby-like in its pursuit of collecting places and experiences that have social value or reflect personal identity, but travel also appeals to professionals who want to learn and make contacts. Any foodie can pursue a 'serious leisure career' that blurs the lines between work and pleasure, and many amateurs have decided to make a living from their hobbies.

Neither 'serious leisure' (nor social world theory, discussed in Chapter 3) makes an explicit connection to travel, in general, or food tourism, in particular. While personal events (e.g. life transitions or achieving goals) are considered within the social-world frame, planned events catering to communities of interest are not explicitly incorporated. According to Stebbins (1993: 8) "each serious leisure activity tends to generate its own social world within which it is pursued and with which participants come to identify, often quite strongly." Stebbins (1993) in *The Barbershop Singer*, concurred with Unruh's conceptualization of social-world as a voluntary, therefore leisure choice. Stebbins (p. 5) also argued that Unruh failed to consider the importance in social worlds of sub-cultures, saying we "find associated with each social world a rich and unique array of special norms, values, beliefs, styles, moral principles, performance standards, and the like".

Bryan (1977: 175) described specialization as "...a continuum of behaviour from the general to the particular, reflected by equipment and skills used in the sport, and activity setting preferences". Bryan hypothesized that as experience in an activity increases, people will progress from more general to specialized behaviour and related patterns of consumption. Applied to foodies, the theory suggests that through experience foodies get more involved and specialized, and that characteristic styles of participation emerge, such as the obvious differences between novice cooks and those with fabulous skills and kitchens to match. It might be extended to suggest that involved and experienced foodies are more likely to travel for food experiences, and in this sense it is close to a serious leisure career in nature. However, we do not have much empirical evidence of this specialization tendency for foodies, and it is even problematic to say what specialization would look like. More research is needed here, but there is some evidence in our research findings that event attendance is linked, with the most involved foodies seeking out learning and competitive events.

Geography

Geographers study human-resource interactions, especially spatial and temporal patterns of human activity and including impacts on the environment. Concepts we are particularly interested in that have a geographical component are food-scapes, terroir, and foodies' relationships with the environment such as a concern for fresh and local, and knowing the provenance of food.

A central theme in this book is the exploration of why foodies travel for food-experiences, and their preferences, so it's essential to consider their travel patterns and destination choices. Only a limited amount of research has been reported on this matter, so we have only bits and pieces of evidence. We will take a traditional view of geography here, emphasizing spatial and temporal patterns of movement and human-environment interactions - all connected to food.

Lists of top foodie destinations are easy to find, although they inevitably reflect the biases and orientation of the bloggers or publishers. The following excerpts from the website Departures is interesting in that their orientation is toward hands-on experiences, often provided in specific establishments (source: www. departures.com/articles/global-foodie-getaways; accessed Nov. 18, 2013).

> *From cheese tastings in Bordeaux with the head chef of Chez Panisse to intimate master classes with Jean-Georges Vongerichten in his kitchen, hands-on culinary trips offer an opportunity to return home with a new-found mastery of cooking's secrets. To experience the flavors of turmeric, lemongrass and coconut milk, Thailand's Four Seasons Chiang Mai offers travellers the opportunity to shop at a local market and then prepare a lunch using local produce. If seafood is the order, Nova Scotia's Trout Point Lodge offers classes in how to cook with lobster, mussels and oysters.*

> *Not all culinary trips have to involve slicing and dicing. Whether a traveler's preference is fine dining and white-table-cloth establishments or charming hidden-gem eateries (and their legendary treats), it's possible to pick epicurean destinations that give an intimate glimpse into a new gourmet world. Take a pilgrimage to Copenhagen, Denmark, to dine at Noma, where foodies clamor to experience Rene Redzepi's revolutionary food experience. Or venture to Tokyo for a personally curated tour of the city's best eats.*

Here is another list, from the website Bunkycooks (www.bunkycooks.com/2013/07/the-ten-best-food-destinations-in-the-world/, accessed Nov. 18, 2013). This one favours cities and regions and embodies the concept of foodscape:

> *The experience around food is what makes a particular meal, dish, or destination unique and able to stand out above all others. It's about the place, the time, and the people and "the best meal" can be found in a fine dining restaurant or in a crowded street market. If you've ever heard the expression, "Food doesn't travel well," it's true. How can you recreate that special moment influenced by place and time and have it be as memorable for someone else as it was for you?*

> *With our current food obsessed culture, culinary travel is becoming the most popular reason to visit many places around the world. While we travel great distances to enjoy unique food, wine, and spirits, it is also important to be educated about the region and its people, learn about the history and architecture, and have time to take in the scenery and the surroundings. Those things have as much impact on the food experience as does the food itself.*

Bunkycooks' top picks are: South of France; Barcelona; Italy; Mexico City; Taipei; Morocco; London; New Orleans; New York City, and Charleston. There might be a little American bias here, but read what they say about Charleston:

Charleston, South Carolina is now the No. 1 travel destination in the world and much of that success is due to its booming food culture and the region's Lowcountry cuisine. This charming coastal town with its stunning architecture has a restaurant nearly every few feet. There is an abundance of incredibly talented chefs, fabulous local produce, and access to some of the freshest seafood on the East Coast. It's a winning combination. While classic Southern dishes, like Shrimp and Grits and a multitude of versions of Fried Chicken, appear on many menus, don't overlook the new generation of chefs making their mark reviving heirloom ingredients, making world class charcuterie, and using the whole animal (from snout to tail) on their menus.

Foodscape is partly a geographic concept and partly a social construction, describing areas where food and consumers meet. It could apply to a restaurant, a district in a city, or a farming area. Similar terms are *winescape* (Bruwer and Lesschaeve 2012) applied to wine regions, and *experiencescape* applied to any environment devoted to leisure, tourism or lifestyle pursuits (O'Dell and Billing, 2005). Everett (2012) referred to 'tastescapes' as areas drawing on the concepts of purity and escape in pursuit of food tourism. The word *servicescape* is found in the marketing literature (Bitner, 1992) and has given rise to the very useful methods of service blueprinting (setting specifications for how customers are to interact with the setting and service providers) and service mapping (an evaluation technique to ensure that blueprinting works).

A food trail could create a foodscape where none had existed by suddenly bringing food tourists directly to the producers within their rural or seacoast landscapes. Attention would have to be given to information and signage, the nature of host-guest contacts, and the provision of both essential services to the visitor and specialist foodie experiences. Whenever travel is involved, there are spatial and temporal dimensions to consider. "How long does it take?"; "Where do people spend a night and eat?"; and "Who is responsible for providing information and services?"

History

An historical perspective on foodies and food tourism should consist of documenting, verifying and explaining the change process: the evolution of ideology and attitudes towards food and travel experiences; the nature and meaning of food celebrations; the evolving nature of foodie cultures; examples set by pioneers, celebrities, proponents; food and social class-precedents for food tourism development; heritage as a resource-cumulative effects of food cultures and food tourism; food and rural landscape conservation and community life-forces and trends affecting the evolution of food cultures and food tourism, and national food policy.

A number of scholarly works have explicitly taken an historical perspective on food in culture. For example, Rotherham (2008, p 48), in a British context, examined how "Food, festival and feast emerge from communities and their landscapes." He considered the influence of landscape on what food was produced, and how it was prepared on the nature of celebration. Great feasts emerged at certain times of the year reflecting the cycle of food production, including those of hunting and fishing. Symbolic representations have been important as well, particularly to reinforce social status. Documenting how the rich and royals ate in comparison to the poor and lowly sheds light on how food and its preparation have always figured in the politics and power structures of society. Over time, however, distinct aspects of local foods disappeared through the industrialization of agriculture, and cities became disconnected from their hinterlands. Only recently has a concern for provenance returned to prominence. Historic links between cuisine and landscape now need to be reinvented, argued Rotherham, which requires finding suitable markets – hence a role for food tourism in landscape conservation and design. A coherent national strategy is required to achieve such a lofty goal. Rotherham concluded by noting how some initiatives like that of the National Trust aim to employ special events to foster a rural renaissance that celebrates local distinction.

Although beyond the scope of this book, also of interest are works by Beardsworth and Kiel (1997), Strong (2003), Grew (2000), and Haber (2007), details of which can be found at the end of the chapter.

■ Economics and business

Macro economics covers global economic conditions, sometimes known as political economy because of the pre-occupation of governments with fostering economic growth and the fact that national economies are heavily influenced by political ideology. Micro-economics applies to the operation of industries and businesses, including marketing and consumer behaviour. The book *Tourism Economics and Policy* by Dwyer et al. (2010) provides all the background theory for explaining the economics of food tourism, and *Event Tourism* by Getz (2013) is also relevant in explaining concepts, strategies and methods that are germane to all special-interest forms of tourism.

Visitors spend money that circulates within an area and generates value or income for residents (jobs), businesses (profits) and governments (through taxes). The aim of any form of special-interest tourism is to attract tourists who would not otherwise travel to a particular place, so in the case of foodies there has to be a special reason to motivate the trip. This differentiates niche marketing from mass marketing, and it requires the kind of market intelligence put forward in this book. If you do not understand what motivates the foodie, you will not be good at attracting them.

Another important point in tourism economics is that niche markets should be high in yield, not necessarily in volume. It is far better to attract a small number of dedicated food tourists willing to spend a lot of money for the right kind of experiences than to generate huge numbers of tourists who each spend very little money. The reasons are several, including the reduction of negative impacts generated by large volumes and related infrastructure, and the fact that many food-related experiences cannot accommodate large numbers (e.g. quality restaurants are often the smallest).

Economically speaking, not all food tourists will be the same. Compare, for example, a family travelling by car, renting a self-catering unit, and cooking for themselves after shopping at the local farm or fish market, with a couple on a short break staying in a luxury spa and spending freely on wine and gourmet meals. Both create value, but there are profound differences in where the money is spent and how it benefits local food producers or service providers and how it might generate tax revenue for different levels of government. Destinations have to understand how different kinds of food-related experiences will impact on their economy and plan accordingly. Some destinations will do better through specialization, such as getting touring families into remote areas, while others might prosper through diverse offerings to foodies.

To extract the maximum spend from each food tourist (while ensuring their satisfaction) requires attention to the supply and value chains. These are inter-related concepts, and both are important to food tourism. These definitions are taken from an online source:www.businessdictionary.com/

Supply chain: Entire network of entities, directly or indirectly interlinked and interdependent in serving the same consumer or customer. It comprises of vendors that supply raw material, producers who convert the material into products, warehouses that store, distribution centers that deliver to the retailers, and retailers who bring the product to the ultimate user. Supply chains underlie value chains as, without them, no producer has the ability to give customers what they want, when and where they want, at the price they want.

Value chain: Interlinked value-adding activities that convert inputs into outputs which, in turn, add to the bottom line and help create competitive advantage. A value chain typically consists of (1) inbound distribution or logistics, (2) manufacturing operations, (3) outbound distribution or logistics, (4) marketing and selling, and (5) after-sales service. These activities are supported by (6) purchasing or procurement, (7) research and development, (8) human resource development, (9) and corporate infrastructure.

Hall and Page (2005, p. 248) identified five culinary supply chain morphologies in Australia and New Zealand including: direct sales; the industrial food supply chain, in which the consumer buys from a retailer, who buys from a wholesaler, who buys from a producer; a cooperative in which a group of producers run a market; a restaurant supply chain in which the consumer purchases meals from the restaurant that obtains supplies from producers, and a network of producers who supply markets as well as restaurants, and who cooperate in promotions as well as sales efforts. Smith and Xiao (2008) conducted research on supply chains for farmers' markets, festivals, and restaurants. They drew the conclusion that insufficient is known about culinary supply chains; governments therefore are disadvantaged when it comes to achieving tourism goals or reacting to shocks to the system. A particular problem they noted was the existence of barriers to chefs who wanted to source local and fresh produce.

Think of supply chains in terms of logistics, or how to connect food tourists with food, meals and food-related experiences. Sometimes the tourists comes to the supplier/producer, which has the great benefit of putting money (i.e. creating value) directly into the hands of food producers and other local businesses, such as tour guides. In many cases the food has to get harvested, processed, moved, stored, retailed, prepared by chefs and served to customers in eating establishments far from the point of origin. In complex supply chains value is dispersed and might very well be minimal for the farmer or fisher. Furthermore, supply chains are often controlled by monopolistic or foreign entities that syphon profits away from the people who most need income while at the same time minimizing or completely avoiding local tax payments. In particular, it cannot be assumed that attracting food tourists to cities will generate substantial value for remote suppliers and producers.

Two principles for food-tourism planning follow:

- Where possible, food tourists should be encouraged and facilitated to disperse widely in their pursuit of fresh and local foods and unique, authentic experiences, thereby creating value for local suppliers and producers.

- In all cases, value-adding activities should be established or facilitated in order to ensure maximum value is created for destination residents and businesses – especially food producers.

Obviously there are issues arising from the first principle, including the need for infrastructure and concerns for possible negative impacts in sensitive cultures and environments. To implement the second principle will necessitate detailed research into how food tourism supply chains operate and where value is created for different links in the chain. How exactly governments and tourism organizations can influence value creation and its allocation is a matter for local politicians and economists, but there are several generic strategies available:

- Incentives to buy local and support national businesses: such as tax reductions, grants, better infrastructure, research, training.

- Penalties for food imports: higher taxes or service fees.

- Restrictions on who can do business (given that food security is of critical national importance).

- Collaboration: forming food-tourism clusters will potentially strengthen the bargaining power and marketing reach of producers and suppliers, thereby enabling them to capture more value.

Consider the following data from Charleston, South Carolina, frequently cited as being a culinary capital in America. While not focused on foodies, the study does reveal the importance of food as an attraction, satisfier, and generator of tourist expenditure.

Summary: 2012 Charleston, South Carolina, Visitor Survey

Prepared by Kevin Smith and Raymond Rhodes Office of Tourism Analysis, Department of Hospitality and Tourism Management, School of Business, College of Charleston, Charleston, SC 29424. Thanks to Dr. Bing Pan.

Charleston visitors were primarily 50 years or older, college educated, married or living with a partner, and have upper-middle income

They were mainly from adjacent states. Most visitors arrived via car, followed by airplane.

More than half of overnight visitors reported staying in hotels, followed by staying in inns and staying with friends and/or family.

The Charleston Area Convention and Visitors Bureau (CACVB) web site still remained the most used online information source for planning a Charleston trip.

Family and friends continued to be strong sources of information and influence for visitors' decision-making, as was personal knowledge acquired from previous trips to Charleston.

The majority of Charleston visitors in 2012 had visited Charleston at least once before just as in 2011, and average traveling party sizes remain consistent year-over-year.

History and local cuisine continued to be among the most important reasons to visit and most enjoyable aspects of a Charleston area visit.

Average total daily spending (per person) by overnight visitors for 2012 was $205 locally in Charleston, an $11 increase from spending in 2011 and a $22 increase over spending in 2010.

Overnight Charleston visitors spent more time in the area with an average length of stay of 4.1 nights, up from 3.4 nights in 2011 and 3.7 nights in 2010. Along with historic sites and the overall historic ambiance, Charleston's food and restaurant scene was also among the top three most enjoyable aspects of visiting Charleston in 2012.

Food tourism has often been identified as a key tool in both urban and rural economic development, and as an important factor influencing patterns of consumption (Henderson, 2004; McMahon, 2005; Tikkanen, 2007). To illustrate this point, (McMahon, 2005) discussed the successful case of New Orleans, Louisiana, which attracts many tourists through 'Cajun bayou culture' and specifically its culinary traditions. But evidence on the economic impacts of food tourism is mostly anecdotal or deduced from non-specific tourist expenditure surveys. To measure food tourism impacts will require highly focused research. The following method is waiting to be tested.

First, consider that food tourism has several measureable value components:

1   *The value of all expenditures made* in an area (and accruing to local businesses) *by dedicated food tourists* (i.e. those who travel primarily for a food-related purpose); this has to be divided into domestic tourism and international. This is measured through the sampling of tourists, selecting only those who have travelled for a food-related experience (e.g. to an event, a destination restaurant, or a market). It will also be useful to estimate the proportion of trip motivation attributable to food experiences, and the importance of food to overall satisfaction with the visit.

   Method: quota samples taken at restaurants, food events, markets, and other places where food lovers are expected to gather. Random sampling is not possible, and it will not be possible to estimate the proportion of all tourists who are food tourists in this way (see below).

2   *The value of all expenditures made by all travellers* within an area, both domestic and international, on food and related purchases, including: restaurant meals; catered events; groceries; beverages; fresh produce (e.g. at farms, ports or markets), and food souvenirs. This is measured by sampling all travellers (taking a representative cross-section) and determining what they spent money on. A large sample of visitors to the area is required, and from this sample it will be possible to estimate the proportion that are dedicated food tourists, then apply to the spending estimates obtained from (a).

3   *The induced, future value of purchases of exported food products* attributable to the favourable influence of food experiences in the area. This is addressed by asking all respondents in (1) and (2) about their satisfaction, brand recognition (i.e. what is from the area, what is it known for), future intentions to purchase the area's products and WOM and social media activity vis-a-vis their experiences. Dedicated food tourists and others can then be compared.

These measures will provide a good estimate of the value of food tourism, but it should be noted that it pertains only to direct expenditures or the 'contribution' of food-tourism. Additional data and analysis would be required to estimate full economic impact including indirect effects. As well, a supply-chain analysis could also be undertaken to determine the backward linkages and foodways associated with restaurant meals, catering and food purchases made in the area.

Forces and trends

Food tourism, like many other lifestyle pursuits, arises from abundance and growing discretionary income. Travellers will always have to eat, but to make a journey solely or mainly because of a love of food or beverages is an indulgence, a luxury. And while that fact engenders criticism, it is no different than many other special interests that generate tourism, including sport, music, and an interest in history. Accordingly, all the forces and trends in leisure and tourism apply to a greater or lesser extent (see Figure 2.3).

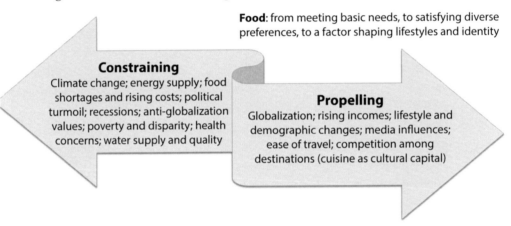

Figure 2.3: Forces propelling and constraining food tourism

Forces propelling growth begin with the complexities of economic and social globalisation which results in a more integrated global economy, rising affluence (but not shared by everyone!), the influence of mass and social media, diaspora or mass migrations, and heavy competition for tourists. As discussed below, there are also demographic and lifestyle forces to consider, and the fact that travel has never been easier or (in relative terms) cheaper.

The 'experience economy' concept popularized by Pine and Gilmore (1999), and their subsequent book on authenticity (Gilmore and Pine, 2007), are highly relevant to food tourism. Food is not a commodity to foodies and food tourists, it is an experience in which authenticity figures prominently; it's also a symbolic experience that involves much more than the food and place, although they do provide meaning. The Pine and Gilmore model stresses four dimensions of experience that clearly cover food: education (the desire to learn, as in taking cooking lessons), aesthetics (all senses being engaged, including the atmosphere), escapism (getting away from routine, finding the romantic, food adventuring) and entertainment (in part the chef and servers as entertainers, or food within entertainment premises and events). And their model makes it clear that the experience is also dependent upon active or passive involvement (the degree to which the foodie is a participant versus a spectator), and immersion or absorption. Absorption means bringing the performance to the customer, as in a stage play, whereas immersion requires the foodie to get mentally into the experience (as in being fully engaged).

There are always constraints on growth, and sooner or later one or more of these constraining forces will become a check on growth, or even halt and reverse it. Most of these apply to tourism in general, especially concerns over energy and global climate change. But health concerns in particular threaten food tourism, including fear: of contaminated foodstuffs, of genetic modification, of unhealthy eating and drinking habits. If a region experiences environmental or health issues of any kind, that can influence perceptions of food safety or quality. On the other hand, countries like Sweden can gain from a food brand that reflects its commitment to sustainability and green tourism.

In general, the diagram summarizes the main trends in food that affect tourism, namely the historic transition from a preoccupation with meeting basic needs (which is still the main issue in many parts of the world!) to an ability to satisfy diverse special preferences, to food as a factor shaping lifestyles and identities. These themes run throughout this book and are supported by research evidence and analysis.

The Barcelona Field Studies Centre identified five key consumer trends affecting culinary tourism (ontarioculinary.com/uncategorized/tasty-tidbits-consumer-trends; accessed Nov. 9, 2013).

The first was called 'trading up', reflecting the tendency for higher levels of affluence to result in more spending on non-essentials. With regard to food, this trend means that when food essentials have been met and consumers can spend more, they spend it on discretionary meals, and pay more attention to getting better quality or food that meets specific dietary requirements. Health has become a key determinant for many, causing rising demand for organic and ecological produce, which tends to mean fresh and local, while other food-lovers indulge special tastes or seeking greater variety.

Second, and linked to the above-mentioned trends, some observers believe that consumers are increasingly rejecting industrial food-production models. Hence, the slow food movement has become more prominent, giving rise to slow villages and slow tourism. The pace of life has accelerated, people are more stressed, and good food experiences can be considered an antidote.

In the third trend, demographics plays a role, with an aging population in many countries, and particularly the baby boomers who are well educated, empty-nesters, with high incomes fuelling demand for all forms of tourism and indulgence, including spas and second homes. Also on the rise have been singles and childless couples with two incomes (i.e., household size is shrinking).

The fourth trend was stated as "growth of the multi-cultured consumer", or multiculturalism, reflecting diaspora (mass migration), globalisation, mass and social media. What this means for food is a willingness and desire to try new things (i.e. novelty seeking), and the assimilation of many new foodstuffs and cuisines into daily life.

Finally, the Barcelona trend spotters identified the roles of celebrity chefs and the media as having a major influence on consumption. This has led to more interest in learning how to cook, trying different cuisines, and perhaps in healthy eating (it depends on who you admire!). In this context, tourism futurist Ian Yeoman (2012) believes food is 'cultural capital' for destinations which now provide cultural experiences; in the future, consuming real food might be a rare luxury.

Another take on trends comes from the website abouTourism: (aboutourism. wordpress.com/tag/culinary-tourism/) accessed Nov. 9. 2013

Facts & stats

- Culinary tourism tends to be largely a domestic tourism activity, with consumers travelling to places to eat and drink specific (usually local) produce.

- A domestic survey of leisure travellers in America found that 17% engaged in culinary related activities.

- The International Culinary Tourism Association predicts that this will grow rapidly in the coming years. According to USA Today (27 Feb 2007), 27 million Americans have made culinary activities part of their travels in the last three years.

- In the UK, food tourism is estimated to be worth nearly $8 billion each year. International culinary tourism is less significant than its domestic counterpart. Whilst consumers do consider food when deciding where to take a holiday, it is not usually the main consideration.

- The growth in popularity of ethnic cuisines like Thai, Indian, North African, Mexican and Chinese throughout the industrialised countries is attributable to a significant degree to tourism where visitors sample local foods and develop a taste for them.

- Food and drink festivals constitute the sole instance where the decision to travel is taken solely on the grounds of the gastronomic experiences offered. These are becoming more prevalent, in particular in Europe. Whilst this segment is growing, at present there are estimated to be no more than one million international culinary tourists travelling each year.

- Gastronomic consumers tend to be couples that have above-average income, are usually professionals and are aged 30 to 50. This correlates closely to the demographics of the cultural tourist.

- The International Culinary Tourism Association states that on average, food travellers spend around $1,200 per trip, with over one-third (36% or $425) of their travel budget going towards food-related activities. Those considered to be "deliberate" food travellers (i.e. where culinary activities are the key reason for the trip) tend to spend a significantly higher amount of their overall travel budget (around 50%) on food-related activities.

2

Summary

To study and understand food tourism, a framework was provided which incorporates the interrelated elements of:

- Core phenomenon (food-tourism experiences and their meanings),
- Antecedents (the motives of food tourism and what it means to be a foodie, including involvement, identity, constraints on behaviour, decision making and social -world influences),
- Outcomes (at the personal, social, environmental and economic levels, including the economic and place-marketing gains that destinations desire),
- Planning and marketing (by destination marketing organizations, suppliers and producers of experiences), and
- The dynamic spatial and temporal patterns and processes that link to geography, history, policy, and knowledge creation.

Look for these elements and themes throughout the book.

The study of foodies and food tourism was examined, particularly in the context of where and how it forms part of food, tourism and hospitality studies. Food studies incorporates the issues of food supplies, sustainable production and security, including the trend towards favouring local foods. In hospitality studies the emphasis is placed on food service, meals, chefs and cooking. Dining out is an experience, usually social, that requires careful design to attract and satisfy foodies. Tourism studies naturally focus on the travel experiences, but also on destination planning, development and marketing. Many individual suppliers and packagers/wholesalers of food-tourism experiences are also important. Food tourism is a rural and urban phenomenon of great importance around the world.

In the social sciences and humanities the study of food, foodies and food tourism is widespread. A good place to start is with cultural anthropology, which concentrates on the importance of food within culture and introduces the important concept of authenticity. We also look at sociology, philosophy, and psychology (all foundation disciplines) and the important contributions of leisure studies - particularly with regard to the nature of leisure experiences and serious leisure. Geography was found to be important in providing insights for various places having special attractiveness to foodies, and this connects to the concept of terroir. The history of food and food tourism is of interest, and some references have been provided. From economics and business studies we get the concepts of supply chains and value chains, which are critical for developing the full economic potential of food tourism. We also looked at how food tourism generates economic benefits, and how to measure them.

This chapter concluded with an examination of the forces shaping food tourism and related trends, arguing that propelling forces will continue to cause growth for some time but that constraining forces - particularly competition - must always be considered.

Study questions

1   Explain the framework for understanding and creating knowledge in food tourism, and illustrate each of the elements.

2   Discuss key issues considered within food studies. Why should we all be concerned about sustainability and security?

3   How can the experiential and social elements of dining out be designed to attract and satisfy foodies?

4   Explain how food tourism fits into agri-tourism and helps in the development of rural and remote areas.

5   Select one of the disciplines or fields of study that are important to the understanding of foodies and food tourism and discuss its main theoretical and/or practical contributions.

6   Discuss the importance of the emergence of gastronomy as a field of study, and particularly its popularity amongst flexible learning mature-aged students.

7   What is cultural authenticity and why is it important in food tourism?

8   Define psychographics and explain its use in segmenting food tourists.

9   What are the components of a leisure experience? How can we use this theory in understanding foodies and food tourism?

10 Give examples from food tourism to explain the meanings of serious leisure and recreation specialization.

11 Define value and supply chains and show their relevance to economic development through food tourism.

12 Discuss the growth of food tourism and its causes, and speculate on which trends will likely continue to be important; give reasons.

Additional reading

Beardsworth, A., & Keil, T. (1997). *Sociology on the Menu: An Invitation to the Study of Food and Society*. London: Routledge.

Boniface, P. (2003). *Tasting Tourism: Travelling For Food and Drink*. Farnham, Surrey: Ashgate Publishing.

Gale Encyclopedia of Food and Culture (2004). Gale Virtual Reference Library: www.gale.com/eBooks.

Grew, R. (2000). *Food in Global History*. Westview Press.

Haber, B. (2007). Culinary history vs. food history. In, A. Smith (ed.), *The Oxford Companion to American Food and Drink*, pp. 179–180. Oxford University Press.

Hjalager, A-M., and Richards, G. (2002). *Tourism and Gastronomy*. London: Routledge.

Long, L., (2003). *Culinary Tourism*. Lexington, KY: University Of Kentucky Press.

Strong, R. (2003). *Feast: A History of Grand Eating*. London: Pimlico.

2

3 The Foodie - Identity, Involvement and Social Worlds

Learning objectives

Readers are expected to learn the following from this chapter:

- What it means to be a foodie in terms of behaviour, personal and social identity
- The concept of ego-involvement and its usefulness in understanding foodies and food tourism.
- The meaning and importance of authenticity and novelty seeking for foodies.
- Social world theory, and how foodie behaviour and travel preferences can be influenced.
- Neophobia and neophilia as personality traits, and how they shape food tourism.
- Food as both a hygiene factor and travel motivator.

Who and what are foodies?

In Chapter 1 we provided a simple definition of a foodie as a 'food lover' and "one who incorporates food, its preparation and enjoyment into their lifestyle". This chapter is an elaboration of the concept of foodie, drawing from multiple authors and our own research in Australia and other countries.

A good starting point is to hear the voices of foodies and food tourists (see Figure 3.1). Many people travel for food and love to share their experiences. Anonymous quotes from various blogs, websites, and our own research tell a story of love, desire, passion and fulfilment! Foodies know they are involved in something special pertaining to their leisure and lifestyle, that it involves their personal and social identity, and that food tourism exists and has significance for them. If there are key words to look for, they are 'passion', 'lover', and 'experience'.

Little research has been conducted on the voices of foodies and food tourists. One example is by Natilli, Pavone and Romano (2012) who did a text analysis of an Italian wine and food blog to determine what topics were being discussed, the language used, and the importance of travelling among those engaging in their on-going discussions. This is passive netnography, similar to the work of Getz and Patterson (2013) on social worlds that included food lovers (which is discussed at the end of this chapter). The Italian researchers found the main themes to be 'food and wine tourism' (34.53% of words), 'gourmet vocabulary in the kitchen' (25.46%), 'recipes' (12.88%), 'critics' food and wine' (11.77%) and 'gastronomic culture' (10.72%). Although the discourse was influenced by the blogger, the analysis shows the prominence of tourism in foodie and wine-lover communities.

A selection of direct but anonymous quotes from websites and research reports

"I am a travelling food lover and I am so excited to be a part of this group. Food makes everything great from travelling to networking and especially during the holidays".

"I am passionate about cooking and travelling but most importantly eating"

"In my searches, I stumbled across an interesting term…Food Tourism (aka Culinary Tourism). Essentially it means experiencing a city's culture through memorable food experiences. I guess I've always known in my heart that I did this, but now I know it has a name. In fact, it even has its own Wikipedia page so it's pretty much a thing now."

"Local food is one of the things I am most interested in when I'm travelling. My journal from my round the world trip mentions what I ate every single day! It's funny how I can remember many of those meals so clearly."

"There are some excellent restaurants delivering the potential of the produce in Tasmania. Others are not so produce-driven. So don't travel around Tasmania expecting every restaurant to deliver beautifully cooked local produce - just like everywhere else in the world you have to know where to eat."

"I prefer going on a wine trail and tasting locally made wine, and my boyfriend is more interested in attending food festivals or shopping gourmet food but we both love cooking classes and dining out for a unique and memorable experience."

"I travel a lot with my wife and we have preferences and enjoy the same things. We always like to eat the local food. We have travelled to destinations for food purposes only. We were in Barcelona last year; just for a city break, and Barcelona is the only city that we would actually go back to for food purposes, and we have been in many destinations in Europe for food. You have Gaudi and other cultural attractions to add on to the food experiences."

Figure 3.1: The voices of foodies and food tourists

Let us now look at some definitions and investigations of what it is to be a foodie.

Watson et al. (2008) said: "The term foodie was coined by Harpers and Queen magazine… but came to prominence in the humorous paperback *The Official Foodie Handbook* by Barr and Levy (1984) who defined foodies this way (p.6):

> *A Foodie is a person who is very very very interested in food. Foodies are the ones talking about food in any gathering – salivating over restaurants, recipes, radicchio. They don't think they are being trivial – Foodies consider food to be an art, on a level with painting or drama.*

According to Watson et al. (2008: 290):

> *Barr and Levy's (1984) definition pointed out the then presumed differences between a gourmet and a foodie: a gourmet was seen typically as an older, upper-class gentleman; foodies were described as 'children of the consumer boom' (p. 7), usually younger couples 'from the ambitious classes' (p. 6), who pronounced judgement on food they had eaten in a restaurant, and attempted to replicate at home. Foodies 'collect' food experiences and visits to celebrated restaurants, much as tourists collect souvenirs.*

Johnston and Baumann (2007; 2009) make an important distinction between two discourses on 'foodies', one reflecting democracy and the other connected to distinction and money. There are advocates who believe foodies are democratic, enjoying all kinds of food, and not snobbish. This is associated with the movement toward healthy eating, favouring local produce, fair trade programmes, and a preference for ecological or organic foods. In other words, being a foodie is part of a major trend that everyone can participate in.

On the other hand, some critics think it is a snobbish, elitist trend - that foodies are privileged, spoiled, up-market gourmets who engage in conspicuous consumption. This resonates with earlier definitions of gastronomy, that were highlighted in Chapter 2. These foodies might be accumulating cultural capital through food consumption, or in other words they are trying to fit into a lifestyle or social group that requires a lot of knowledge and talk about great food experiences that only the educated and rich can afford.

Both of these discourses have some merit, and you can probably find foodies who seem to fit into one or the other categories. But behaviour, whether it be conspicuous consumption at a five-star restaurant or weekly trips to the farmers' market, does not define the foodie. Being a foodie is a matter of personal identity, or how one feels about oneself. This self-identification theme is important, and it leads to our employment of ego-involvement theory to help segment and understand foodies and food tourism. The next discussion highlights this critical point.

Foodies as omnivores

An omnivore is a creature who eats just about anything, but in the discourses on culture, food and social status, and on elitism versus democratization, it means something else. The basic argument is in contrast to Bourdieu's (1979) contention that social status, and habitus (that is the place in which one is acculturated), determines taste and utilizes judgements of good taste in exercising power. The elite might eat better, or more, or different from the rest of us, but is their understanding of what is good food or good taste necessarily relevant to the rest of us? The 'omnivore' thesis claims that you can no longer be identified by what you do, whether it is the music you listen to or what you eat. According to the critic Shamus Khan (2010, pp 731–32), in reviewing the Johnston and Baumann (2009) book,

> Whereas Pierre Bourdieu's distinction was an exclusionary one, wherein different classes had distinct tastes, today's distinction is more democratic, wherein different groups have overlapping tastes, yet wherein the particular conglomeration and articulation of tastes can reveal distinctions nonetheless. These overlaps can create the appearance of democracy while the particular conglomeration of the elite omnivore helps maintain a reality of inequality.

To extend this reasoning, consider the recent phenomenon of selling 'gourmet' hamburgers and hot dogs - what does it mean? And why have certain food styles, like TexMex caught on around the world? Will foodies eat anything? Does consumption of a hot dog, however gourmet, indicate that foodies are being democratic (because, presumably, this is a food associated with the 'working class' or 'rednecks') or that they are seeking distinction (a kind of snobbery) because the lowly hot dog has now been elevated to gourmet status? In short, observing behaviours alone can be deceptive and does not give a full account of what it constitutes to be a foodie.

Identity and involvement

Foodies cannot be solely identified by looking at them, nor by studying their behaviour - although important clues will be presented. Foodies identify themselves, and anyone can claim to be one. We need to examine that proposition in detail, through theory and research findings, and see exactly how it leads to food tourism.

Even if a person feels they are a foodie, just how involved are they? Are they beginners, just looking for other foodies to connect with? Or are they highly-involved sophisticates with plenty of experience under their belts? Most people who are involved with any leisure or lifestyle pursuit can easily determine whether they are a little bit involved, or a lot, but we employ involvement scales to get at the various dimensions of involvement, then we use levels of involvement to analyse food-tourism behaviour and preferences.

■ Identity

Benckendorff and Pearce (2012, p. 175) have stated "Social psychology offers two dominant theories of identity: social identity theory and identity theory."

Identity theory is based on McCall and Simmons' (1966) role identity theory. Individuals will base their actions on "...how they would like to see themselves and how they like to be seen by others." So in the context of events, identity is seen as being internal "...and consisting of internalised meanings and expectations associated with a role." There are two components: the role itself, and the identity associated with the role. "Identity theory suggests that event attendees define themselves by attending events that carry symbolic significance." (Benckendorff and Pearce, p. 172).

Social identity theory is derived from Festinger (1954). It focuses on the ways in which individuals perceive and categorise themselves, most often relative to relationships with groups. Identities are shaped by group membership and identity is a function of attachment to a group, including how people feel they are perceived by group members. Identity may foster communitas, social prestige, and self esteem. This theory has been applied to crowd behaviour at events, and collective identities of sport fans (e.g. the sport spectator identification scale by Branscombe and Wann, 1992).

Communitas is a concept established in the works of anthropologist Victor Turner (1969: 96) who said it was an unstructured togetherness and a feeling of equality. People sharing a common interest often desire to meet with one another in a spirit of sharing and celebration which we can call communitas. The desire to belong, related to social identity, is something that many foodies feel - whether on a tour, at home with friends for dinner, or at a festival. In other words foodies frequently yearn for the opportunity to affirm or express their identity in social contexts.

Consumption of event or travel experiences therefore involves the absorption of symbolic meanings which link to one's identity. For example, attending a food festival might meet generic needs for entertainment and socializing, but attending a cooking class offered by a chef, or travelling to Tuscany for a food experience, offers high symbolic meaning to aficionados.

Specific to foodies, Johnston and Baumann (2009) observed that media coverage and the ways for foodies to connect with each other and to share their passions have all multiplied, making food-related activities and culinary tourism an important, postmodern consumer phenomenon. Liu et al. (2012) have even stud-ied the phenomena of foodie communities proliferating online via the medium of food photography sharing site Flickr.com. Cairns, Johnston and Baumann (2010) proposed that a new culture has evolved wherein a consumer now views food as an essential aspect of their identity. They also believe that gender roles are being negotiated through food, and that being a foodie has different implications for men and women within foodie culture. Leal and Arellanoe (2012) explored Consumers' Identity Projects related to being a foodie with a view to gaining insights on how these consumers construct a self-identity based on symbols and meanings provided by the marketplace (after Arnould and Thompson, 2005).

Carins et al. (2010) showed that a foodie positions him/herself as a cultural connoisseur who is knowledgeable in the realm of cutting edge culinary trends, while Baumann and Johnston (2009) believed that a foodie upholds a cultural sophistication with a preference for a genuine and original experience. They also believed that foodie identity is reflected in performances in which the foodie demonstrates knowledge and expertise.

■ Involvement

Havitz and Dimanche (1997: 246) defined ego-involvement as "…an unobservable state of motivation, arousal or interest toward a recreational activity or associated product, evoked by a particular stimulus or situation, and which has drive prop-erties". With regard to leisure, travel and lifestyle pursuits, it has been confirmed that people's preferences, behaviour and satisfaction are affected by their level of involvement with products and pursuits, including wine. How one actually becomes involved is another question, and more difficult to answer. Havitz and Dimanche (1999), based on a meta-analysis of 53 leisure involvement studies, concluded that strong support has been found for involvement as a mediator of purchases and participation. The evidence they cited contained little about the link between recreational involvement and travel.

Hu (2010), undertaking doctoral-level research in China, studied visitors to a food festival with a focus on their expenditures. Most respondents were young, with more females than males, and predominantly locals in groups. So they do not constitute a real tourism sample, and indeed, their main motivations were generic (social and family related) rather than food-specific. They were however, judged to be somewhat more highly involved with food than general food con-sumers, with special interests in cooking and taste judging. With regard to food involvement, the visitors were relatively more highly involved with food than general food consumers; in particular, they were highly interested in 'Cooking' and 'Taste judging'.

Involvement is a much researched and applied construct in the consumer behaviour literature (Gross & Brown, 2008). Early research developing the construct investigated an individual's involvement with a product focused on the medium of communication, and the product it represented, at a moment in time. For example, product involvement has been applied to understanding wine purchases (Dodd, 1998; Charters & Pettigrew, 2006).

Attention has shifted to personal or ego involvement - that is how an individual's life revolves around a product or an activity (Zaichkowsky, 1985). This was based on the logic that consumer behaviour was predicated on involvement with a passion, pastime or product in everyday life. Thus an individual's involvement could be measured as high or low. In a review of how involvement was applied in leisure studies, Havitz and Dimanche (1999) found that involvement had a clear relationship with behaviour, in terms of both participation and purchase. This approach, otherwise known as ego-involvement, has also been applied to wine consumers in a tourism context (Brown, Havitz & Getz, 2007), who found that highly involved wine lovers were also wine tourists and food lovers.

It was low involvement, and its consequences, that first attracted the interest of researchers of food consumption. Neophobia and low food involvement were significant barriers to nutritional wellbeing, health and performance and productivity in institutional contexts. Bell and Marshall (2003) developed a food involvement scale (FIS) to enable the identification of food habits, in the specific context of the American military. Their scale development was structurally undergirded by a social anthropological food lifecycle theory (Goody, 1982).

Goody proposed five stages in the lifecycle of food: acquisition, preparation, cooking, eating, and disposal. Economically, the acquisition of food related to primary production, but in a mature market economy is more likely to be purchase and choice making. This also involves the acquisition of knowledge related to informing food choices. Preparation represents the transformation of foods in readiness for cookery or presentation. Goody's fourth stage is eating, which can occur in domains, whether domestic, public or commercial (Lashley, Lynch and Morrison, 2007). Eating itself, and the consumptive aspects of food, have attracted by far the majority of researcher attention. Indeed, previous research suggests that the recall of the food, or specific dishes, actually consumed during memorable dining experiences can be surprisingly low (Lashley, Morrison and Randall, 2004). Finally, the disposal stage involves the cleaning and hygiene elements of food production and consumption. Given the various domains in which food might be eaten, and broader contemporary sustainability and environmental issues, the after-meal experience needs greater examination. For example, what are foodies' attitudes toward recycling? Moreover, particularly in the commercial domain, the after-meal experience may include the collection of stimuli for the recall of memorable occasions. The 'souveniring' of dining experience artefacts, for example menus, is a case in point. Thus, considering reflective contemplation in the after-meal experience is worthy of greater investigation.

Bell and Marshall (2003) applied involvement theory to food, reflecting on the value of this construct in relation to brand loyalty, product information search processing, responses to advertising communications, diffusion of innovations, and product choice.

Bell and Marshall (2003) subsequently developed a succession of items structured by Goody's five stages of the food lifecycle and tested its validity, reliability and mediating effect against several established involvement and dietary scales including a food neophobia scale (FNS). Their food involvement scale (FIS) successfully discriminated between high and low food involvement. This instrument has been reapplied in domestic (Marshall & Bell, 2004) and social contexts (Kim, Suh and Eves, 2010). Kim et al. (2010) found that in the context of food festivals, visitor satisfaction was lowest for individuals with high food neophobia.

However, the foodie involvement scale that Robinson and Getz (2013) employed in their Australian research, and that was used in the multi-country survey, owes more to the leisure literature, specifically Kyle et al. (2007) who developed a modified involvement scale (MIS). Leveraging the application of social network theory, as it had been applied in leisure contexts (Scott and Godbey, 1992), and thus implicitly applying Stebbins' serious leisure concept, the MIS consolidated a range of leisure involvement studies. Kyle et al. distilled involvement to five dimensions: 'centrality', 'attraction', 'social bonding', 'identity affirmation' and 'identity expression'. Although 'risk' was a dimension validated by many other involvement studies it did not match the context of their study. 'Risk' refers to the notion that people who are highly involved in something, like sport competition, are much more concerned about making the right decision. It however, is a construct central to food studies and goes beyond the safety issues of hygiene (e.g. Tikkanen, 2007). Considering this an important aspect of high food involvement, it was incorporated into the development of the scale discussed below.

Development of this foodie involvement scale can be traced back to earlier work on wine lovers and wine tourists, which is described in an article by Brown, Havitz and Getz (2007). Their research involved a focus group with self-proclaimed wine lovers, followed by a survey of wine-club members and people attending wine tastings. It concluded that segmentation of wine tourists could be based on levels of involvement, with highly-involved wine lovers being experienced wine tourists. As already mentioned, that research also determined that wine lovers were also food lovers, and their wine-tourism experiences had to include good food and wine experiences.

For the Australian research, a series of in-depth interviews was conducted with self-identified, highly involved foodies whose professional food careers all blurred into their personal food-related passions. These interviews were undertaken in parallel with the instrument development and refinement process. By talking to experts Robinson and Getz (2013) gained an appreciation of how passion and employment go together, and this is also reflected in their research results which include many respondents with some work experience related to food, hospitality or tourism.

■ The Australian food involvement scale

3

A 44-item involvement scale was constructed for the Australian research. Table 3.1 ranks the 44 items by means, with the scale being 1-7. Means of 5 and above are considered to be a high level of agreement with the statement, while 3 and below are low levels of agreement. The statements were designed so that high levels of agreement are interpreted as high levels of involvement on most of them, although there are a few opposites where disagreement was expected, and there is no single item that on its own is a complete indicator of involvement. Analysis was required to isolate the main dimensions of food involvement.

Table 3.1: The Australian Involvement Scale. Adapted from Robinson and Getz (2013)

Involvement items	Cases	Mean#	Std. Deviation
I really hate having a bad meal experience	541	6.26	1.209
I like to experiment with food from different cultures	541	5.87	1.227
Being careful not to waste food is important to me	541	5.83	1.118
My special family occasions are often marked with a truly great meal	541	5.76	1.211
A well equipped kitchen is important to me	541	5.73	1.145
Table etiquette says a lot about a person	541	5.63	1.271
Nothing satisfies me more than eating a splendid meal	541	5.60	1.378
Dining out is one of the most enjoyable things I do	541	5.60	1.287
My kitchen and equipment are always clean	541	5.59	1.372
Sharing memorable dining experiences bonds me with my friends	541	5.58	1.199
Healthy eating is absolutely essential to me	541	5.43	1.318
Food experiences prompt me to learn more about other cultures	541	5.43	1.327
I love cooking for my friends	541	5.33	1.532
Cooking is one of life's great pleasures	541	5.30	1.540
I consult people who 'know' food about where to eat out	541	5.20	1.459
Most of my friends are food lovers	541	5.11	1.366
I feel proud of my knowledge of food and cooking	541	5.04	1.551

I cook with local produce whenever possible	541	5.04	1.522
I often reminisce about food experiences with family and friends	541	4.96	1.595
My friends and I enjoy discussing TV cookery programs	541	4.85	1.704
My cooking skills help express who I am	541	4.79	1.593
I express my creativity in the way I use 'leftovers'	541	4.74	1.515
I only use suppliers I can trust	541	4.61	1.443
I organise my day so that I can enjoy my meals	541	4.59	1.465
It's important to me to seek novel food choices	541	4.58	1.417
I am considered a real 'foodie' by others	541	4.55	1.726
The kitchen is my favourite space in my home	541	4.50	1.623
Acquiring food for domestic meals occupies a central role in my life	541	4.49	1.666
My craving for new food experiences defines who I am	541	4.47	1.535
Others value my opinion on where to get good produce	541	4.46	1.543
People know me as a gourmet	541	4.28	1.690
I select restaurants to dine in that feature regional produce	541	4.26	1.494
I spare little expense in getting the best produce	541	4.24	1.492
I enjoy spending longer than needed in the kitchen when cooking	541	4.21	1.757
Shopping for produce is one of the most enjoyable things in my life	541	4.16	1.618
I use the best cooking equipment in order to prevent kitchen disasters	541	4.06	1.620
I hate cooking in unfamiliar kitchens	541	3.96	1.620
My fondest childhood memories are cooking with my family	541	3.94	1.730
I often cook with my friends	541	3.89	1.716
I spend a great deal of my disposable income on dining out	541	3.84	1.739
Purchasing organic produce says a lot about me	541	3.44	1.638
I try not to shop for my food in supermarkets	541	3.33	1.826
I collect food-related 'trophies' e.g. souvenir menus, packaging	541	2.86	1.796
I give little thought to planning meals	541	2.80	1.575

Having said that, note that the highest mean (6.26) was given to the statement "I really hate having a bad meal experience." This is a 'risk' item and aligns with theory, in that people who love food the most are the ones who most hate a bad meal. This same finding was made in research on highly involved mountain bikers (Getz and McConnell, 2011) who really hated a bad event experience. Not too much can be made of it, however, because it does not differentiate levels of involvement within the sample; it would be useful in telling apart food lovers from people who have little concern for what they eat.

Table 3.2: Four dimensions of being a foodie revealed through factor analysis. Adapted from Robinson and Getz (2013)

Involvement dimensions		Item	Factor loading	Composite variable mean	Total Initial eigenvalues	Cronbach alpha
	Food-related identity	I feel proud of my knowledge of food and cooking	.824	5.00	5.821	.900
		I am considered a real 'foodie' by others	.760			
		Cooking is one of life's great pleasures	.731			
		My cooking skills help express who I am	.720			
		I love cooking for my friends	.713			
Food quality		I cook with local produce whenever possible	.617	4.01	1.977	.677
		I try not to shop for my food in supermarkets	.607			
		Purchasing organic produce says a lot about me	.548			
		I spare little expense in getting the best produce	.473			
Social bonding		I spend a great deal of my disposable income on dining out	.669	4.77	1.749	.726
		My craving for new food experiences defines who I am	.648			
		I consult people who 'know' food about where to eat out	.546			
		Sharing memorable dining experiences bonds me with my friends	.543			
Food con- sciousness		Being careful not to waste food is important to me	.729	5.39	1.323	.673
		I express my creativity in the way I use 'leftovers'	.579			
		Healthy eating is absolutely essential to me	.513			
		My kitchen and equipment are always clean	.438			

Our factor analysis from the Australian data (Table 3.2) demonstrates that these four dimensions are crucial to self-identification as a foodie:

1 **Food-related identity:** First is the importance of cooking to self and social identity. Foodies, first and foremost, love to cook; naturally that is reflected in their kitchens, their expenditure on cooking-related materials, and their constant desire to learn more.

2 **Social bonding**: Eating is pleasure, but this is largely about the social context; foodies like to please and entertain others, to join others in a great food experience; to seek novelty.

3 **Quality**: Quality is paramount, both in terms of the produce foodies buy and the meals they purchase.

4   **Conscientiousness**: Foodies are likely to be fastidious about how they buy, use and dispose of food.

We believe these dimensions are central to the foodie / food lover concept and have incorporated them into our definition in Chapter 1.

■   Involvement analysis from the multi-country research

The involvement scale utilized in the international research was different, but in part derived from the Australian research. We believe it covers all four dimensions of being a foodie and although much shorter it performs well in differentiating respondents on the basis of their level of ego-involvement with food. The specific need was to enable a clear distinction between highly involved and the lesser involved, then use high involvement as the dependent variable in various correlations related to food tourism, and in segmentation.

In Table 3.3 the 12 involvement items are listed and results given by country.

Table 3.3: Involvement results from the multi-country research: means (out of 7) by country. Adapted from Vujicic et al (2013).

Involvement Items	Germany	UK	Norway	Italy	Other	Ave.
Cooking is one of life's great pleasures	5.41	5.63	5.14	5.69	5.63	5.54
Sharing memorable dining experiences bonds me with my friends	5.15	5.49	5.51	5.71	5.49	5.53
I feel proud of my knowledge of food and cooking	5.05	5.02	4.56	5.08	5.02	5.00
I spend a great deal of my disposable income dining out	3.54	3.79	3.53	3.64	3.79	3.72
Shopping for fresh food is one of the most enjoyable things in my life	5.18	4.78	5.37	5.66	4.78	5.26
I like to experiment with food from different cultures	5.14	5.56	4.94	5.63	5.56	5.37
My good cooking expresses who I am	4.17	4.81	4.07	5.19	4.81	4.65
Healthy eating is essential to me	5.54	5.31	5.20	5.95	5.31	5.48
I give little thought to planning meals	2.78	3.04	3.09	3.93	3.04	3.21
I am considered a real 'foodie' by others	4.34	4.12	3.60	4.55	4.12	4.28
I love cooking for my friends	5.02	4.90	4.88	5.33	4.90	5.09
People know me as a gourmet	4.18	3.75	3.67	4.24	3.75	4.10

In interpreting the results, means of over 5 are considered to be high levels of agreement with the statements; means of under 3 are low; 3-5 are medium or neutral. For all statements except "I give little thought to planning meals", which is negatively worded, higher agreement is considered to reflect greater involvement.

Of the four target countries, Italians were the most highly involved foodies.

Norwegians recorded the lowest means, indicating lesser involvement; this could be a national trait or an artefact of the sampling. 'Others' (not from the 4 target countries) are highest in involvement, and this is considered to be a validity check on the scale, as the 'others' were all voluntary respondents who were not offered an incentive and were not members of marketing panels. Accordingly, it is possible to suggest that our overall means are somewhat less than one would expect from a purposeful sampling of food tourists (as opposed to self-declared food lovers).

3

▪ Identifying and profiling the highly involved foodies

One can almost tell at a glance which items are best at identifying the highly involved. No-one but the most involved would reply with a high level of agreement to these statements that relate to self and social identity: "people know me as a gourmet"; "I am considered a real foodie by others"; "my good cooking expresses who I am". On the other hand, most respondents love cooking, sharing food experiences, and trying foods from different cultures. Note that spending a lot on dining out is not necessarily a firm indicator of being a foodie - this behaviour depends more on jobs, disposable incomes and life stage.

However, we wanted an actual number of respondents to call Highly Involved Foodies (HIFs) in order to perform some correlational analysis with other variables. They are the top 11 per cent of respondents as measured by addition of their individual mean scores. In other words, we assumed that those who gave the highest scores across all the statements, excluding the one negative item ("I give little thought to planning meals"), were a distinct category. The truth is that involvement is not absolute, as in yes or no, high or low; it is relative and evolutionary, changing over time. Statistical analysis, reported below, reveals significant differences between the HiFs and others, so this technique does have validity and utility.

Why 11 and not 10 per cent? It is somewhat arbitrary, and could just as easily have been 5 or 20 per cent, but 11 per cent resulted in a sufficient number of HiFs to perform the analysis.

We established that the top 11 per cent of respondents, those we call HiFs, is clearly distinguishable from the remainder of the 'Foodies' in our large sample of over 3,000.

Furthermore, what gives us more confidence is that according to the majority of the demographic characteristics that we identified for comparison, our sample is remarkably consistent with the characteristics of foodies in previous research reported in the literature.

In terms of differences between the two groups according to country, we see a higher than average representation of HiFs from Italy, perhaps reflective of their passion for food and its integral role in their social and cultural life. Similarly, the 'Other' category had a disproportionately high number of HiFs, and this is perfectly logical since we did not actively pursue responses from countries outside of the four target countries, so it is likely that only highly involved food lovers would have been interested in completing the survey.

The HiFs are clearly differentiated from the normal 'Foodies' according to a range of socio-demographic characteristics. HiFs are significantly more likely to be female, to be younger, to be married, to have children, to be 'wage earners' and to have higher incomes when compared to the other 'Foodies'. Current and former chefs, current and former restaurant and catering workers and current and former tourism/hospitality professionals are over-represented among HiFs. Current agriculture and other food production workers are also over-represented among HiFs.

In later chapters we return to the highly involved for more detailed analyses.

The social worlds of foodies

Anyone engaged in a 'serious leisure' pursuit (defined later), or following a certain lifestyle (defined earlier), is likely to find him or herself increasingly engaging with others who share the same interests. Today, this process of belonging and sharing within a social world is not confined to face-to-face relationships, and therefore localities, but is truly global in scope and organization. This new reality has occurred through mass media, the internet, and social networking (e.g. Liu et al., 2012). As a test, the reader can pick any interest (a sport, form of art, hobby or activity) and instantly find established networks for that interest through a simple web search.

Unruh (1979, 1980) explained the nature of a social world, including aspects of individual involvement, structural features, and levels of analysis. These social worlds occur without a powerful centralized authority structure and are seen as, "...amorphous and diffuse constellations of actors, organizations, events, and practices which have coalesced into spheres of interest and involvement for participants" (Unruh 1979, p. 115).

Actors

Actors are people who belong to a variety of social worlds in a fluid, evolving process over their lifetimes. Within social worlds there are four kinds of social actors, each identified by their relative closeness to the activities and knowledge that are vital to the continuance of the social world.

Closest in proximity are the *insiders* who organize the activities and hold the knowledge that is central to their social world. Who are these insiders in the realm of foodies? No doubt on a global scale they include celebrity chefs, bloggers, travel writers and others who influence opinion and behaviour. More locally, some foodies will always be held in high esteem, and therefore be viewed as insiders, because of their knowledge, sophistication or extensive experience.

Regulars are the consistent participants committed to the continuation of their social world, that is foodies who get involved in clubs, blogging, holding dinner parties, etc.

Further out from the core are the *tourists* who limit their involvement in the social world to entertainment, profit, and diversion.

Finally, at the periphery, are *strangers* who influence some aspect of the social world, however they are not involved in the interests of the social world (Unruh, 1979).

All this is a matter of perspective, of course, because for those who take no interest in being a foodie or in food tourism it will all seem invisible and irrelevant. As well, foodies are not always so narrow in their interests that they do nothing but eat, cook and travel! As we discovered in the research, they have diverse interests and might belong to multiple social worlds.

Events

Events are personal occurrences that are important to people who are involved in a social world, such as the antecedents to their becoming a foodie (e.g., learning to cook at home, while young; visiting the market or a farm), or in terms of a first dinner party or club meeting with insiders. However, these can also be planned events that participants attend, such as a cooking class, wine and food pairing, food festival or tour. Foodies may participate in a social world that is structured, like sports and other hobbies or art forms, in which case there will be more events and social occasions to attend. Or, within the more amorphous frame of living a food-lover lifestyle, foodies may recreate and travel mostly on their own or within very small family and friendship groups. There is always scope for both, but as one gets more involved it seems likely that formal events and more networking arise.

Practices

Members of social worlds meet, participate in clubs, correspond, travel to events, and buy and sell items of value. There is also a symbolic and ritualistic dimension to their practices, reflecting the values or ethos of the social world. This includes signs of membership and status, and prescribed or desired ways of speaking and doing things. Foodies have their own language, and to be an insider means learning and using the 'lingo'. For example, when a foodie says she always favours "fresh and local" it is both acknowledgement of a key buzzword used by foodies everywhere and a hint that shopping is done at farmers' markets, not the big-chain superstores.

Sub-cultures and other communities of interest tend to develop their own language or to adopt jargonistic terminology that can be an indicator of insider status. It is also clear that events are produced by the insiders themselves, as in the case examined by Green and Chalip (1998) with regard to the sub-cultural identity of female flag footballers.

Formal organizations

Many organizations can play roles in shaping social worlds and facilitating networking among members: governing bodies and associations that are often hierarchical in nature; corporations that are intent on building brand communities for their own marketing purposes; clubs and teams; tourist organizations attempting to attract groups; events catering to special interests, and publications focused on special interests.

Unruh also produced an analysis of the different levels of social worlds. A local or regional social world might have boundaries, but that is not what defines them - it only shapes their scale and scope. Globally dispersed social worlds have grown enormously since Unruh's treatise, facilitated by travel, a proliferation of planned events (periodic and one-off), and the power of the internet and other forms of social media that bring like-minded people together.

Netnographic analysis was conducted by Getz and Patterson (2013) on several serious-leisure pursuits, employing the social-world frame of Unruh and making an explicit connection to tourism. One of these was food, and the researchers specifically searched for blogs where people talked about food and being a foodie. The 20 selected websites for foodies included Foodbuzz which was found to be an online community that aims to connect foodies "with search and discovery for everyone". Furthermore, Must Love Food is a social network for foodies to chat and share their knowledge about favourite foods, recipes, or wine pairings. Other sites concentrated on the link between health and organic foods, e.g., "Food is a brilliant way to do your bit for the planet – and to become more healthy!" Vegans and vegetarians have their own sites as do those on special diets (gluten and lactose free, Kosher, low salt, low fat, etc.). There are also numerous sites for lovers of particular types of foods (chocolate, pizza, and sushi), or styles of cuisine (Cajun, French, African-American), or ways of cooking (BBQ, baking, slow food, and raw food).

Many sites were found to be completely open, while others had certain membership restrictions. On one site, members posted bios that were only open to their friends, while in other food-related blogs they openly discussed their passions and other specific interests. The eating dimension was reflected in the following statement, "Food is good and we all know it. Blogging about food makes eating food a more attentive experience". The cooking dimension was also reflected in the quote: "Passionate about cooking and travelling but mostly importantly eating." One blogger stated a personal goal: "I am a chef on a culinary quest to transform myself from a foodie wannabe into an all-round gourmet guru."

Another website was specifically targeted at food lovers, to discuss, share, and learn about the art of food preparation. "This is a group for people who love to cook and share recipes". The cultural dimension was also important with the statement, "As a foodie, I find food and travel to be interrelated which is where our 'gourmantic' concept comes from. I love food! I especially love experiencing how food is prepared and eaten in different countries". Another blog was created by the 'Food Lover' who described herself as a 'culinary adventuress' who discovered her love of food and cooking through studying the French language, living in France and travelling extensively. Her desire is to chronicle and share her personal experiences in the kitchen. The travel connection was strong across many food-related interests, for example: "I organize cooking holidays in Israel", and "I am a travelling food lover and so excited to be part of this group".

Here is an example of a private company in the social networking business:

FoodiesLikeUs.com is a Scottsdale-based food-centric company that brings the Valley foodie community together, and provides unique and affordable culinary adventures to the home cook. Hinged on uniting people who enjoy food, and who center their social activity around it, we introduce food lovers to new and affordable culinary experiences. We host a mix of events each month including a social at various eclectic restaurants and wine bars throughout the Phoenix area.

The link between involvement and participation in a formal social network is somewhat tenuous, and certainly has not been reported on extensively in the research literature (for an exception see Liu et al., 2012). One can choose their level of engagement, being more or less social at any point in time. One could even be a 'secret foodie'! You just need a kitchen for that.

Infinite possibilities for involvement

Foodies can define and distinguish themselves in many ways, in terms of values, both personal and social identities, lifestyles and the activities or interests they pursue. There is no one model, no stereotypical or ultimate foodie. It's a matter of choice - many choices.

Drawing from our research and the many voices of foodies we can say that being a foodie enables a person to find one or more aspects of lifestyle that appeal to them, and these can evolve over time. A foodie can specialize on one aspect, or pursue diverse interests. A foodie can on one trip be a frugal self-caterer, shopping at local markets and cooking for the family, or book a famous restaurant a year in advance and splurge on the best meal ever. You could be one kind of foodie today and happy to boast of being another person a year from now.

We can see, however, that there is an apparent dichotomy of lifestyles, or perhaps it's a spectrum of choices, ranging from the frugal, health and environ-ment-conscious foodie on one hand to the globe-trotting, self-indulgent, luxury-favouring foodie on the other. One foodie might reject the notion of travel for food experiences on the basis of an ethical position on consumption and waste, while another might feel unfulfilled without such cultural experiences and related taste discoveries. Who is to say which model of foodie is better?

If you say "I am a foodie" it means that one or more of these elements are important to you. You can get involved by way of specialization (e.g. a preoccupa-tion with organic food and healthy cooking) or diversify over time. A foodie can be a lone ranger, or a social maven; stay at home, or be a globe trotter. The choices are almost infinite when you consider the permutations of food with cooking, socializing, lifestyle and travel. We have framed these choices as opposites, but they might actually be alternatives for some foodies who prefer to experiment.

- *Choices in food interests*: local, organic, ecological and sustainable practices are in sharp contrast to globe-trotting 'gastronauts' seeking adventure and novel food experiences.

- *Choices in cooking:* a state-of-the art kitchen has appeal, but why spend all that money when simple cooking gets good results?

- *Choices in socializing*: private dinner parties versus ever-expanding social worlds defined by one or more food interests; you can be a foodie all by your-self, who needs company? Connect through social media and ever-expanding food frontiers are opened to you, or join an online blog devoted to one topic you have great interest in.

- *Lifestyle choices*: amateur versus professional cook; spending large sums of money on kitchens, shopping for the best food, dining out and food tourism, versus being frugal about all aspects of your food-related budget.

- *Travel choices*: stay at home and read about other places or 'collect' destination restaurants and famous food regions; plan your own trips or join an escorted tour, cruise or other food-themed group experience.

What counts the most for marketers, therefore, is profiling and segmentation that reveals the most likely food tourists to be attracted to specific destinations, for specific experiences. This makes it essential to collect original market intelligence. Otherwise, communications and products will be made in a 'shotgun' fashion, hoping to hit some potential clients.

▪ Food as hygiene factor (satisfaction of tourists)

Bad food experiences can make for unsatisfied tourists, even if it was not an attraction for them (Pendergast, 2006). The researchers Correia et al. (2008) determined that three factors (price and quality, gastronomy and satisfaction) were "highly related manifestations of a single factor (gastronomy satisfaction)", and that "satisfaction with gastronomy in Portugal was very much related with local courses, originality and exoticness, and the presentation of food and staff".

However, some studies have revealed impediments to experiencing local cuisine, which tourists encounter even when they are seeking it. Cohen and Avieli (2004) identified hygiene standards, health considerations, communication gaps, and the limited knowledge of tourists concerning the local culinary offerings as impediments which should be considered by destinations. MacLaurin (2001) argued that visitors could have anxiety and uncertainty feelings when they travel and experience different cuisines. Indeed, information about local food safety significantly impacts on tourists' destination choices (MacLaurin, 2004).

Beside the above themes, tourists' behaviour, especially tourists' satisfaction and loyalty has been investigated in many studies. For example, tourists' satisfaction in terms of the relationships with local food tourism, local destinations, tourists' behavioural intention and quality of services have taken researchers' attention (Crotts, Pan, & Raschid, 2008; Ling, Karim, & Othman, 2010; Nield, Kozak, & LeGrys, 2000; Robinson & Clifford, 2012; Smith & Costello, 2009a).

Research note on satisfaction

Ling, L., Karim, M. & Othman, M. (2010). Relationships between Malaysian food image, tourist satisfaction and behavioural intention. *World Applied Sciences Journal*, **10**, 164-171.

This study aims to examine tourists' satisfaction towards Malaysian food and their future behavioural intentions. A survey was carried out at the Kuala Lumpur International Airport (KLIA) and Low Cost Carrier Terminal (LCCT) in Malaysia. A sample of 392 tourists was obtained at the respective departure halls using systematic sampling approach. The findings indicated that Malaysia has the potential of being a food tourism destination as the country is viewed as a melting pot of cultural food variety at reasonable price. In addition, the results reveal that image has a direct effect on satisfaction and tourists' satisfaction towards Malaysian food has a direct effect on behavioural intention. The findings, strengthens the notion of repeat visitation to experience the unique food culture. Practical and theoretical contributions are discussed, with future research suggested.

■   Neophobia (risk), novelty-seeking and neophilia

Are food lovers psychologically pre-disposed to seeking out new tastes and new food-tourism experiences? Quan and Wang (2004) argued that food consumption in tourism can be either the peak touristic experience or the supporting consumer experience, dependent upon specific circumstances. To these theorists, peak food experiences are derived from both motivation (novelty seeking) and memorability. Often food is a medium for peak social experiences.

Presumably sensation-seeking is similar to neophilia, and the only research available concerns wine tourists. In their study of wine tourists, Galloway et al. (2008) determined that "sensation seeking was observed to be significantly related to spending on wine, and wine drinking, as well as to the frequency of visits to wineries and the number of activities engaged in at wineries, the use of the internet as a source of information about wineries, venturing off the beaten track during a visit to a wine region, and the strength of opportunity for learning, stimulation, or indulgence as incentives to visit a wine region." Gyimóthy and Mykletun (2009) found that food in a tourism context had a "challenging culinary trophy" element with an association of novelty (Mykletun and Gyimóthy, 2010).

Research note: scary food and traditions

Mykletun, R., & Gyimóthy, S. (2010). Beyond the renaissance of the traditional Voss sheep's-head meal: Tradition, culinary art, scariness and entrepreneurship. *Tourism Management*, **31**(3), 434-446.

Attempts have been made to make traditional local foods a part of the tourists' experiences, but few have caught great interest among the tourist and leisure consumers. An exception is the Norwegian traditional Sheep's-head meal. This article focuses on driving factors behind this success. Sheep's heads have been continuously available and used at private meals, albeit the status of the meals has changed from everyday food to party food, and a festival and commercial meals with unique ceremonies have developed. Participation in these may give a sense of symbolic proximity to traditions and historical 'roots'. The culinary qualities of the product are important especially for the experienced sheep's-head meal participants. The scariness of the product itself and the measures taken to make the meal an enjoyable adventure trigger the feelings of courage, mastery and inclusion in the 'in-group' of sheep's-head eaters. Most important for the success were the individual entrepreneurships and entrepreneurial networks which were the number one drivers behind the rejuvenation of these unique meal experiences. This case illustrates the significance of the individual and network entrepreneurial processes in the branding and development of tourism destinations.

Food is certainly a risk factor for tourists (Lepp and Gibson, 2003), sometimes leading to sickness or to disappointment owing to a large gap between perceived value and cost. Kim, Suh and Eves (2010) found that neophobia, or the fear of new foods, had a negative relationship with visitor satisfaction, but despite discussing the food involvement literature at length they used only two established measures from Bell and Marshall (2003). Logically, an actual fear of strange foods, or perhaps purchased meals, will tend to keep people at home, or will encourage them to visit only those establishments perceived to be familiar and/or safe. But a person who feels food neophobia could conceivably be a foodie – only with a narrow range of likes or tolerances. This constraint on food tourism, from a supplier's point of view, will also apply to those with special dietary requirements and preferences, including those related to religion and health. Increasingly, food tourism, and travel suppliers in general, have to accommodate greater diversity in demands, and greater respect for allergies and other dietary restrictions.

Summary

This chapter went into detail on the nature of being a foodie, starting with the voices of self-described foodies and then questioning whether being a foodie has a positive of negative connotation. Psychological theory was brought to bear on personal and social identity, which is essential to understanding any leisure or lifestyle pursuit. Only the individual can decide if they are a foodie, because they identify with what it means; it cannot be determined solely by appearances or behaviour. And what it means to them is always in part a reflection of social considerations including the possibility that foodies are part of a loose or tight social world devoted to like-minded people. In that social context the concept of communitas is important, wherein people get together at events and through social networking to celebrate their interests in an atmosphere of sharing and belonging.

The social-psychological construct called involvement (or ego-involvement) was then examined, drawing from leisure studies where many pursuits have been examined through this theoretical lens. Involvement is reflected only in part by behaviour (such as spending, time commitments, travel) and is otherwise a matter of self-identification and attitudes. Highly involved foodies make food a central part of their lifestyle and take all food-related activities very seriously. This is where the connection to serious leisure theory is important.

Based on a lengthy food involvement scale for Australian research, which constituted a test, we then utilized a much shorter and more efficient scale for the multi-country online survey. The Australian findings made it clear, through factor analysis, that foodie involvement embodies four important dimensions:

food-related identity (e.g. I feel proud of my knowledge of food and cooking), food quality (e.g. I cook with local produce whenever possible), social bonding (e.g. sharing memorable dining experiences bonds me with my friends), and food consciousness (e.g. being careful not to waste food is important to me). These dimensions are central to any discussion or definition of foodie, and they are themes running through this book.

We have no doubts about the efficaciousness of our reduced involvement scale, as utilized in the multi-country online survey, in detecting levels of involvement. This enabled us to isolate the Highly Involved and statistically correlate their characteristics with those who had travelled for food. It is now clear that a high level of involvement with food is closely associated with food tourism and with certain preferences that are important to destination developers and marketers. This does not imply, however, that foodies will always get more involved over time, nor that all highly-involved foodies will become food tourists. It does mean that marketers should seek, and now have the tools to identify the highly-involved foodies who are most likely to visit their destination for food-related experiences.

This chapter includes a discussion of social worlds, starting with theory and closing with implications drawn from netnographic research. Evidence exists to support the contention that online social networking through blogs and other websites influences foodies and encourages food-related travel. Celebrities and experts can influence the decision-making process, attracting foodies to specific areas and getting them interested in particular foods and experiences.

Ending the chapter is consideration of the infinite possibilities or choices in being a foodie. If you believe you are a foodie, it does not necessarily brand you as the being the same as all the others. That means careful attention is required by marketers to all the nuances of self and social identity. A short discussion was included on food as a hygiene factor, either causing illness or leading to satisfaction/dissatisfaction with travel experiences. Novelty-seeking or neophilia was then compared with neophobia, or the fear of different things, as it relates to the foodie and food-tourist experience.

Study questions

1   Define foodie within the context of personal and social identity, ego-involvement, and serious leisure.

2   Can a foodie be identified by appearances or behaviour?

3   What is being an omnivore got to do with foodies?

4   How is involvement measured?

5   Describe the four key dimensions of being a foodie.

6   What are the various choices for foodies, in terms of getting involved?

7   Are all highly involved foodies also food tourists? Why or why not?

8   What is the foodie social world, and how does participation influence food tourism?

9   Define neophobia and neophilia. How are these personality traits important in understanding food and tourism relationships?

10   Why is food both a hygiene factor and an attraction?

Further reading

Johnston, J., & Baumann, S. (2009). *Foodies: Democracy and Distinction In The Gourmet Foodscape*. London: Routledge.

Unruh, D. (1980). The nature of social worlds. *Pacific Sociological Review*, **23**(3), 271-296.

Stebbins, R. (1992). *Amateurs, Professionals, and Serious Leisure*. Montreal: McGill: Queen's University Press.

4 Foodies and Tourism

Learning objectives

Readers are expected to learn the following from this chapter:

■ How seeking and escaping theory relates to the motivations to travel and benefits sought by foodies; push and pull factors

■ Destination attractiveness in the context of food tourism

■ The meaning and importance of perceived authenticity

■ Why foodies want tactile experiences

■ Who exactly travels for food-related experiences

■ Photo elicitation as a technique for exploring preferred experiences

■ Willingness to pay as a measure of involvement and preference

■ Preferences and styles of travel by foodies for international food-related trips

Motivation and benefits sought

In this chapter actual food tourism is examined, mostly through our research data. We present material from a number of major surveys and our own work. The first section examines motivation in theory and with regard to the specific benefits sought by foodies. The benefits obviously focus on food-related experiences, but foodies are also often looking for authentic cultural experiences, and they do combine food experiences with other activities.

Seeking-escaping theory is a theoretical way of looking at travel motivation. According to Mannell and Iso-Ahola (1987), people engage in leisure and travel in order to simultaneously escape from aspects of their personal and interpersonal environments (perhaps boredom or stress) and to seek specific benefits. These benefits could be expressed in terms of fundamental needs, namely to find rewarding social experiences and for self development. In the tourism literature escaping is often expressed as the 'push factors' while seeking is called the 'pull factors'. Anything that acts as an attraction is a pull factor in this context.

Heldke (2003) used the term 'food adventuring' to describe foodies in pursuit of new experiences. This is an example of how foodies might describe their travel, and theoretically we should ask why some people feel the need for adventure or novel experiences. Is their life boring, or do they find personal growth and identity through food adventuring? Along these lines, Kim et al. (2010) studied food-event motivations and identified three push factors (knowledge and learning, fun and new experiences, and relaxation with family) and three pull factors: area quality and value, quality of events, and food variety.

Any travel experience might satisfy generic needs, such as relaxing and social bonding with family, or specific needs related to a special interest, like food quality and variety. The more involved with food one is, the more likely it is that motivations will be very specific. This is confirmed when we examine the highly-involved foodie.

Specific pull factors, or attractions that appeal to foodies have been identified through research. Park et al. (2008) determined that one of the major factors that motivated visitors to go to wine and food festival is tasting new wine and food. Kim et al. (2009) argued that tasting local food and beverage not only satisfies visitors' appetites but also offers them local cultural experiences. Exploration of indigenous culture through food has been emphasized as an attraction by Molz (2007), while opportunities to discover new taste sensations and gain access to well-coordinated culinary experiences was identified by Kivela and Crotts (2006).

In Australia, Sparks et al. (2005 p. vi) explored wine and food tourism. "The Good Living Tourism project focused on the lifestyle aspects of food and wine tourism. The project comprised several studies including regional case studies and consumer research." Based on focus groups with experienced wine tourists, the researchers identified 'enhancement factors' that make a visit to a wine and food region more enjoyable, namely: authenticity of the experience, value for money, service interactions, the setting or surroundings, product offerings, information dissemination, personal growth and indulgence. "The food and wine tourist is rarely just interested in wine tasting; the total experience is of greatest importance." (p.vi). A survey was also conducted, with 828 completed questionnaires - approximately 87% being female respondents and mostly from one state, Queensland. "Results demonstrated that, when taking a holiday, the four most important themes were 'enjoyment and pleasure', 'being pampered', 'beautiful/undiscovered surroundings' and 'inspirational' experiences... Respondents reported that they sought a lifestyle that was characterized by comfort, health, harmony, relaxation and fun. Activities that most provided enjoyment to this group were 'getting away', 'food' and 'art'. Almost half the group indicated an intention to take a holiday revolving around food and wine within the next twelve-month period." (p. vi).

A Korean food festival study by Kim et al. (2009) examined motivational factors (exciting experience, escape from routine, health concern, learning knowledge, authentic experience, togetherness, prestige, sensory appeal, and physical environment) and food neophilia versus neophobia among tourists with regard to consuming local food and beverages. Interviews were conducted with 20 travellers. This exploratory research does not address the issue of food-tourist destination choices or desired experiences but reveals something of basic motivations and factors influencing food consumption while travelling.

Tikkanen's (2007) study in Finland linked food tourism to Maslow's hierarchy of needs. Physiological needs can be the main motivation for food tourism in the case of alcohol-oriented cruises and cross-border shopping. Safety needs relate to hygiene concerns, but translate into motivation in the case of conferences on this theme. Social needs relate experiences where food is part of the social mix, including vineyard tourism and food event tourism. Esteem needs motivate travel for cultural food experiences. "Self-actualizing needs become realized in the form of trade fairs and conferences that increase the visitor's knowledge and competences related to food, and which heightens his/her self-respect." (Tikkanen, 2007: 731).

Kivela and Crotts (2005) studied gastronomic tourists in Hong Kong, finding them to be a substantial segment, more males than females, and more of a regional (Asian) market. Cultural differences were determined to be important, separating Asians from, for example, North Americans. They concluded that a major challenge is to make dining experiences more memorable – perhaps by active participation to broaden their knowledge and try different tastes.

■ Perceived authenticity (from the food tourists' perspective)

It is often said that foodies search for authentic cultural experiences, including regional and national cuisines, but what is authenticity and how do food tourists determine that their experience was indeed authentic? Exactly what is 'authentic' is almost always open to interpretation.

Kuznesof et al. (1997) said there are personal factors including the cultural awareness and knowledge of consumers that influence perceptions of authenticity. Personal factors might emerge as an individual connection between the produced and the consumed, which may be based on ethnicity for example (Johnston and Baumann, 2007) or simply the contemplative process (Beer, 2008) so the food just tastes 'right'. Perceived authenticity depends much on self-identity, personality, personal goals, lifestyle and values.

Johnston and Baumann (2007: 179) emphasized that authenticity is a social construction, with their review of the literature suggesting that "Qualities that lend themselves to the social construction of authenticity include creation by hand rather than by industrial processes; local settings and anticommercialism;

sincere expression distant from calculation or strategy; honesty, integrity, or dedication to core principles; and closeness to nature combined with distance from institutionalized power sources." By analysing what food writers said about food authenticity they concluded that there are four qualities used to frame a food or cuisine as being authentic: geographic specificity; simplicity; personal connections and historicism. Geographical references relate to provenance and can also suggest ethnic or cultural origins. Simplicity embodies the notions of hand-made, traditional, and non-industrial, sometimes with connotations of rusticity and non-pretentious dining. Personal connections relates to "food with a face", the opposite of impersonal. The face can be that of a celebrity chef, or a family artisanal tradition. Historicism refers to tradition and the test of time, as opposed to faddism. It should be noted that these observations themselves might reflect the fads of travel and food writing, as what is interesting to foodies changes with familiarity.

Where the food is consumed embodies authenticity, whether this be in the family home (Moisio et al., 2004), in a culturally ambient restaurant with a plethora of authenticity 'signifiers' (Lu and Fine, 1995) or in a commercial tourist precinct which communicates authenticity by a range of product signifiers other than food (Carroll and Torfason, 2011).

■ Activities and experiences

Activities, such as dining or picking produce, are often featured in tourism advertising and there is a general assumption that activities equal experiences. This is wrong, or at least confusing, because activities are only one of three experiential components that must be measured: cognitive (mental processes), affective (emotions or feelings), and conative (behaviour or activities). Leisure researchers have long employed experiential sampling and other methods to determine the nature of leisure, and these can be applied to food tourism. Similarly, ethnographic methods will be effective, including participant observation and netnography.

An exhaustive list cannot be compiled but Figure 4.1 provides a number of obvious examples that require examination. In the left-side column are three categories of higher-order, experiential outcomes that are believed to be sought by food tourists. They cover mental, emotional and physical domains and connect directly to social needs, esteem, and self-development or actualization (Maslow, 1954; 1962). Lower-order physiological needs are met by eating, but food tourists also know that food consumption can simultaneously be an aesthetic, intellectual, as well as a social experience.

In the right-side column are associated activities that can be packaged and sold. How activities lead to experiences, and particularly to memorable or even transforming experiences, remains a major research and theoretical challenge.

Successful entrepreneurs who design experiences become skilled at knowing what will satisfy their customers, but academics need theories that can be applied in many possible situations; these can only be developed through systematic research. We take up this theme again in Chapter 8 in which experience marketing for foodies is detailed.

Figure 4.1: Experiential outcomes linked to activities for food tourists

Higher-order experiential outcomes	Associated activities
Intellectual development ♦ learning new things ♦ aesthetic appreciation ♦ problem solving ♦ reasoning	♦ experiential learning through participation in demonstrations, cooking classes, formal education and training; being mentored by experts ♦ learning through interpretive stories and themes attached to food-tourism experiences ♦ discovery and development of talent through hands-on, creative cooking
Mastery (adventure and meeting challenges heightens enjoyment and self esteem) a) technical: how to do things b) creative or artistic c) physically demanding (overcoming obstacles or pain)	a) technical mastery gained by experiential learning: through cooking, planting, harvesting, tasting, smelling, etc. b) creative mastery gained by experiential learning: through menu and serving design, design of meals or consumption settings, etc. c) physical mastery through exertion, endurance or applied motor skills (e.g., picking fresh produce, preparing, cooking, and serving a meal)
Emotional satisfaction ♦ memorable and transforming experiences ♦ satisfaction with experiences (value for money) ♦ communitas (belonging and sharing) ♦ anticipation and remembering (before and after travel)	♦ gained through personally relevant experiences, co-created with suppliers, leading to higher levels of emotional engagement; celebration of things valued ♦ perceived authenticity and uniqueness of the experience adds value and increases satisfaction ♦ suppliers facilitate valued social experiences (with friends, family, affinity groups) such as events and tours ♦ facilitated social worlds (employing social media)

Analysis of the 2007 TAMS, conducted by Smith et al (2010), concentrated on visitors to Ontario (residents and out-of-province visitors) who reported engaging in at least three of a specified set of food-related activities on a trip in the last two years. This segment of food tourists were subdivided into a number of clusters:

■ Dining (40.2%) high-end restaurants, menus featuring local ingredients, cafés

■ Celebrating (24.6%) attending food festivals

■ Sampling (16.4%) winery or brewery visits

■ Rural experiences (12.9%) farm gate sales, picking, farmers' markets

■ Learning (5.7%) cooking schools, wine classes

Shenoy (2005) examined 341 tourists visiting the four coastal counties of South Carolina. She concluded that food tourism is composed of five dimensions of activities: dining at restaurants known for local cuisines; purchasing local food products; consuming local beverages; dining at high quality restaurants, and dining at familiar chain restaurants. Segmentation generated three clusters, with the so-called culinary tourist identified as the ones who frequently dined and purchased local food, consumed local beverages, dined at high-class restaurants, and rarely ate at chain restaurants; they were more educated, earned higher income, and engaged in variety-seeking (i.e., the absence of food neophobia).

■ Large-scale surveys of American food tourists

The most directly pertinent and substantial research comes from the Travel Industry Association of America (2006). Their *Profile of Culinary Travellers, 2006 Edition* stems from the first-ever, national research study on the culinary travel market in the USA. A survey was completed by 2,364 leisure travellers, from which the 'culinary traveller' was profiled. This segment (17% of the total leisure travellers) had participated in one or more of: cooking classes, dining out for a unique and memorable experience, visiting farmers' markets, gourmet food shopping, attending food festivals, or undertaking some wine tourist activity. Here are some highlights:

- Culinary tourists are younger, more affluent, better educated travellers.
- They are motivated by unique experiences, reinforcing the benefits of focusing on a destination's individual environmental and cultural elements.
- They are a more desirable prospect pool across all aspects of the travel experience, culinary and non-culinary.
- Total interest was found to be growing, and is significantly higher among women (65%) than men (50%), and is lowest among those over 65 (38%).

What is popular? Going to restaurants for unique and memorable experiences and local/regional cuisine topped the list, and many also reported they were interested in visiting farmers markets (83%), sampling traditional artisan products (81%), attending culinary festivals (77%), tasting locally made wines (72%) or touring wineries (71%).

Three market segments were profiled, with the 'deliberate' culinary travellers being food tourists who travel specifically for food experiences. The accidental culinary tourists were, on average, less educated with lower incomes.

- 'Deliberate' Culinary Travellers: "The availability of culinary activities was a key reason I chose to take the trip or destination."
- 'Opportunistic' Culinary Travellers: "I sought out culinary activities on my travels but they were not necessarily a factor in making a choice."

- 'Accidental' Culinary Travellers: "I participated in culinary/wine related activities, simply because they were available."

Serious culinary travellers are also more likely to participate in a wide variety of other trip activities ranging from shopping and spa services to cultural and heritage-related activities to outdoor/nature-based experiences. They are more likely to select a destination to experience local culture and cuisine, and spend more money per trip - especially for food and wine. For marketers, it was found that they are active information seekers, relying heavily on word of mouth and a variety of print publications, as well as using online information resources. The study pinpointed a range of specific attractions, or pull factors: learning about the local culture and cuisines; trying regional cuisines, culinary specialties and local wines and spirits, and bringing back regional foods, recipes, wines etc. from places they have visited to share with family and friends.

In 2013, The American Culinary Traveler study was replicated by consultants Mandala Research and a summary was posted by the Arizona Office of Tourism (www.azot.gov/system/files/1051/original/The%20American%20Culinary, accessed Jan. 13, 2014). This update examined a sample of leisure travelers and then focused on those who had a culinary experience during the trip. The method entailed 2,113 Web interviews conducted between May 2 and May 10, 2013. The average age of respondents was 44 years old; 82% were Caucasians; 93% had some college or above; 51% were female.

They were asked: "Thinking about all the trips you have taken over the past three years in which you participated in culinary activities (cooking classes, dining out for an unique and memorable experience, farmers' markets, gourmet food shopping, etc.) or attended food festivals, which if any, of the following applies to you? (Please select all that apply)."

Highlights:

- Three quarters of all leisure travellers (77%, representing 131 million Americans) can be classified as Culinary travellers, having participated in the specified culinary activities within the past three years.

- About half of all leisure travellers travel to learn about or enjoy unique and memorable eating and drinking experiences (51%), a notable gain from 2006 when 40% said they travelled for these reasons.

- Culinary travellers overall (62%), and Deliberates (87%) and Opportunistics (77%) in particular, are especially likely to travel for unique and memorable culinary experiences. "Deliberates" answered yes to one of these options:

  ❑ I took one or more trips where the availability of culinary activities was a key reason I chose to take the trip

  ❑ I took one or more trips where the availability of culinary activities helped me choose between potential destinations

- Gen Y and Gen X are more interested in culinary travel than Baby Boomers and Matures.
- Most travel with a spouse/significant other; 20% with friends, 15% with family and/or children.
- Approximately 47% fly while 50% drive their own personal vehicle.
- Culinary travellers stay an average of four nights away from home.
- They seek out unique foods and atmosphere, gourmet foods, farmers markets, wine and beer.
- Culinary travellers spend more per trip compared to $1,200 for all leisure travellers.

U.S. Wine & Culinary Enthusiasts: A special analysis of the Travel Activities and Motivation Survey (TAMS).

Prepared for: The Canadian Tourism Commission (CTC) 2000

Another large-scale survey was commissioned by the Canadian Tourism Commission. The Travel Activities and Motivation Survey (TAMS) was completed first in 2001 and repeated in 2007. The 2001 research by Lang Research, developed a Cuisine and Wine Interest Index as part of the analysis of both Americans and Canadians. The index consisted of answers to questions about motivations for, and activities during vacation experiences taken in the previous two years. The most notable and predictable conclusion of TAMS was that interest in, and travel for wine and food experiences is highly correlated (in North America) with education and income levels. But of course, this applies to tourism in general. Childless couples were identified as a prime target market, from the Canadian perspective. A subsequent analysis of TAMS by the Economic Planning Group of Canada revealed that a number of general motivational factors, namely personal indulgence, exploration, romance and relaxation, influenced the target markets. Wine and food tourism was closely tied to entertainment and cultural activities.

'Wine & culinary enthusiasts' were those Americans who had some recent Canadian tourism experience and who exhibited a particular interest in fine foods and wine. They had engaged in the following activities on these trips. Any one of the following:

- Stay at cooking school
- Stay at wine tasting school
- Stay at gourmet restaurant with accommodation on the premises

Or any two of the following:

- Tour a region's wineries
- Go to wineries for day visits
- Dine at internationally acclaimed restaurants

These American enthusiasts were better educated and had higher incomes than other pleasure travellers. They were more likely to be couples without children at home. Of the activities used to define wine & culinary enthusiasts, day visits to wineries had the largest following. Over 8 in 10 of these enthusiasts claim to have participated in this activity on a leisure trip in the past couple of years. Other popular defining activities include touring a region's wineries and dining in internationally acclaimed restaurants.

Activities engaged in by wine & culinary enthusiasts

- Go to wineries for day visits (85%)
- Tour a region's wineries (74%)
- Dine at internationally acclaimed restaurants (70%)
- Stay at gourmet restaurant (12%)
- Stay at wine tasting school (5%)
- Stay at a cooking school (3%)

4

Past and projected travel

Probably the most important indicator for measuring and predicting demand is that of previous travel for food experiences, so in our own research we asked about past food-related trips and future plans for international food tourism.

From Australian research

Results suggest that there is only a minority that combine their passion for food with a high level of travel, especially internationally, and this is entirely expected given the costs and commitment required to become an international food tourist (it is obviously much easier in Europe to cross borders). It is reasonable to assume that a degree of involvement with food or any other lifestyle or leisure pursuit does not automatically generate travel demand.

Respondents mostly agreed that food and tourism go together in a fulfilling manner, and food tourism is primarily a social experience – often shared with partners. While travelling, new and exciting meals are sought. Importance is assigned to cultural events and authentic food experiences, food trails, and combining food tourism with other cultural experiences.

In response to the question "In the past 12 months have you travelled within Australia for a food-related experience?" 54% of our sample replied that they had done so. 26% (n=141) had done so once, 17% (92) had travelled twice, and 11% (61) had travelled within Australia for a food-related experience three or more times. Regarding plans for future domestic food tourism, 34% (179) responded that they were planning a trip. While it is not possible to categorically state that food was the primary or sole motivating factor for all these reported trips, some comments suggest it is often the case. This direct quotation from a respondent is pertinent:

"We're flying to Melbourne next week for the Good Food and Wine Festival because we heard it's amazing there. This is our first actual flight for a food experience"

30% of the sample over the past 12 months had travelled internationally for a food related experience. Regarding plans for future travel for an international food experience, 29% (n=152) were planning such a trip. Responses were suggestive of the types of international food-related experiences respondents sought:

"My dream is to eat at as many restaurants as possible in the 'top 50 restaurants in the world'. I have done 5 so far."

"[I'm] interested in participating in cooking schools in Vietnam."

"I've already travelled a lot for food - most recently Thailand and India".

This high number of international travellers is likely attributable to several factors: a) sampling bias in favour of better-educated food lovers; b) the high general propensity to travel abroad among Australians, and c) a high correlation between being a food lover and international food tourism. Our cross-country comparison, discussed next, also reflects this strong propensity of foodies to engage in domestic and international food tourism.

■ Preferred food destinations of Australians

Participants were asked to list their top-three preferred food experience destinations. Overall, there was a high degree of Euro-centricity apparent in destinations of choice with Italy and France the two clear preferences. This is identical to that of Canadian wine tourists in a previous study's findings (Getz and Brown, 2006). Spain and other Mediterranean climate destinations such as Greece and Morocco registered some choices. Australia's proximity to Asia influenced moderate responses for Thailand and Vietnam, with neighbours Cambodia and Laos also figuring in responses. Singapore, Taiwan and Hong Kong also registered some support.

Table 4.1 : Most-mentioned desired food-experience destinations (by Australians). Source: Robinson & Getz (2012).

Food destination	Frequency (Valid % n=111)	Food related reasons
Italy	47%	Traditional/local/regionalism, lessons/learning, pasta (wine)
France	40%	Culinary heritage/authenticity, techniques, cheeses (wine)
Vietnam	14%	Authentic, freshness, technique, cooking school, street food
South America	12%	Authentic, rustic, spices
Thailand	10%	Authentic/traditional, natural/fresh cuisine, learn to cook
Spain	9%	Tapas, destination restaurants
Australia	27%	Local producers, restaurants

Authenticity, tradition and cuisine specific to the country/region were frequently mentioned as reasons for preferences. Taking lessons, or learning to cook, seemed to cut across preferred destinations, while naturalness and freshness appeared to be a factor for south-east Asian destinations. Interestingly, for the European destinations, there was an association with old world wine producing countries, and indeed, specific wine producing regions like Champagne. 27% (n=30) of the valid respondents listed domestic destinations, and in Australia there was a definite overlap of wine and food in well-known regions like the Barossa, Hunter Valley and Margaret River.

■ Multi-country research

As discussed in the previous chapter, High Involvement is correlated significantly with past travel for food-related experiences. With further analysis using a regression model it was also found that Gender and Income were statistically significant predictors of international travel for food in the next 12 months with food as the main reason. Males and higher-income respondents had a higher propensity to plan food-related trips.

Highly involved foodies (HiFs) prefer active and hands-on food experiences, for example farmers' markets, food festivals, meeting and learning from chefs, and food trails. The remainder of the foodies sample prefer sedentary (eating) food experiences, for example good food while at a harbour, romantic dinners and regional cuisine at local restaurants; also hiking and viewing wildlife, experiencing an outdoor concert and staying at a spa.

HiFs reported a willingness to *spend more* for *both* the active experiences and the sedentary eating experiences. In terms of non-food related Swedish experiences, the HiFs preferred visiting art galleries and museums, tripping to the islands, visiting historical and archaeological sites, experiencing a winter resort and staying at a spa. The HiFs were prepared to pay significantly more than the other foodies for all these experiences that they might enjoy 'between meals'. They are definitely 'up-market' and likely to be high-yield visitors, if only a destination can attract them.

The highly involved foodies were significantly more likely than normal foodies to book package tours online and to make all their accommodation and travel bookings online. It might seem contradictory, but this self-reliance of HiFs also means they are more likely to stay in budget accommodation and fly on discount airlines. The reason is simply that they travel much more than average; they are veterans and rather sophisticated at finding good deals.

Attendance at food-related events was found to be much higher by the HiFs. So strong is this relationship between High Involvement and event attendance that it has been used as the basis for developing three segments (see Chapter 7).

Respondents were asked about travel internationally, first for leisure or holiday purposes, then for food-specific purposes. 65% of the overall sample had travelled between one and three times internationally for leisure or holiday in the last 12 months. More importantly, 34% of the respondents had travelled at least one time internationally with food as the main reason (see Table 4.2). Germans had been the most travelled for food (45% had done so), followed by Norwegians (41%), Italians (35%) and British (28%). The 'Other' category was also well travelled for food experiences, at 49%.

We did not examine the details of these trips, but other evidence strongly suggests that the main lures for such travel would be food events, destination restaurants, and cities or regions famous for cuisine.

Table 4.2: Frequency of previous food-related international travel, by country. Source: Vujicic et al (2013).

Country	None	1-3 times	4-6 times	7-9 times	10+	Sample size
Germany	55%	41%	3%	1%	1%	714
Italy	65%	31%	4%	1%	0%	733
Norway	59%	36%	3%	1%	1%	611
Uk	72%	25%	2%	1%	0%	644
Other	51%	38%	7%	2%	2%	400
Average	61%	34%	4%	1%	1%	
						N= 3102

(Q: How many times have you travelled internationally in the last 12 months with food as the main reason?)

■ The importance of food in travel decisions

Boyne et al. (2003) proposed a four-fold taxonomy describing types of consumers according to the level of importance of food and gastronomy in their destination decision-making processes. Gastronomy is an important element of the Type 1 holiday experience and they actively seek information relating to an area's gastronomic heritage and/or the nature of the supply of locally-produced or quality food in the area. For Type 2 gastronomy is also important, however they require exposure to food-related tourism information before taking action; they welcome it, but do not actively seek it. Their Type 3 consumers do not attach importance to gastronomy in the holiday experience, but might do so in the future if they have an enjoyable food experience. And Type 4 consumers have no gastronomic interests at all, and cannot be influenced to make it important in travel decisions.

This kind of typology makes some sense, intuitively, but can it be backed up by evidence? And does it provide reasonable guidance for segmentation and related communications? There are no permanent types when you consider how foodie involvement evolves, and generalizations such as this distort the potential to engage more and more people with food experiences when travelling. Plus, the market is certainly growing, so static conceptualizations should be rejected. What is clear is the fact that many people are travelling out of an interest in food, and food experiencescapes are tourist attractions.

When it came to the importance of food in making travel decisions the multi-country research determined that the UK sample was least motivated, and the 'Other' (mean: 5.25 out of 7) were most motivated by food. Looking back on their last holiday trip, respondents were asked how important the food experience was for their total satisfaction and the 'Other' category again demonstrated the priority they gave food with a mean of 5.64 out of 7. As noted elsewhere, this 'Other' category consists of those who responded to the general online call for respondents, without reward, and they appear to be more highly involved foodies. But note that across the four countries food was indeed an important factor in trip satisfaction, with all means above 5.0.

Type of group

More than half of the respondents travelled 'with my partner' (56%), 30% travelled 'with my family and children', 20% were in a 'self-organized group of family and friends', 15% travelled alone, and 5% travelled 'with a group tour'. Travelling with a partner is preferred (which reflects the demographics of the sample), and Germans were highest at 50% . Few travelled with a tour group, with Italians being the highest (only 6%). Italians were also the highest in travelling with a self-organised group of family and friends (20%).

Experiences and benefits sought

In this section we utilize analysis from the multi-country survey to further explore the nature of food-tourism experiences sought by foodies. It begins with data from a photo-elicitation exercise, combined with questions on willingness to pay for various travel experiences.

■ Photo elicitation and willingness to pay

Small versions of the photos used in this exercise are given on the next two pages. To view the original photos in colour, visit this site where the Executive Food Tourism Report can be downloaded:

http://www.experiencec.com/En/Page.asp?PageId=276

Or visit the Goodfellow site for this book:

http://www.goodfellowpublishers.com/academic-publishing.php?promoCode=&partnerID=&content=story&storyID=328

4

Photo credits

Emil Fagander: A; Mikael Almse: B, I, N, R;
Goran Assner: C, D, H, J, K, T; Janolof Fritze: F;
Lisa Nestorson: G; Jennie Lund: O; Thomas Northcut: Q;
Jamie Grill: U

Using photographs for tourism purposes is quite common. Many of the demand-side studies identify how people interpret the messages in photographs and have been used for purposes of market segmentation. Age and income have been found to influence interpretation (MacKay and Fesenmaier, 1997), and Vujicic (2008) concluded that gender has an influence in determining whether potential tourists interpret photographic messages according to the producers' intentions. As well, Vujicic found that past travel frequency influences whether potential tourists interpret photographic messages according to the producers' intentions; this is important because photos in advertising and promotions are expected to help sell the destination or package. Nationality is also a factor that influences people's interpretation of visual messages (Vujicic, 2008).

In the initial, qualitative stage, focus groups were conducted in Germany, England, Italy, and with a group of Norwegians visiting Sweden in order to test the usefulness of pictures for the subsequent online survey, and to obtain constructive feedback regarding questions to use in the survey. The participants in the focus groups were chosen through food and travel networks, as well as through university colleagues. Each focus group took between one to two hours and were mostly held in conference rooms at hotels. One or two moderators held the focus group sessions.

The researchers selected twenty-one colour photos that were judged to represent a wide range of possible Swedish experiences, including food in different settings. This selection was purposeful and expert, in the sense that the researchers had a clear, a priori understanding of what Sweden could offer a foreign tourist, and of what food lovers would potentially seek in food-related experiences while travelling abroad.

No such selection can cover all possibilities, so it was necessary to achieve a variety that would appeal to a potentially global sample. In effect, this selection is a representation of touristic experiences available in Sweden, although respondents were never informed of the country or origin. The selection omits cityscapes (which might have given away the country), but includes activities that are obviously urban in setting.

Each photo was given a short caption by the researchers to describe the experience, and respondents were given written instructions. The respondents were asked to pick three activities they preferred when travelling on a trip or short break to another country. The same respondents where then asked to pick three more activities they preferred assuming they had more time and money. The participants were also asked to indicate what the amount of money per person and per day they would be willing to pay for each experience, and that data will be analysed elsewhere.

Captions employed action verbs, namely "attend, enjoy, go, take, and experience", and attempted to make clear the nature of the experience. The focus groups revealed that the photos achieved the desired responses in terms of eliciting comments of an experiential nature. In other words, respondents were to put themselves into the pictures and imagine they could be doing what was depicted. Feedback was not sought on the quality or composition of the photo itself, and respondents understood this difference. Some of the comments received from participants are quoted below, to provide additional insights.

First-choice picture preferences

A simple ranking of preferences is presented in Table 4.3, by country and totals, indicating the percentage of respondents who selected each photo as one of their three first-round picks. The exact captions are provided, but this is not the order in which photos were presented to respondents.

It is evident from the table and the first column, Total, that pictures with food related motifs are attractive, and three out of the top four are in one way or another alluding to food experiences. The most popular picture "Enjoy regional cuisine in a local restaurant" depicts a young couple eating seafood at a restaurant and the second most attractive "Enjoy a farmer's market to look for and buy fresh food" depicts a customer savouring delicacies at a food market.

Some quotations from the focus groups shed light on these dominant preferences.

Regarding the photo captioned "enjoying regional cuisine in a local restaurant":

...the regional kitchen, visiting local restaurant. This is what I like to do." (female, age 28, Germany)

...I like to experience the local food." (male, 61, U.K.).

...I like to try the local food when visiting a new place". (female, 52, Norway)

Some of the respondents in the focus groups who chose "enjoy a farmers' market to look for and buy fresh food" described their choices as follow:

...I usually like to go to places where you can buy fresh food but where you also can eat. I like to walk around and see what people are selling." (female, 60, U.K.)

...We have a farmers' market close to where I live, which I go to regularly. It is really nice to have local produce." (male, 74, U.K.)

Table 4.3: Percentage of respondents that selected each photo in their top three picks. Source: Vujicic et al (2013).

Country	Total	Germany	Italy	Norway	Other	UK
M: Enjoy regional cuisine in a local restaurant	32%	33%	30%	23%	39%	37%
D: Enjoy a farmer's market to look for & buy fresh food	29%	29%	29%	24%	34%	32%
B: Take a trip to the islands and stay in a cottage	25%	27%	33%	15%	17%	28%
L: Experience a nice romantic dinner	21%	24%	17%	22%	24%	20%
C: Go hiking and view the wildlife in nature	19%	21%	22%	19%	16%	17%
I: Attend a food festival	18%	20%	24%	12%	21%	15%
O: Experience historic and archaeological sites	16%	15%	19%	10%	15%	19%
S: Staying at a spa	14%	16%	16%	13%	14%	13%
G: Enjoy some good food by the harbour while yachting	13%	15%	9%	20%	11%	12%
A: Enjoy a visit to art galleries and museums	13%	10%	22%	8%	13%	14%
U: Follow a food trail by car	10%	12%	11%	8%	14%	8%
J: Experience an outdoor music concert	6%	8%	5%	8%	3%	6%
Q: Experience a winter resort	6%	6%	6%	5%	5%	6%
E: Go shopping in the city to buy designer fashion	5%	4%	7%	5%	4%	4%
P: Meeting and learning from chefs	5%	5%	5%	4%	8%	3%
N: Experience an indoor music performance	4%	5%	1%	6%	4%	4%
T: Fishing	3%	2%	3%	5%	3%	2%
H: Playing golf	2%	2%	1%	1%	3%	3%
K: Enjoy a traditional dance performance	2%	2%	3%	1%	1%	1%
F: Experience a fashion show	2%	3%	2%	1%	1%	1%
R: Shopping for interior design	1%	1%	1%	1%	1%	2%

There is a divide between the first eleven pictures, and the remaining ten which were all selected by less than 10% of the respondents. Among the first eleven pictures there are two pictures with people eating and four more pictures with food as an important motif. Furthermore 'food trail' is part of the caption for picture U. The less attractive pictures only include one picture related to food, namely: "Meeting and learning from chefs".

Apart from food activities, nature activities such as "Take a trip to the islands and stay in a cottage" and "Go hiking and view the wildlife in nature" are high on the list, whereas shopping activities all are on the bottom half of the ranking. The less attractive ten pictures seem to be less attractive for all nationalities. It is however interesting to note that the segment 'Other' were significantly more attracted by "Meeting and learning from chefs".

If we look at the first eleven as being highly attractive and the remaining ten as less attractive, some interesting differences emerge. Table 4.3 indicates that the food pictures are much more frequent among the highly attractive pictures, whereas pictures of shopping activities are all considered less attractive.

It might be asked if people should have been shown in all the photos, but our analysis found that it does not seem to make any difference in making the picture more or less attractive to our sample of food lovers.

Second choice picture preferences

After having selected the top three photos, respondents were then asked to pick three more pictures (i.e. to select pictures ranked 4-6):

1   Experience a nice romantic dinner (19%)
2   Attend a food festival (17%)
3   Enjoy regional cuisine in a local restaurant (16%)
4   Staying at a spa (15%)
5   Enjoy some good food by the harbour while yachting (14%)
6   Enjoy a farmers' market to look for and buy fresh food (12%) and experience historic and archaeological sites (12%).

Variations between country preferences are evident, particularly when all six selected photos are considered, pointing to the need for careful segmentation and marketing. In particular, Norwegians were not at all interested in festivals, and Italians favoured archaeological sites while ignoring a spa experience.

Preferences of experienced food tourists

Respondents were asked how many times they had travelled in the previous 12 months for food-related reasons. In total, 39% had done so, and it was confirmed that the most travelled (i.e. 4 or more times in the past 12 months) are very similar in characteristics (statistically significant) to the 11% of the sample we determined to be highly involved through analysis of the involvement scale. Therefore, we can conclude that frequent food-related travel is a good surrogate measure for ego involvement, and that highly-involved foodies are indeed food tourists.

In Table 4.4 the first-choice preferences of experienced food tourists are shown. Pictures describing nature experiences as well as music performances and cultural tourism are significantly more attractive to less frequent food travellers. "Experience historic and archaeological sites" is unattractive for frequent food travellers. Enjoying regional cuisine remains the top choice for all, but the most frequent food tourists were significantly more inclined toward food festivals and meeting and learning from chefs. They were significantly less interested in the island visit, wildlife, archaeological sites, and musical performances. Following a food trail is not very popular among this segment, perhaps owing to a propensity to fly for short breaks. And dining in the harbour while yachting is also a minority preference across the sample, quite likely because of the cost of yachting.

Table 4.4: Percentage of respondents, categorised according to respondents' travel frequency with food as the main reason, that selected a picture as one out of their three top choices. Source: Vujicic et al (2013).

Food travel: How many times have you travelled internationally in the last 12 months with food as the main reason?	No time	1 to 3 times	4 or more times	Total	Sign.
M: Enjoy regional cuisine in a local restaurant	32%	32%	31%	32%	ns
D: Enjoy a farmer's market to look for and buy fresh food	26%	36%	31%	29%	0.001
B: Take a trip to the islands and stay in a cottage	27%	22%	20%	25%	0.05
L: Experience a nice romantic dinner	20%	22%	25%	21%	ns
C: Go hiking and view the wildlife in nature	21%	17%	15%	20%	0.001
I: Attend a food festival	15%	24%	26%	19%	0.001
O: Experience historic- and archaeological sites	19%	12%	3%	16%	0.001
S: Staying at a spa	15%	15%	10%	15%	ns
A: Enjoy a visit to art galleries and museums	14%	13%	11%	14%	ns
G: Enjoy some good food by the harbour while yachting	13%	14%	14%	13%	ns
U: Follow a food trail by car	10%	11%	13%	10%	
Q: Experience a winter resort	6%	5%	4%	6%	
J: Experience an outdoor music concert	8%	5%	1%	6%	0.001
P: Meeting and learning from chefs	3%	6%	10%	5%	0.001
E: Go shopping in the city to buy designer fashion	5%	5%	4%	5%	
N: Experience an indoor music performance	5%	2%	2%	4%	0.001
T: Fishing	3%	2%	4%	3%	
K: Enjoy a traditional dance performance	2%	1%	3%	2%	
H: Playing golf	2%	2%	4%	2%	ns
F: Experience a fashion show	1%	2%	2%	2%	ns
R: Shopping for interior design	1%	1%	1%	1%	ns

Three of these experiences appealed significantly more to the experienced food tourists, namely:

■ A farmers' market to look for and buy fresh food

■ Attend a food festival

■ Meeting and learning from chefs

Comparing the differences in preferred experiences among HiFs and Foodies (their three first-round photo choices), Table 4.5 shows that the HiFs preferred "to enjoy a farmer's market to look for and buy fresh food" (47%) more than the remainder of the respondents (28%). The HiFs also preferred "attending a food festival" (33%), "meeting and learning from chefs" (10%) and "following a food trail by car" (9%). These are active experiences, tactile, and hands-on.

Table 4.5: Highly Involved Foodies (HiFs) compared to the remainder (Foodies): First choice of photos, and willingness to pay (WtP, in Euros). Source: Vujicic et al (2013).

	High Involvement (HiFs)			Foodies			Total		
	WtP(€)	N	Vote	WtP(€)	N	Vote	WtP(€)	N	Vote
A: Enjoy a visit to art galleries and museums	75.80	41	12%	46.27	378	14%	49.16	419	14%
B: Take a trip to the islands and stay in a cottage	143.51	72	21%	93.31	705	26%	97.96	777	25%
C: Go hiking and view the wildlife in nature	76.94	49	14%	74.60	556	20%	74.79	605	20%
D: Enjoy a farmer's market to look for and buy fresh food	124.66	163	47%	59.72	755	28%	71.25	918	30%
E: Go shopping in the city to buy designer fashion	148.87	15	4%	189.87	135	5%	185.77	150	5%
F: Experience a fashion show	44.78	9	3%	63.78	41	2%	60.36	50	2%
G: Enjoy some good food by the harbour while yachting	127.69	39	11%	109.94	378	14%	111.60	417	14%
H: Playing golf	116.00	5	1%	106.44	54	2%	107.25	59	2%
I: Attend a food festival	90.47	114	33%	68.45	463	17%	72.80	577	19%
J: Experience an outdoor music concert	68.89	9	3%	82.38	190	7%	81.77	199	6%
K: Enjoy a traditional dance performance	56.67	3	1%	69.69	54	2%	69.00	57	2%
L: Experience a nice romantic dinner	176.36	66	19%	108.20	588	22%	115.08	654	21%
M: Enjoy regional cuisine in a local restaurant	95.81	98	28%	71.32	899	33%	73.73	997	32%
N: Experience an indoor music performance	283.33	3	1%	97.30	121	4%	101.80	124	4%
O: Experience historic- and archaeological sites	111.88	24	7%	61.55	460	17%	64.05	484	16%
P: Meeting and learning from chefs	105.24	33	10%	119.73	113	4%	116.46	146	5%
Q: Experience a winter resort	195.33	15	4%	137.70	165	6%	142.50	180	6%
R: Shopping for interior design	357.33	3	1%	137.56	27	1%	159.53	30	1%
S: Staying at a spa	207.28	25	7%	164.94	442	16%	167.20	467	15%
T: Fishing	105.08	12	3%	111.09	117	4%	110.53	129	4%
U: Follow a food trail by car	113.80	30	9%	111.89	157	6%	112.20	187	6%

Note: "Vote" is calculated as number of respondents (N) divided by total number of HiFs (346), Foodies (2771) and Total (3117) respectively.

4

By contrast most of the activities that the lower-involved foodies preferred significantly more than the HiFs do not involve food: for example hiking and viewing wildlife, experiencing an outdoor concert and staying at a spa. In general the HiFs are prepared to pay more (in Euros) for these experiences even though the lower-involved foodies prefer them more. For example the HiFs are prepared to pay €207.28 for a spa experience while the 'Foodies' are prepared to pay €164.94.

What is also apparent in the table is that the HiFs were prepared to spend up to twice the amount of euros to enjoy these experiences. For example, the HiFs were prepared to pay €124.66 for a farmers' market experience while the lower-involved foodies would only pay €59.72. The one exception was 'meeting and learning from chefs', and it can be surmised that the HiFs were more likely to be experienced in terms of the real cost of this experience. There were interesting results for the three 'eating' activities ("enjoy some good food by the harbour while yachting", "experience a romantic dinner", and "enjoy regional cuisine in a local restaurant". Eating, being a sedentary activity, appealed as much to the Foodies as to the HiFs as shown on the 'Vote' columns. However, the HiFs were willing to pay much more for these passive eating experiences.

What we can conclude from these findings is that overall the HiFs prefer tactile, hands-on and active food experiences over sedentary and passive experiences (i.e. eating). Almost without exception they valued experiences more, in terms of their willingness to pay. These findings reveal the highly-involved foodies to be higher-yielding tourists.

Summary

This chapter assesses the strong connection between being a self identified, and especially a highly-involved foodie and international travel for food-related experiences. It began with a discussion of motivation, employing seeking and escaping theory - a construct similar to the so-called push and pull factors that destination marketers often talk about. An attractive food-tourism destination in this context is one that both satisfies generic needs, such as escapism, hedonism, socializing, or relaxation with family, but also has food-specific allure. A successful food-tourism destination must pay attention to the concept of authenticity and what it means to foodies. Authenticity is a theme running through the book, with some primary considerations being the links to traditional food sources and cuisine, the ways in which food is served, terroir, provenance, and of course marketing and communication.

Activities and experiences were then discussed, stressing the need to involve foodies throughf all three experiential realms of cognition, behaviour and emotion. Examples were provided of things to do (i.e. activities) and ways in which the foodie can be engaged intellectually and emotionally in experiences, including aesthetics and physical mastery. A summary of some major foodie surveys revealed their dominant and preferred activities and experiences, in which socializing, celebrating and learning figure prominently. Ensuring that tourists have a truly memorable food experience becomes a top goal for destination developers and marketers, as well as innkeepers, caterers and restaurateurs.

Who exactly travels for food-related experiences has been examined through the summaries of major foodie surveys and our own Australian and multi-country research. Findings cannot be generalized across the globe, but the available evidence can certainly be used as the starting point in gaining market intelligence for any city or region. Data from North America demonstrate that food tourists tend to be younger, better educated, and more affluent. They spend more and tend to combine food and other cultural experiences with shopping. Food and wine are often combined, so wine regions have an advantage. Festivals and events are attractive, as are unique foods and atmosphere, gourmet foods, farmers markets, wine and beer. Most travel as couples, or with family or friends, and many travel by air. They are information-seekers and relatively high-yield visitors.

The North American surveys are somewhat misleading in that they did not focus on foodies in as precise a way as our Australian and multi-country surveys. As shown in the Appendix, we only wanted to sample self-declared foodies, then analyse them according to travel and involvement. Australian foodies were found to be very highly travelled for food experiences, demonstrating a high level of involvement. They had in mind a number of specific destinations and experiences to motivate them, favouring traditional wine countries in Europe and nearer Asian countries. Authenticity, tradition, cuisine specific to the country, taking lessons or learning to cook applied to all preferred destinations, while naturalness and freshness appeared to be a factor for south-east Asian destinations.

In the multi-country research it was found that 39% had taken a food-related international trip in the previous 12 months. Males and higher-income respondents had a higher propensity to plan future food-related trips. Photo elicitation was employed as a technique for exploring preferred experiences of food tourists. In this way respondents could imagine themselves within an experiencescape such as the number one overall pick - a couple dining casually by the seaside. Highly involved foodies (HiFs) preferred active and hands-on food experiences, for example farmers' markets, food festivals, meeting and learning from chefs, and food trails, and they were willing to pay more for most experiences. The remainder of the foodies preferred sedentary (eating) food experiences, for example good food while at a harbour, romantic dinners and regional cuisine at local restaurants; also hiking and viewing wildlife, experiencing an outdoor concert and staying at a spa.

Study questions

1   Explain what it is that motivates foodies to leave home and pursue specific experiences abroad? What is food "adventuring" in this context?

2   How do food tourists know that something is authentic? Does it matter? Give some examples related to food experiences.

3   What is the difference between activities and experiences in the context of food tourism? How can suppliers and destinations ensure a memorable, satisfying experience for food tourists?

4   Define and give examples of tactile food experiences. Who provides them?

5   Why do most foodies prefer to travel in couples of family groups? Refer both to demographics and identity theory.

6   Explain how photo elicitation can be used to determine the experience preferences of foodies and others with special interests. What are the limitations of this method?

7   Why are highly-involved foodies prepared to pay more for their food-related experiences? Why are their preferred experiences different from other foodies? Does this make them high-yield tourists?

Further reading

Heldke, L. (2003). *Exotic Appetites: Ruminations of a Food Adventurer.* London: Routledge.

5 Planning and Developing Tourism for Foodies

Learning objectives

Readers are expected to learn the following from this chapter:

- How to put foodies at the core of food tourism planning, development and marketing
- How to conduct a self-diagnosis of food tourism development and potential
- Preparing and using key performance indicators
- The meaning, purpose and process of developing food tourism clusters
- The application of the cluster concept to rural and urban areas
- Destination concepts for food tourism focused on experiences for foodies
- The meaning and co-creation of authenticity in food tourism
- How provenance is connected to the concept of authenticity and why it is important to foodies

Planning and development: foodies at the core

Based on a sound understanding of the foodie and food tourists, this chapter outlines a planning and development process that puts foodies at the core. It is true that destinations and businesses cannot usually ignore the local resident market, nor the tourist who wants a good food experience while travelling for other purposes. The point is simply this: if you want to grow food tourism you really have to design experiences and your marketing specifically for foodies.

In Chapter 6 we provide case studies and examples to illustrate food tourism planning and development at all levels, from country and region to city and individual enterprise, all with foodies as the focus. In Chapter 7 planned events are featured, owing to their pivotal role in food tourism; and in Chapter 8 marketing and communications to foodies are the subject.

This chapter begins with a general discussion of planning and developing food tourism, but not in the usual supply-side manner. Rather, we stress planning for foodies and those highly-involved, experienced food tourists who will constitute the highest-yield food tourists - and the most demanding.

Most of the conventional wisdom on food tourism, as reflected in articles and textbooks, is really about supply-side development or traditional planning and marketing approaches. For example Mykletun and Gyimóthy (2010) stressed the significance of networking entrepreneurial processes in the branding and development of tourism destinations. Ottenbacher and Harrington (2013) illustrated six key elements that closely link to successful culinary tourism strategy, namely: the strategy itself, cooperation among stakeholders, leadership issues, regional products/services, communicating quality standards, promoting regions as perceived by tourists. Of course these elements are all important, but should not be the starting point.

In this book the emphasis is placed on keeping the foodie at the core, and this is in line with experience marketing and service-dominant logic. In other words, the starting point is not with what you have (however great or unique you think your food is) but with an understanding of the foodies and food tourists. Kivela and Crotts (2006) were on this track when they said that DMOs (Destination Marketing Organizations) are to create visitors' desires of local destinations through educating tourists about why the local cuisine and culture are special and unique.

Until recently, however, there has been insufficient knowledge of foodies and food tourists to make this approach realistic. Hall et al. (2003) in their book *Food Tourism around the World: Development, Management and Markets*, mostly examined the potential of food tourism and the supply/development aspects. They did consider motivations, with the proposition that food tourists can be separated into a continuum of increasing special interest: from 'culinary' to 'gastronomic' to 'gourmet' tourism. They acknowledged, "there is little published research on how this market is constructed" (p. 62).

■ A demand-side approach

Various published typologies have been based on the assumption that a high interest in food generates the fewest number of visitors. They also assumed that these highly motivated food tourists seek out restaurants, markets or wineries, and that all or nearly all of their activities are food-related. This might or might not be true, it depends on the location and the types of visitors being attracted.

Here is a new typology, based on aggressive food tourism development goals:

■ Large numbers of *dedicated food tourists* visit the destination because of its reputation for high-quality and diverse food-related experiences; they are high-yield tourists as they are willing to spend more for the customized, hands-on experiences they seek; they spread the word that this destination is worth a visit, and a repeat visit, contributing to its overall reputation as an attractive destination.

- Many other *cultural tourists* are attracted, and while they are not dedicated food tourists they are food lovers and they expect high-quality food experiences because of the destination's established reputation.

- *All visitors*, most of whom are not foodies, receive high-quality food experiences and this contributes to a globally successful destination brand.

This simple typology reflects reasonable goals for food tourism development, in concert with overall destination branding. There is no need to assume that dedicated food tourists will be small in numbers, indeed that is probably what happens when there is no understanding of what foodies need and the 'product' on offer is not appealing. On the other hand, as mentioned elsewhere in this book, it is generally better to attract a small number of high-yield food tourists than large numbers of tourists seeking low-cost experiences.

Our process does not assume that all foodies become food tourists, nor that all food tourists are potential customers for any particular destination or service. But it requires market intelligence based on original research into the target segments, not a reliance on data about who is already coming to a given place and what they are spending their money on. That common approach to tourism research leads to superficial understanding of the foodie and inappropriate communications or product development. For example, a common market segmentation approach is based on demographics or socio-economic variables (e.g. upwardly-mobile singles; two-income couples without children; active seniors) and while these factors do affect tourism in general, they say nothing about food tourism motivation or foodie identity and involvement. The same critique applies to all special-interest tourist segments.

A model is provided in Figure 5.1 which illustrates the demand-side approach, and while planning can begin at any stage in this process we start by considering market intelligence.

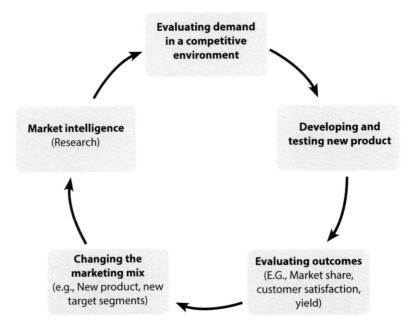

Figure 5.1: A demand-side approach to food tourism planning and development

Market intelligence

There is a growing body of research-based knowledge available on the foodie and food tourists, as summarized in this book, but data and analysis does not automatically yield intelligence. It is best to customize research and analysis, including market segmentation, for the exact needs and purposes of the city, destination or product to be marketed. What we have been able to do in this book is give examples of how research leads to implications for Australia and Sweden, but the data could be applied to the other countries from which we obtained large samples of foodies.

Refer to Figure 5.2 which provides a comprehensive self-diagnostic for destinations interested in progressing their food tourism development and marketing. It includes specific types of necessary market intelligence and appropriate research methods.

Evaluating demand in a competitive environment

Everything done to develop and market food tourism has to be in the context of evolving supply and demand conditions. Will foodies travel to a city if they hold a poor comparative image of its food distinctiveness, price or quality? It can never be assumed that having good product or doing a lot of branding and marketing will result in increased food tourism. Regular evaluations of competitors are required, including gaining a detailed understanding of why foodies make their choices.

Developing and testing new product (co-creation)

A supply-side approach begins with what a destination or provider has to offer, then proceeds to 'selling' it. That has limited growth potential. In the experience marketing approach (or demand-led marketing) the target foodies have to be involved in co-creating experiences suited to their preferences. Again, this requires customized market intelligence, plus innovative entrepreneurs and a willingness to take risks.

Evaluating outcomes

It is a widespread problem that tourism data do not provide sufficient detail on special-interest segments like foodies, neither their motivations, activities nor expenditures. That means special surveys are required to isolate dedicated food tourists and separate them from others consuming food products. If a destination wants to know the value of food tourism, it is going to be a difficult challenge requiring one of two methods:

1 Incorporate special-interest questions into regular intercept and exit surveys (e.g., what specifically attracted you? what have you spent on food, dining out, other food-related experiences?)

2 Conduct special surveys to find dedicated food tourists, such as at destination restaurants, food-related experiences and events; the key is to be able to estimate overall food tourism expenditures on the basis of a sample, which means making some assumptions about averages and applying that to an estimate of the total number of dedicated food tourists visiting an area in a period of time.

Changing the marketing mix

The fundamental principle of a customer-oriented approach is that products, prices, promotions and packages be geared specifically to the needs and preferences of the target segment. This marketing mix, including focused communications, has to change in response to competition.

The whole process is cyclical and can be started at any point. However, if starting from scratch, its always wise to begin with available market intelligence and knowledge of what competitors or successful food destinations/providers are already doing.

■   Comparative and competitive advantages

In their book, *The Competitive Destination: A Sustainable Tourism Perspective,* Ritchie and Crouch (2003) explain how both comparative and competitive advantages must be cultivated. Comparative advantages accrue from what you inherit; they include location, geography, climate, natural resources, culture, and events and organizations that have evolved along with historical development of an area.

A destination cannot rely on its endowments; it must at least match its competitors with intelligence, planning, investments and targeted marketing if it hopes to find advantage. Monitoring and learning from competitors, and if possible formal benchmarking, is always a good idea. Fostering entrepreneurship and innovation through a bottom-up planning and development approach will also generate advantages.

In Figure 5.2 specific ideas on comparative and competitive advantages related to food tourism are listed. These can be used in destination diagnostics, considering the importance of each item and how well the destination is doing in exploiting or developing the attributes.

Note that every comparative advantage listed in the figure implies a disadvantage if you do not have it. When doing a competitive SWOT analysis (strengths, weaknesses, opportunities and threats) these have to be taken into account. It should also be emphasized that some disadvantages can be dealt with, but some cannot be overcome or reversed - you cannot easily turn from a winter to a summer destination. This suggests that in some areas it is best to make do with what you have - build on it.

	Comparative advantages What destinations inherit	**Competitive advantages** How destinations compete
Location and accessibility	♦ proximity to large cities; good access to, and within the destination	♦ investment in transport infrastructure ♦ cultivation of resident demand for food experiences ♦ develop food trails and tours ♦ cluster services and attractions
Climate and natural resources	♦ a climate attractive to tourists and favorable for certain activities/events ♦ fresh and local produce available seasonally or all year ♦ oceans and fresh water for fishing and seafood ♦ unique food products	♦ investment in fishing, farming, and food/ beverage processing ♦ sustainable food production practices
Accommo- dation	♦ a range of quality accommodations for international tourists ♦ hotels, spas and resorts stressing food, beverages, food events	♦ develop urban and rural food tourism clusters and packages
Export- ready food experiences	♦ existing quality restaurants, farms, fishing fleets, tours, events	♦ develop a portfolio of food events, both hallmark and iconic ♦ foster entrepreneurship and innovation in food and tourism ♦ invest in mass, social and online communications to foodies ♦ quality assurance schemes
Culture	♦ friendly and hospitable for visitors ♦ attractive traditional cuisine and beverages	♦ food culture cultivated through the work of chefs, cooking schools, media management ♦ develop food precincts in towns and cities ♦ set and enforce high quality standards

Economy	• cost advantages; low inflation • strong agriculture and fishery sectors	• develop the food brand • supply-chain management; adding value through food tourism cluster development • create a positive investment climate for food, hospitality and tourism • invest in market intelligence on foodies and benchmarking of other food destinations
Social conditions	• a substantial population able to cultivate food and beverage interests (i.e., lifestyle)	• promote healthy eating; encourage fresh and local markets
Health conditions	• healthy food and healthy eating • high food saftey standards and enforcement	• position the destination for healthy eating
Professional-ism	• proven leadership • a strong destination marketing organization • education/training available for event management and event tourism • professional associations and standards	• constant efforts to improve strategy, planning, marketing and investment • industry-education linkages strengthened • mentorship and apprenticeship programs • a programme of research and evaluation to support food tourism
Food events	• existing food events that are popular with residents and tourists alike • a healthy portfolio of permanent local and regional food events • a successful track record in hosting events	• build on local strengths to create hallmark food events • build iconic events for foodie segments • sophisticated portfolio creation and management • learning organizations employing market intelligence

Figure 5.2: Comparative and competitive advantages in food tourism

■ Self-diagnostics and strategic planning

Most strategic planning begins with environmental scanning, including a competitive SWOT evaluation. The strengths and weaknesses compared to competitors will suggest strategies, as will a more internal-looking assessment of opportunities – such as resources and synergies to build upon. Threats can come from within or externally, so the section on propelling and constraining forces offers some guidelines on what to monitor.

Figure 5.3 has been prepared specifically for food tourism planning and development, including the marketing and communications components of strategy and implementation. A country, city, or resort can start with these self-diagnostic tools and work towards the strategies and action plans best suited to its needs and ambitions.

There are eight major dimensions to this process; it is not a linear model in which things get done in sequence. Three pertain to outcomes in a triple-bottom-line approach: economic, environmental, and social/cultural. While most tourism development planning concentrates on the economic dimension (notably measured in terms of attracting tourist expenditure and creating jobs), it is better to frame any tourism strategy in more comprehensive terms so that all stakeholders and the community will support the strategy. The other five dimensions relate to process, starting with various plans, evaluation of the product and experiences, quality evaluation and controls, branding along with image and reputation management, and the research and evaluation systems needed to support the entire process.

Key Performance Indicators (KPIs) can be interpreted and utilized in several ways. Specific goals and objectives can be employed, or performance measures articulated. In this table the KPIs are deliberately general. For examples, under plans, the KPIs are to establish various plans – users can go beyond this to formulate specific goals, objectives and measures.

Methods are specified for each dimension, but again in general terms. Planning requires visioning, stakeholder consultations, setting goals and objectives, all supported by market intelligence. The creation of food tourism clusters (as examined in the ensuing section) is highly recommended, with the specific aim of maximizing collaboration and tourist attractiveness where the greatest potential exists.

Major dimensions	KPIs: key performance indicators	Methods
Plans	Establish the following: ♦ cluster concept ♦ strategic plan ♦ marketing plan ♦ targeted communications plan	♦ strategic visioning involving all stakeholders; setting goals and objectives ♦ forming a food tourism cluster through collaboration among all stakeholders ♦ through research determine the best media and messages to reach your target markets
Product	♦ export-ready and communicated internationally ♦ customizing potential for co-created food experiences ♦ restaurants: number, variety, reputation, awards (e.g., Michelin) ♦ chefs: professionalism; prizes (e.g., Bocuse d'Or) ♦ events: designed especially for food lovers; number, size, reserved tickets for tours and online booking ♦ tours: food and wine trails; tour companies specializing in food; combined urban/rural; ♦ packages: for food lovers; food plus culture, nature, shopping ♦ other experiences: at hotels and resorts; food/fish markets with guides	♦ inventory and SWOT evaluation of existing product and experiences, relative to the competition ♦ bottom-up approach to evaluating potential (i.e., stakeholder engagement through cluster development) ♦ expert opinion (e.g., from wholesalers, agents, travel writers and bloggers)

Research and evaluation	• market intelligence is regularly obtained through regular visitor surveys constructed especially to measure food satisfaction, food as travel motivation, and to permit foodie segmentation; through online research (e.g., netnography) and in target market areas • comprehensive evaluation systems are in place : of product/experience quality; stakeholder satisfaction; public opinion; outcomes (economic, social/cultural, environmental)	• establish a research and evaluation system or employ experts • work with research/academic establishments • join food and food tourism industry organizations
Quality of the experience	• customer satisfaction: regular measures of importance and performance, satisfaction with all food experiences • quality control: systems in place to ensure product and experience quality and continuous improvement	• implement a TQM program for food, hospitality and tourism sectors • periodic visitor surveys
Brand, image and reputation	• brand values and design: ensure that the destination has its own, but also reflects higher-level food-brand values; develop a distinctive design and competitive positioning • reputation monitoring: monitor media to detect issues with food reputation; combat negative images and messages • media management: communicating messages and images that build and reinforce the brand	• media monitoring • consult external experts • test all elements of branding
Economic outcomes	• increase food tourist numbers and expenditure • demonstrate economic benefits including jobs • set and meet growth targets	• conduct economic impact assessments
Social and cultural outcomes	• demonstrate benefits to the host community: new choices for food and entertainment; preservation of traditions (e.g., distinctive cuisine); opportunities to participate in events or create new ones	• employ various forms of public input • monitor residents' engagement with food events and other food-related experiences
Environmental outcomes	• implement green policies for the entire supply chain • measure the ecological footprint of food tourism and compare with other industries and tourism sectors	• get certified by appropriate environmental agencies • work with all stakeholders to identify and ameliorate problems • conduct surveys to measure energy consumption, waste, conservation practices

Figure 5-3: A diagnostic process for food tourism planning and development

■   The evolution of food tourism: Hjalager's typology of value added in gastronomy tourism

Hjalager (2002) proposed a categorization that has relevance for both an evolutionary perspective on the development of food tourism (not that a deterministic model of progression is suggested) and as guidelines for destination and cluster development. Her 'first order' category consists of food tourism based on enjoying the produce of an area. Food might be promoted as an attraction, and there might be food events to enjoy, but this is supply-side food tourism based on what the region has to offer.

In the 'second order' of gastronomy tourism, Hjalager proposed that understanding the food should be more important. The destination engages in development through quality controls and certification, preserving culinary traditions, and bringing the service sector to the fore (as opposed to solely relying on producers). In this scenario high cooperation must be achieved across the entire supply chain.

In the 'third order', experiences are paramount. Entrepreneurial resources must be mobilized in order to meet the needs of discriminating food tourists who value unique, authentic experiences. New organizations might be required, and the destination develops trails, attractions, events, cooking classes, holidays for foodies, and the opening of production sites (like farms and factories) to visitors. This category resembles the highly-advanced food destinations of today – those that realize they are catering to sophisticated foodies with special requirements.

Finally, and perhaps nowhere is this yet evident, the 'fourth order' concentrates on knowledge as the main resource. In other words, highly successful food destinations can profit by sharing their expertise. To do so they might require new structures that have a global reach, and they must invest in research and development plus demonstration projects.

Food tourism clusters

According to Michael Porter (1990, 1998, 2000) location is not as important as it once was, nor are the comparative advantages traditionally enjoyed by cities and nations who relied upon natural endowments or good access to markets. His popular notion of business clusters and agglomerations helps explain why certain areas have flourished.

> *A business cluster is a geographic concentration of interconnected businesses, suppliers, and associated institutions in a particular field. Clusters are considered to increase the productivity with which companies can compete, nationally and globally. In urban studies, the term agglomeration is used.* (Porter, 1998; 2000)

A number of food and wine tourism clusters have emerged in various countries, with or without planning and intervention. This concentration of attractions and services can evolve naturally, based on unique terroir and pioneering entrepreneurship, but if a country really wants to grow food tourism there will have to be a concerted effort to establish more of them.

From a supply side, the logical starting point is where the food, wine or other produce originates. If there is sufficient supply and will power, then why not take the next step and develop food tourism to its maximum potential? Essentially, this means building the value chain to include tourist consumption and (hopefully) resulting exports. But from a demand-side point of view, there is much more potential within cities, resorts and other places where visitors naturally concentrate. To the extent possible, clusters should incorporate both urban and rural (even remote) partners.

The cluster concept brings all stakeholders together in specific cities and regions for their mutual benefit and for synergies that require full co-operation. The main functions (and goals) of clusters are:

- Attract and hold dedicated food tourists; increase their spending and loyalty; add value through quality, authentic food experiences for all visitors.

- Minimize leakages by stressing 'fresh and local' produce; grow the value chain to the benefit of local and regional suppliers.

- Brand the cluster, reinforcing the national food brand.

- Increase marketing reach and effectiveness of the cluster; gain new and larger export markets.

- Improve network efficiencies; bring all stakeholders together.

- Develop tourist experiences; continuously improve quality.

According to Mossberg et al. (2014: 340) "A successful food tourism model should be grounded in a bottom up approach as most innovation comes from local community driven networks and collaboration." This was the approach taken by Failte Ireland in promoting its food tourism strategy, involving primarily social media and food champions.

Figure 5.4 is an illustration of the food tourism cluster concept, stressing key stakeholders and their roles. Start with agriculture and fisheries, because a food tourism cluster rests on a foundation of good produce: fresh, local, organic and ecological are accepted brand values. This particularly applies when meal providers (from chefs to the catering at convention centres and food festivals) can rely on local producers for top quality. The provenance of food needs to be explained to foodies, and can be provided to them as souvenir-style information booklets.

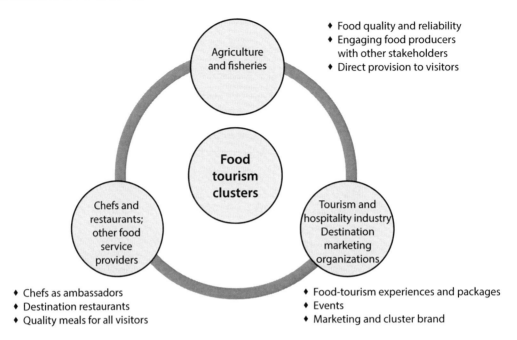

Figure 5.4: Food tourism cluster concept

Although fishers and farmers can sell directly to tourists, and export through various intermediaries, they need to be convinced of the advantages of working more closely with providers of meals and the tourism and hospitality sectors in general. Farmers can diversify their revenue base in numerous ways, as farm stay or agri-tourism destinations and educational hubs, many of which can be developed in partnership with other regional cultural and natural endowments. Moreover, research suggests these farmers' produce can attract premium prices and even be resilient in declining markets. When communities collaborate these benefits diffuse throughout regions, both adding value to local brands but also keeping land in production and settling land use disputes.

Chefs, restaurants and other food-service providers are key players in the cluster concept. Their primary responsibility (to the concept) is to ensure that every visitor has a quality food experience, hence the importance of programmes that stress constant improvement and certification. This is partly because of the hygiene factor, namely that bad food experiences are likely to discourage existing and potential tourists. It is also important to realize that food is the one cultural experience that all visitors have in a city or country and so they should at least have the option of purchasing fresh and local and authentic recipes.

Those establishments with the potential to attract food tourists have added roles to play, as they are likely to be the focal points for media and foodie reviews, at the hub of tourist districts, and flagships for the food brand. Chefs also have an important role to play as ambassadors of the food brand and authentic cuisine.

Destination marketing organizations (DMO) must develop distinct cluster brands, and market to potential food tourists. This can only be done when there is confidence in local and regional produce. The tourism/hospitality industry and marketing organizations have the additional role of creating innovative food tourism events and other experiences, some of which will require the active participation of food producers.

■ Rural cluster

Clusters can be developed in rural or remote areas, centred around fishing ports, a town or villages within farm districts, or at resorts. In this context, a resort could be a self-contained property where people spend their holidays (e.g. skiing, seaside/lakeside, spa) or a town that caters to all the needs of visitors (i.e. accommodation, meals, transport, entertainment, recreation). In the cases of fishing and farm-based food tourism clusters the emphasis is on fresh and local produce, whereas at resorts (and cities) the food has to be largely brought to the tourists.

■ Urban cluster (or agglomeration)

What we see developing naturally in many cities are entertainment and food/drinking districts. Agglomeration benefits businesses who can pool their marketing and parking, rely on higher levels of public transport and police security, and generally benefit from the tendency of residents and visitors alike to spend time in areas where there are lots of choices and plenty of activity. Cities often label these districts and develop them through various regulations.

Top foodie cities

Any ranking is going to be subjective, but what is interesting is how various 'experts' or 'enthusiasts' compare destinations with foodies in mind. The following excerpts are from Gregory Cartier, Fine Living Correspondent at the website Ask Men (ca.askmen.com/fine_living/wine_dine_archive_60/87_wine_dine.html) accessed Nov. 10, 2013:

> *People take food seriously, perhaps none more so than I. As a result, I can understand if you disagree with some of the choices below. But before you read on, here are some of the factors I chose to single out in my quest to find the ultimate world food capitals.*
>
> ***Food history:*** *Does the city have a history or reputation as a culinary hotbed?*
> ***Food variety:*** *Does the city have a diverse food landscape? Is this a city with a unique mix of cultures and as a result, culinary styles?*
> ***Food price:*** *Does the city accommodate a host of budgets with not just good, but superior cuisine?*
> ***Food soul:*** *As intangible a quality as there is, but nonetheless, does the city exude a soul and a passion for food? Do the residents as a collective care about food?*

To Gregory Cartier, Melbourne, Australia "...can lay claim to some of the most inventive cuisine in the world", while New York City, USA is a "food mecca" with "...just about every kind of cuisine imaginable to accommodate every budget." Montreal, Canada has old-world charm and its real allure comes from "...those neighborhood jewels that ooze with hospitality and charm (and allow you to bring your own wine to boot)." San Francisco, USA "...is a gorgeous paradise for food lovers and presents a feast of impossible choices to gourmands game enough to take on the challenge."

Its rather difficult for all but a few major world cities to get on to lists like this, implying the need for hierarchical considerations of countries, major cities, minor cities, rural regions and small towns or villages. Not every food tourist goes to major cities and even if they do they are potential visitors to the world's most out-of-the-way places as well.

Creative Cities of Gastronomy is a UNESCO movement. From its website (www.unesco.org/new/en/culture/themes/creativity/creative-cities-network/gastronomy/) we find criteria for joining:

■ Well-developed gastronomy, characteristic of the urban centre and/or region;
■ Vibrant gastronomy community with numerous traditional restaurants and/or chefs;
■ Endogenous ingredients used in traditional cooking;
■ Local know-how, traditional culinary practices and methods of cooking that have survived industrial/technological advancement;
■ Traditional food markets and traditional food industry;
■ Tradition of hosting gastronomic festivals, awards, contests and other broadly-targeted means of recognition;
■ Respect for the environment and promotion of sustainable local products;
■ Murturing of public appreciation, promotion of nutrition in educational institutions and inclusion of biodiversity conservation programmes in cooking schools curricula.

Délice: Good Food Cities of the World "...is an international network of like minded cities engaged in promoting the benefits of culinary excellence and good food. Created in 2007 by the City of Lyon (France), Délice gathers today 19 cities from 4 continents and offers a platform to exchange and meet with chefs and gastronomy professionals." (delice-network.org)

The activities and events of Délice revolve around five main themes:
■ City marketing
■ Education and transmission
■ Local products
■ Health and nutrition
■ Excellence of chefs.

Destination development concepts

Resources are the foundations of food tourism development, whether they be natural (e.g. gathering wild foods, fishing or hunting), farmed (including pick-your-own places) or manufactured (as in beverages and processed foods). Resources for eating have to be packaged and marketed in order to become tourism products. To become experiences, more value must be added through co-creation and interpretation.

Attractions are places, businesses and experiencescapes that can motivate a trip. They are the pull factors, or whatever food tourists are seeking. Resources become attractions only when the tourist can find out about them, get to them, and find a way to enjoy them. That means attractions are mediated experiences, with managers actively seeking visitors and facilitating their experiences.

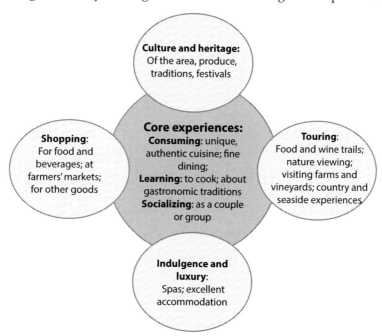

Figure 5.5: A destination concept for food tourism

■ Export-ready

To be an 'export-ready' attraction means the experience is available for purchase outside the region or country, as through travel agents, tours companies and other wholesalers, and online bookings. Information has to be easily accessed by potential visitors and the advance purchase made simple. In food tourism, examples are few and far between (see the New Zealand example on p. 134), which is a major limitation on growth.

■ What Australian foodies want in a domestic destination

We have learned that the food tourism experience must be multi-dimensional. Since it can be expected that food tourists seek out very specific information about preferred destinations, and might respond to highly targeted messages that convey special food-lover meanings, the lure has to consider what else foodies want from their travel. These augmentations must be part of the communication, and they must be available for the autonomous traveller.

First and foremost are the elements of culture and heritage that go together best with the food experience, including shopping (e.g. farmers' markets; direct from farm or fisher), and cultural events featuring food and other local traditions (see Figure 5.5). Touring in food and wine regions is valued, but there must be access to farms, vineyards, country inns and other unique dining experiences. A well-designed food or wine trail (preferably combined) will offer the food tourist much more than sightseeing, and should be thought of as an interpretive tool. Indeed, all aspects of the food tourist experience will be greatly augmented with a variety of interpretive mechanisms - from available group tours to individual learning opportunities. Similar to wine lovers, the food tourist wants other shopping and nature-oriented experiences. They are, after all, educated, sophisticated and experienced travellers.

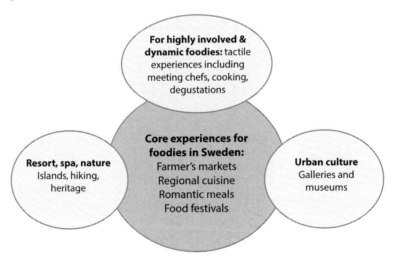

Figure 5.6: A destination concept for food tourism in Sweden

■ Destination preferences from the multi-country research

Although the Australian and multi-country research projects yielded similar patterns and preferences, the two illustrations of destinations are different. Figure 5.6 was prepared for Sweden, based on the results, so it shows what experiences they need to offer as the core for foodies, and what augmentations make the most sense given our findings. Highly-involved foodies will want the same core experiences as others (markets, festivals, romantic meals and regional cuisine) plus a variety of specialist, mostly tactile (i.e. hands-on) opportunities including meeting chefs, cooking classes and attending degustations. Sweden (and many other countries) have good potential to combine food tourism with resort and spa packages, nature-base experiences (e.g. the islands), and urban culture.

Concept for urban or resort-based food tourism

Resorts, or accommodation establishments within cities, can develop their own concepts, packages and promotions for food tourism, although it is probably wise to fit these into broader food tourism strategies. Figure 5.7 illustrates such a concept, for an urban accommodation establishment or a stand-alone resort. The foundation principle is that visitors can purchase (export-ready) an all-inclusive package, or customize a food tourism experience with the resort as 'base camp'.

Logical partners are local chefs and restaurants, periodic events, and experience suppliers within the city and surrounding region.

5

Authenticity as a resource

Perceived authenticity, and the search for authentic food and cultural experiences, has already been considered in our discussion of what foodies want. But who provides or certifies authenticity? What is deemed to be authentic within a destination's planning for food tourism?

A recurring theme since the earliest tourism studies is authenticity and it persists as a hot topic in tourism's foremost journals (Robinson and Clifford, 2007). From a purely scientific perspective the compositional integrity and authenticity of foodstuffs is important, yet if food is considered a cultural artefact then it is clear there is an integral relationship between food and tourism. Heldke (2003) identifies three key aspects of authenticity in food. The most common usage is for a food that is simply different, or novel, which is distinct from native authenticity – that is a food experience produced by and in a specific culture. Contrarily, replicable authenticity is an effort made by the cook to produce food as it is somewhere else, or sometime else. Food then is a medium that can allow an immediate authentic relationship with a culture or tradition.

A number of dimensions of food authenticity are apparent in the literature. First, is its naming. As Groves (2001: 246) notes, "the authenticity of foods… is frequently used to refer to a genuine version of a product in relation to a specific place, region or country". The dish or product name conveys authenticity by association; to geographic place, to a time and to a tradition even if mythologised.

Product or dish labelling connote trustworthiness, often by association with an authority, and these are increasingly being ratified by law. Tellstrom et al., (2006) add that labels marketed since medieval times mature into brands with nostalgic value.

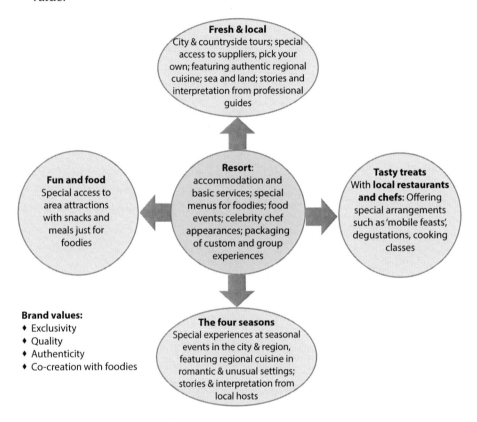

Figure 5.7: A concept for urban or resort-based food tourism

Central to food authenticity are ingredients, locally sourced and unique. Standalone ingredients, or those that compose a dish, are reflective of a culinary heritage and the foodstuff's historicism, although the composition itself might be contemporary (Hughes, 1995). Alternatively, food authenticity, Abarca (2004) argues, can be reduced to two determinants: the authenticity of the cook and the authenticity of the process. What binds the process is the foodstuff's production, which for Kuznesof et al., (1997) represents the situational factors. On the one hand the authenticity of the production process is elevated by its method's simplicity and naturalness and on the other being reflected in the small-scale or non-commercial characteristics of the producing organisation. The integrity of the cook too confers authenticity as do celebrity status or product endorsement (Johnston and Baumann, 2007).

Research note on authenticity

Sims, R. (2009). Food, place and authenticity: Local food and the sustainable tourism experience. *Journal of Sustainable Tourism*, **17**, 321-336.

In recent years, attempts to improve the economic and environmental sustainability of both tourism and agriculture have been linked to the development of 'alternative' food networks and a renewed enthusiasm for food products that are perceived to be traditional and local. This paper draws on research from two UK regions, the Lake District and Exmoor, to argue that local food can play an important role in the sustainable tourism experience because it appeals to the visitor's desire for authenticity within the holiday experience. Using evidence from qualitative interviews with tourists and food producers, the paper records ways in which local foods are conceptualised as 'authentic' products that symbolize the place and culture of the destination. By engaging with debates surrounding the meaning of locality and authenticity, the paper challenges existing understandings of these concepts and offers a new way forward for tourism research by arguing that 'local food' has the potential to enhance the visitor experience by connecting consumers to the region and its perceived culture and heritage.

5

■   Provenance

A concept related to authenticity, fresh and local, is that of 'provenance':

> *Provenance: place of origin; derivation; The records or documents authenticating such an object or the history of its ownership.*   (TheFreeDictionary)

Signifying authenticity, and potentially enabling the food tourist to seek out the origins of food consumed in dining establishments, some businesses provide souvenir material that tells diners where the foodstuff originates and why it is special. Diners at the Hastings' Europa Hotel in Belfast find a provenance brochure on their table, and it can be downloaded for free at this site: http://www.hastingshotels.com/food-provenance.html. From the website of Hastings Hotels in Northern Ireland comes this description:

> *We're talking about local produce. Only the finest will do, and where possible, only local Northern Ireland Cuisine will do. In terms of quality and freshness, it makes all the difference to our dishes. It also means our award-winning chefs can serve up the best in traditional and contemporary cuisine. In each Hastings Hotel Northern Ireland, the menu is fresh, exciting and seasonal. We also like to offer guests a taste of Northern Ireland, with creative spins on classics such as Champ, Irish Stew and the good old Ulster Fry.*

■ Distinctiveness for competitive advantage

In the following research note two theoretical perspectives are utilized to provide practical advice to rural food tourism operators wanting to achieve distinctiveness for competitive advantage.

Research note on rural food tourism and distinctiveness

Sidali, K., Kastenholz, E., & Bianchi, R. (2013). Food tourism, niche markets and products in rural tourism: Combining the intimacy model and the experience economy as a rural development strategy, *Journal of Sustainable Tourism*. DOI: 10.1080/09669582.2013.836210.

Focusing on food consumption in rural tourism, this article illustrates a framework for identifying the dimensions that underpin the potential perception of food products as effective market niches that appeal both to novelty-seeking tourists as well as to more politicized, alternative tourists. The framework merges two theoretical approaches, the experience economy and the intimacy model, and we suggest seven dimensions as examples that elevate a food product to a culinary niche...

1   **Coherence:** The memory of the experience is provided through the 'sense of belonging' that stems from both the contact of the tourists with the host or food producer and among the tourists themselves.

2   **Anti-capitalistic attitude:** Tourists are attracted by the ambivalent nature of rural entrepreneurs: the latter show a strong sense of belonging to the community in which they are 'embedded'... anti-capitalistic attitude may create a strong bid for attention that reinforces tourists' sympathy toward the host or food producer...

3   **Struggle against extinction:** ...small-scale facilities scattered in rural territories that are difficult to reach can turn these 'drawbacks' into a major attraction for tourists who perceive the challenge of discovering a producer and his/her surrounding as a major draw.

4   **Personal signature:** The home-made character of many food specialties creates memories which are difficult to forget.

5   **Mutual disclosure:** A mutual communication is the basis for a close relationship among individuals. Sharing family recipes with guests, showing the working environment and/or lodging tourists in one's own home are but some of the practices that signal the entrepreneur's willingness to establish a closer relationship with the guest.

6   **Rituals of spatial and physical proximity:** "Breaking-bread-together practices" are ....a way to elicit unforgettable experiences.

7   **Sustainability-related practices**...signalling a system of values that unites both responsible consumers and alternative supply chain actors.

Summary

The key to planning, developing and marketing food tourism is to understand foodies and to place their needs and preferences – manifested as co-created experiences – at the core. As the starting point, a planning and development process with foodies at the core was presented, basically directing destinations and suppliers to develop their marketing mix in response to market intelligence on the food tourists they wish to attract. Product must be developed and tested, keeping in mind that there is a big difference between what is usually considered supply (e.g., meals, restaurants, food festivals) and the actual experiences co-created with foodies. The competition must always be considered when setting strategy, and outcomes continuously monitored – especially the reaction of visitors to their experiences and of target markets to communications.

Goals follow, including these: attract high-yield, dedicated food tourists; satisfy cultural tourists with food experiences in combination with other attractions; provide all visitors with exceptional food. A self-diagnostic checklist was then provided, and this can be used by suppliers and destinations to reveal strengths and weaknesses relative to the competition. An entire set of Key Performance Indicators is included, and methods suggested for undertaking the evaluation.

When it comes to actual development, the food tourism cluster concept is recommended. The supply and value-chain concepts are pertinent here, and deliberate networking and collaboration must be fostered among all the stakeholders. The starting point could be farmers and fishers, or chefs and caterers, it does not really matter. The aims will be to: attract and hold dedicated food tourists; increase their spending and loyalty; add value through quality, authentic food experiences for all visitors; minimize leakages by stressing 'fresh and local' produce; grow the value chain to the benefit of local and regional suppliers; brand the cluster, reinforcing the national food brand; increase marketing reach and effectiveness of the cluster; gain new and larger export markets; improve network efficiencies; bring all stakeholders together; develop tourist experiences, and continuously improve quality.

Then two destination development concepts were illustrated, one based on the Australian research and the second based on the multi-country research and customized for Sweden. In both cases the model is based on what research told us that foodies and potential food tourists want in a destination experience. The Australian-based model placed consuming, learning and socializing at the core, surrounded by packaging ideas. The model based on multicountry research placed more specific 'products' at the core, namely farmers' markets, regional cuisine, romantic dinners and food festivals. These can be packaged with nature, spa and resort experiences, or in an urban context with galleries and museums.

5

Specific tactile experiences wanted by the highly-involved foodies are emphasized in this model, such as meeting chefs and taking cooking classes. A third model was presented for urban and resort-based settings, given that many hotels and resorts are keen to attract food tourists. This concept suggests brand values to emphasize in marketing and specific ideas for product development and packaging, with accommodation as the base.

Provenance and authenticity are the final topics in this chapter. They are closely related to the notion of fresh and local, and resonate well with foodies seeking unique, cultural experiences. What exactly is authentic is open to interpretation, and therefore understanding the mind-set of foodies is critical.

Study questions

1   Placing foodies at the core of food tourism planning, development and marketing, what is the meaning of product testing and co-creation?

2   Define comparative and competitive advantages and discuss what you think are the key actions needed for food tourism development.

3   Define 'key performance indicators'.

4   In conducting a self-diagnosis of food tourism development and potential, suggest key performance indicators for competitive advantage and economic outcomes.

5   Describe the meaning, purpose and process of developing food tourism clusters.

6   How can the cluster concept be applied to rural and urban areas?

7   Integrate the two destination concepts for food tourism focused on experiences for foodies.

8   Discuss the meaning and importance of export-ready products in food tourism.

9   Define authenticity in food tourism from the food tourists' perspective.

10   How is provenance connected to the concept of authenticity, and why it is important to foodies?

Further reading

Hall, C. M. (2005). Rural wine and food tourism cluster and network development. In, D. Hall, I. Kirkpatrick and M. Mitchell (eds.), *Rural Tourism and Sustainable Business*, 149-164. Bristol: Channel View.

Ritchie, J. B., & Crouch, G. (2003). *The Competitive Destination: A Sustainable Tourism Perspective*. Wallingford UK: CABI.

6 The Destination

Learning objectives

Readers are expected to learn the following from this chapter:

- How to apply or adapt the knowledge from real-world food tourism examples to new ventures.
- Challenges facing countries and cities in developing food tourism
- How destinations develop and promote food tourism domestically and internationally
- Comparative approaches from Scandinavia, Scotland, Ireland, Italy, and Canada
- Specific products/experiences for food tourism and their development: food trails and tours; chefs, restaurants and cooking schools, markets.

6

Introduction

This chapter provides examples of food tourism development and marketing from several countries. It is unreasonable to think that every city or country can be a mecca for food tourists, but it is probable that every destination can develop some degree of food tourism. Casciola, Laurin and Wolf (2014: 225) presented a concept that classifies destinations according to the strength of food and drink motivations relative to other reasons for tourists to visit. This is a premise that needs testing through actual visitor surveys, but the categories range from primary food/beverage destination to emerging food tourism destinations.

If the starting point is a recognition of the potential of food tourism, than one test of development and marketing effectiveness will be to monitor the growth in the number of dedicated food tourists – that is, the aim is to attract more and more people coming just for food or food and beverages. However, other performance measures can be suggested depending on the vision and aims of food tourism strategies:

- Growth in the number of food tours.
- Higher spending on food in restaurants and commercial accommodations

- Increased food-event attendance.

- Higher proportions of visitors expressing satisfaction with food and resulting word-of-mouth recommendations.

- Image and reputation improvements (compared to a base point and to competitors).

The key point is that objectives and performance measures must realistically fit the destination's nature and its stage of food tourism development.

We start with a discussion of New Nordic Cuisine which is a multi-country branding concept, with specific reference to Goteborg Sweden and Copenhagen Denmark. This is followed by profiles of Scotland and Ireland. Dr Alessio Cavicchi has contributed a profile of Italy, which follows. The chapter concludes with a short section on specific products or experiences for destinations to develop, including food trails and tours, chefs, restaurants and cooking schools, and markets.

New Nordic cuisine

In this section we have consulted, and quote from a number of Nordic experts:

- Claes Bjerkne, Senior Adviser Bjerkne & Co, Chairman at Visita – Swedish Hospitality Industry, Former CEO of Gothenburg & Co (DMO)

- Ditte Furstrand Nytofte, Project Manager International Marketing, Wonderful Copenhagen

- Claus Meyer, Associate Professor at CPH University Department of Food Science, cofounder of the restaurant Noma, owner of the Meyer Group (http://www.clausmeyer.dk/en/the_new_nordic_cuisine_/manifesto_.html)

- Mats Nordström, Chef at Restaurant Wasa Allé , Gothenburg

- Bengt Linde, Restaurateur and Chairman of the Board at the Gothenburg Restaurant Association

The New Nordic Cuisine Manifesto is provided on the website of Claus Meyer, co-founder of the famous Noma restaurant in Copenhagen (www.clausmeyer.dk/en/the_new_nordic_cuisine_/manifesto_.html)

"As Nordic chefs we find that the time has now come for us to create a New Nordic Kitchen, which in virtue of its good taste and special character compares favourably with the standard of the greatest kitchens of the world.

The aims of New Nordic Cuisine are:

1. To express the purity, freshness, simplicity and ethics we wish to associate with our region.

2. *To reflect the changing of the seasons in the meals we make.*

3. *To base our cooking on ingredients and produce whose characteristics are particularly excellent in our climates, landscapes and waters.*

4. *To combine the demand for good taste with modern knowledge of health and well-being.*

5. *To promote Nordic products and the variety of Nordic producers – and to spread the word about their underlying cultures.*

6. *To promote animal welfare and a sound production process in our seas, on our farmland and in the wild.*

7. *To develop potentially new applications of traditional Nordic food products.*

8. *To combine the best in Nordic cookery and culinary traditions with impulses from abroad.*

9. *To combine local self-sufficiency with regional sharing of high-quality products.*

10. *To join forces with consumer representatives, other cooking craftsmen, agriculture, the fishing, food , retail and wholesale industries, researchers, teachers, politicians and authorities on this project for the benefit and advantage of everyone in the Nordic countries.*

Byrkjeflot et al. (2013) have documented the evolution and legitimation of the New Nordic Cuisine movement in the context of 'gastronationalism' which has been used as a source of national branding and identity expression. In the last decade, the five Scandinavian countries (Denmark, Finland, Iceland, Norway, and Sweden) have attempted to brand themselves as the world's new culinary Mecca. As a brand it was launched with a manifesto endorsed by chefs at a culinary symposium in Copenhagen, Denmark, in 2004. Whether it has worked or not remains to be seen, as data on actual results expressed in food tourist increases are not available. Results of our own multi-country research suggest that it has not done much to change the stereotyped images of Swedish food, although that is not to say there have not been other successes.

■ Sweden and Gothenburg

In the document *Sweden The New Culinary Nation* (2009, Ministry of Agriculture), the Swedish advantage is put forward:

■ Sweden has unique nature that supplies unique produce. The combination of nature and produce also offers opportunities for an exclusive culinary experience.

■ The sea gives the west coast its shellfish, which are world famous for their flavour; there are mussels and farmed oysters, and of course fresh fish caught every day. The great forests and wildernesses offer not just peace and quiet, but also game: an ingredient that holds a special place in Swedish cuisine.

- Growing tourism gives Culinary Sweden a chance to develop further. Culinary experiences form a major part of tourists' experience and image of Sweden.

- Sweden has a diversity of produce and manufacturing methods, blending Swedish culinary traditions with inspiration from other countries.

- Swedish chefs are renowned the world over for their ability to make the best of this blend of tradition and innovation.

- Sweden has a growing food industry that is of major importance to rural areas. Entrepreneurial spirit and ventures are a strong contributing factor to a living countryside. This creates a regional food culture and a local identity.

Mossberg et al. (2014: 344) said that the West Sweden Tourist Board provides a case study on how to use different types of food strategically in destination development. Seafood is at the core of their branding, as each shellfish is "imbued with its own myths" meaning that their consumption holds symbolic significance. The concept 'Seafood Safari' was developed, and in 2009 the theme "All of Bohuslän on one plate" was promoted (www.skaldjursresan.se).

Gothenburg (Göteborg) in West Sweden has used food as a tool for destination development for over ten years. According to Claes Bjerkne, the former CEO at Gothenburg & Co (the city's DMO), the company "....used food as an enticer for site inspections, airline lobbying, when bidding for big events and conferences, both when visiting Gothenburg and internationally". Famous Swedish chefs from the city travelled with DMO staff when bidding for events in order to cook fantastic dinners and impress their hosts.

In order to attract foodies, Gothenburg promotes itself as a city with four Michelin star restaurants for trendy eaters, top-class seafood, and a vivid agricultural landscape. More casually, the city offers street food and many cafes where people 'fika', that is, drink coffee or tea and have some sweets. Gothenburg also offers local and organic produce like its artisan cheese, jams and sourdough bread, but of course, Gothenburg has world-class seafood such as fresh shrimps, crayfish and oysters. At the restaurant Wasa Allé the chefs are sourcing local-regional foods in order to emphasize West Swedish produce. Gothenburg is also famous for its farmers' markets like Briggens Market Hall, and Fiskekörka - the fish market nicknamed Fish Church for its design. (http://www.goteborg.com/en/Eat/Gothenburg-for-foodies/)

Chef Mats Nordström states that "the new trends now are to do less fine dining and have more small dishes at a faster pace...The focus are on good quality produce". He also hopes that the new trend of produce based on seasonality and local produce will keep on for years and years.

Restaurateur Bengt Linde adds, "today, you have to know what you get when you come to a restaurant. You need a complete concept like being a sports restaurant, French restaurant...you can't just be a restaurant. You cannot emanate from the restaurant, you have to emanate from the guest, that is, how long the guest wants to stay, how much he/she would like to eat". He continues by saying that "we need competence, knowledge and uniqueness when it comes to food in order to succeed regardless of your chosen concept". A restaurant does not look the same on a Monday as on a Thursday or Saturday, rather restaurant owners have to know who the guest is and what the guest that specific day wants and needs. Linde thinks that Gothenburg has done a great job promoting its food brand, with Göteborg & Co at the front and with top politicians in the city always speaking Gothenburg about the importance of food. However, Linde says that "a challenge for us is to attract quality employees in the future. One way to accomplish this is to improve the collaboration with the restaurant schools. They really need to enhance the way the schools work and educate. This development is influencing the image and brand of Gothenburg and Sweden".

Mats Nordström describes the poor image of Sweden as a food nation in this way: "there are not many Swedish restaurants around the world like you have Italian, French restaurants in almost every city in the world. When Swedish chefs start opening up Swedish restaurants around the world, I think that will change. However, among chefs, Sweden has a great reputation, specially after all the international awards like the World's Championships, Olympics etc. So, I think the image of Swedish food is very high but among people in the industry". Nordström also thinks that "we can improve the Swedish food image through events, that is, create food events that put Göteborg on the map".

Bengt Linde thinks that the poor Swedish image as a food nation can be explained this way:

> We have not decided as a nation how we should work with food. Norway has
> their salmon. We have at least ten world-class chefs, but each one of them works
> individually; we have not jointly decided what we want to do, what we want
> to emphasise when it comes to promoting Swedish food. With all due respect to
> VisitSweden and the fact that they have considered food and the restaurant industry
> as a focus area for international promotion, I think we need a stronger theme for
> promoting food. It would be appropriate if the restaurant industry is included in the
> decisions as to what the key values should be and what the essence of Swedish food
> should be and then start working.

Linde concludes: "I do not think that food tourism in Gothenburg will grow until the key values in a food concept are organised".

As to the future, Mats Nordström thinks that people will do more short breaks for food. He also thinks that "....you can be a food combo, that is, you are interested in food but also interested in history for instance". Nordström hopes that "we will be more Swedish in what we do, that is, that the Swedish chefs use more Swedish produce when cooking....I hope that we will have more Swedish restaurants, from street food to fine dining, that we have good middle class Swedish restaurants as well. What I mean with different classes is a different price range".

■ Copenhagen

A decade ago people were not exactly talking about Copenhagen as a food destination, but thanks to the award winning restaurant Noma it all changed. Today Copenhagen has many choices from bistros to Michelin starred restaurants (15 of them) and they all focus on high quality and seasonal produce. Other famous restaurants in Copenhagen are AOC, Geranium and Sollerod. (http://www.visit-copenhagen.com/copenhagen/restaurants/eat-your-heart-out)

Ditte Nytofte at Wonderful Copenhagen describes what they have done with promoting Copenhagen as a food city:

> Wonderful Copenhagen has used gastronomy to promote Copenhagen, but that happened after food in Copenhagen became popular and of good quality. I think it was Claus Meyer who started to boost up the food in the city, and that foreign media and foodies got noticed about us. Rumours spread and a great deal of focus has been on the Nordic cuisine, specially due to the restaurant Noma.

However, Ditte also notes that: "we have not done any analysis of food tourism or foodies. We know that Copenhagen is known for its food and has become popular and price worthy, but we have not found any evidence that tourists come to Copenhagen specifically for food. For that reason, we do not use food as a strategic theme in our marketing, rather as a unique selling point (USP)".

According to Claus Meyer the Noma restaurant and the New Nordic Cuisine movement speak for themselves when it comes to what Copenhagen has done to develop a food brand and a positive image food tourism image. Claus says that: "I make sure I get a couple of research projects made on this subject". Claus is the co-founder of MAD and Sydhavsøernes Frugtfestival, and he has produced more than 100 food events himself. MAD is a food symposium with Rene Redzepi at Noma, and has been going on for a couple of years. Claus has focused on events/ festivals because "I think it is a strong instrument".

Scotland

Everett (2012) believed that Scotland had been worried about a poor, long-standing reputation for food, so the Taste of Scotland campaign was introduced to revitalize traditions and make food tourism feasible. Their efforts, including an 'Eat Scotland' campaign, seems to have worked - the International Culinary Tourism Association (2010) cited Scotland as one of the planet's most 'unique, memorable and interesting places' for food and drink. As an example, the 'Isle of Arran Taste Trail' has been hailed as an exemplar of best practice (Boyne et al. 2002). The establishment of the 'Taste of Arran' brand confirmed Arran's presence on the Scottish food map, winning the 2006 Food Tourism Award at the Highland and Islands Food & Drink Awards.

■ A Taste for Events

EventScotland has published a guide for producing food events and enhancing the food experience at events (http://www.eventscotland.org/funding-and-resources/event-planning-resources/a-taste-for-events/) A Taste for Events (accessed Nov. 11, 2013). The basic premise is this: "There is a clear business opportunity for both tourism businesses and producers across Scotland to increase their income by offering visitors more quality, local produce." The guide

> ...aims to help event organisers, tourism businesses and food producers to make the most of this outstanding opportunity. Each year over 15 million visitors enjoy holidays and short breaks in Scotland and spend over £4 billion. Just over 80% of our visitors come from the UK and they account for over two thirds of all visitor spend in Scotland. Detailed surveys tell us what these visitors spend their money on. Their biggest expenditure item is accommodation; second is food and drink. Food and drink is a vital element of the overall visitor experience of Scotland and, in total, our visitors spend well over £1/2 billion a year on eating and drinking. VisitScotland research shows that over 70% of visitors to our country say they want to enjoy traditional dishes, regional specialities and fresh, local produce while they are in Scotland. Even better, the majority of visitors say they are prepared to pay a little more for locally produced Scottish food as they expect it to be fresher, better tasting and to give them a more genuine feel for the area they are visiting. More detailed research undertaken by Scottish Enterprise through the Experiencing Scotland project indicates that, on average, visitors are willing to pay between 7-8% extra for fresh, quality, local Scottish food.

Ireland

Two key agencies are responsible for developing strategy: Bord Bia, the Irish State Food Agency, and Fáilte Ireland (the National Tourism Development Authority). According to O'Donovan et al. (2012) there are also interest groups in Ireland of producers and practitioners who strongly advocate the promotion and development of more sustainable approaches to food supply chains.

Failte Ireland determined that tourist expenditure on food and drink in 2009 was close to €2 billion, representing the largest single component of individual visitor expenditure (2010.p.5). This recognition has led to the development of a food tourism strategy which aims first and foremost to develop a strong, positive brand for Irish food. In developing its National Food Tourism Implementation Framework, Fáilte Ireland (2010) proposed a strategy for food tourism based upon the twin aims of promoting a local food culture and expanding the number and variety of authentic, high quality food experiences in key destinations across the country.

Key stakeholders must collaborate to undertake the priority tasks which are grouped into four key themes:

1   Brand development and promotion to communicate a clear message to the consumer as to Ireland's product offering (this is considered in greater detail in the next chapter).

2   Quality and value which are the cornerstones of visitor satisfaction.

3   Business and sector supports to enhance skill capability and encourage innovation.

4   Research and benchmarking to ensure the group have up to date and accurate information on which decisions can be based.

The National Food Tourism Implementation Framework was developed in line with a Visitor Experiential Model which is concerned with ensuring that food-related experiences in Ireland are of a world class standing, particularly with regard to three critical dimensions:

■   **Quality** and **value** – Ensuring that the quality of food and service offered to visitors across a wide variety of outlets is of a consistently high standard and competitively priced. Equally, the overall quality of the visitor experience provided at food festivals, events and activities is also important.

■   **Availability** – Expanding the number and variety of food-related experiences through community-driven activity to ensure that an attractive mix of high-quality offerings is available which maximises the potential for visitors to sample locally produced food. This, in turn will create new business opportunities and routes to market for local producers.

■   **Authenticity** – Ensuring that all food experiences promoted to visitors offer a unique and distinctive Irish flavour and are reflective of our image as a natural, unspoilt and hospitable destination.

Targeting reflects market intelligence concerning both domestic and overseas visitors.

"Tourism Ireland research would suggest that experiencing local food/drink/ cuisine while on holiday is ranked very highly in top source markets of Britain and US, while countries such as France, Germany and Italy, which have a strong gastronomy culture, ranked this activity lower in importance but still relatively high compared to other activities."

Italy: A synonym of good food?

By Dr. Alessio Cavicchi, Assistant Professor, University of Macerata (Italy). Co-editor of *Food and Wine Events in Europe: a Stakeholder Approach*, Routledge, 2014.

Why does Italy come out on top among preferred destinations by so many foodies? Is their reputation based on fact or myth? The official website for tourism in Italy, sponsored by the Italian Government (http://www.italia.it/en/travel-ideas/gastronomy.html) provides a colourful and succulent answer:

> "Visitors cannot miss the culinary and wine itineraries - journeys through Italy's enogastronomic culture, in search of ancient recipes, genuine products, and simple food inspired by classic Italian cooking and innovative creations. World-renowned products such as Parmigiano Reggiano (Parmesan) cheese, Parma and San Daniele ham, Modena balsamic vinegar, Genoa's pesto, buffalo mozzarella from Campania, Alba truffles, and cured meats are just some of the symbols that make Italy the land of good food. And how could anyone forget pasta and pizza, universal synonyms for Italy? … The pleasure of tasting a fine wine in its native environment is unparalleled - a glass of Chianti or Brunello di Montalcino in Tuscany, of Barbera or Barolo from Piedmont, of Prosecco di Valdobbiadene in Veneto, of Lambrusco from Emilia Romagna, or the Sicilian wines or the white wines in Friuli and Trentino-Alto Adige…".

6

This reputation has been confirmed by the UNWTO Global Report on Food Tourism (2012) which acknowledged the primary role of Italy as an influential destination for food lovers. This vanguard position has been recently recognized by the inclusion of the Mediterranean diet in the UNESCO's list of Intangible Cultural Heritage of Humanity. Furthermore, the UNESCO recognizes the role of food and wine festivals as part of the intangible cultural heritage: during festivals product knowledge is spread among participants and local communities and local products become a powerful tool for disseminating the culture of a place.

In Italy, according to a leading portal for the HORECA sector, www.italiaatavola.net, there are an estimated 7,000 plus food and wine festivals covering all the seasons, from North to South (Santini et al., 2013). This is a huge number of events, even if it is impossible to exactly define how many authentic food and wine festivals take place due to the lack of an official register of events at a national level. And it is just one side of the multifaceted supply, offered by a titanic and unrivalled presence of gastronomic associations, movements and organizations.

Local food production brings to the market more than 4,400 traditional food products officially registered by the Ministry of Agriculture, among which we can find 332 quality wines produced in designated regions plus 118 wines with a typical geographical indication, as well as 265 protected designations of origin (PDO) and protected geographical indications (PGI) for food products.

Many public bodies are gathered under the umbrella of 'Res Tipica', a national organization founded in 2003 by the National Association of Municipalities (ANCI) with the aim of coordinating the activities taking place at local level. Today (at the end of April 2014) it is possible to find about 531 wine cities, 354 olive oil cities, 225 almond cities, 192 organic farming cities, just to cite few examples. Considering the whole bundle of food and wine cities the total number of public bodies involved is 2022.

Then, a widespread presence of local associations working on a volunteer basis, called 'pro loco', is relevant for the events and performances they are able to organize. UNPLI stands for "Unione Nazionale Pro Loco Italiane" and indicates the National Association for the promotion of local areas. In Italy the Pro Loco number almost 6,000 well diffused even in small villages; there are 650,000 members and 20,000 organised events and performances (Santini et al., 2013).

Farmers' unions bring their contribution to foodies through their specific associations devoted to the promotion of food and wine tourism in rural areas: Terranostra (Coldiretti) is a national association that groups 18 regional and 96 provincial associations through the guide for rural tourism published on a yearly basis; Turismo Verde is an association created in 1981 by the Italian agricultural confederation that promotes hundreds of farms through its guide Agriturismo in Italia. Turismo Verde also has some regional websites for promoting educational farms and 'open farms' operations, Agriturist is the oldest rural tourism association, created in 1965, promoting around 200 farms.

Slow Food is well known at global level: a non-profit, member-supported eco-gastronomic organization which was founded in 1989 to counteract fast food and fast life, the disappearance of local food traditions and people's dwindling interest in the food they eat, where it comes from, how it tastes and how food choices affect the rest of the world.

Wine routes or Strade del Vino became widespread in Italy. Gatti and Incerti (1998) define a wine route as a kind of cultural itinerary; along a sign-posted itinerary visitors can discover products and wines in a certain region by visiting wineries. Once a wine route is established in a certain area, wineries can decide to join the wine route network. As well as wine routes, the Strade dei Sapori – which literally means Flavor Routes – provide tourists with a gastronomic itinerary. In some areas, under the aegis of regional administration, the Strade del Vino and the Strade dei Sapori are jointly promoted.

The Movimento Turismo del Vino (Wine Tourism Movement) was established in 1993 with the aim of encouraging "Italian wineries to open their doors to visitors". The main event is Cantine Aperte (open cellars), which is organised every year in Italy during the last Sunday of May (Santini et al., 2011).

This census is far from complete but it can be considered a first rough picture to understand the incredible bundle of opportunities that foodies have in Italy to satisfy their expectations.

Foodies in Italy: the growth of a sleeping giant

A strong culinary tradition is diffused in Italian families and during recent years those who can be defined as foodies have reached 5 million, with an increase of 250,000 per year (Episteme, 2013). Even in this case it is very difficult to exactly define the boundaries of this emerging trend. For this reason, analogously to what has been said in relation to rural tourism in Italy, we can call it a 'sleeping giant'. The first research carried out to understand the phenomenon in Italy was performed in 2009 by GPF research for the agri-food company Negroni. They discovered that 4.5 million Italians, corresponding to 9% of the whole population (65% men, 35% women), could be considered foodies. The iden-tikit revealed a class of medium-high income and a higher education qualification. And, if for almost half (53%) the foodie is married with children, the concentration is above average among singles and couples without children, mostly living in the northwest of the country and with a low penetration in central Italy. Interested in the new and the cuisine of other countries, the foodies are sensitive to the multi-sensory experience of food, they give importance to the impression that they get looking, touching and feeling the flavours of food (Mark-up, 2009).

According to Unioncamere (2013), international tourists who travel to Italy with food and wine as their main motivation are 9% of arrivals. This proportion has almost doubled during the last 10 years. The main origins of food and wine tourists are The Netherlands, Germany, Spain and Switzerland. They rate their experience with an average 8.1 on a scale from 1 to 10, and the most relevant factors that increase their enogastronomic experience are: the atmosphere linked to local identity; the cordiality and friendliness of local people, and satisfaction with food and wine quality.

During recent years many initiatives for foodies have been mainly promoted through the Web, with many committed food bloggers who became ambassadors of dedicated appointments. Furthermore, the publishing industry, well developed in Italy with hundreds of wine, food and restaurant guides published every year, has followed this trend and launched new products. The most relevant is the *Foodies' Guide to Italy*, that the groups Negroni and Gambero Rosso launched in 2011. The authors recognize that foodies find the Internet and word-of-mouth far more reliable sources of information than traditional gourmet guides. Thus, this book is differently structured: it is a sort of travel guide that shows readers where to find the best bakeries, cheese specialists, wine merchants, chocolate stores, gourmet deli, farmers markets, and a lot more throughout Italy with more than 1200 addresses. As stated by the vice-executive director of Gambero Rosso, Laura Mantovano, a foodie is different from a gourmet, in that, "without any pre-conceived notion, he/she wants to learn everything about food, both the best and the ordinary, and about the science, industry, and personalities surrounding food".

6

In light of this arising interest shown by both a huge part of the Italian population and by international tourists, in 2007 there has been the launch of a new kind of shopping experience in Turin: EATALY. Founded by an entrepreneur, Oscar Farinetti, formerly owner of a chain of consumer electronics products, this place is a food market/mall including restaurants, foods, bakeries, wine tasting rooms where the Italian quality products are promoted and sold. It has been defined by Tardi (2007) as a 'megastore' that "combines elements of a bustling European open market, a Whole-Foods-style supermarket, a high-end food court and a New Age learning center". After the inauguration, several shops have been launched worldwide and currently there are nine in Italy (Rome, Florence, Milan and other important cities), two in the US (Chicago and New York), one Japan, one in Turkey and one in Dubai (www.eataly.it). Supported by SlowFood and developed with a specific focus on educational and cultural values of food, this chain actually represents a flagship for the Italian food system and for its agricultural sector.

It is worth underlining that in 2015 Expo Milano will revolve around the Feeding the Planet, Energy for Life theme. The main purpose of this Universal Exposition is to stimulate major debate on nutrition and food. This challenging event is another great opportunity to promote the vast culinary heritage of Italy and to address the Foodies.

References

Agriturismo-Sicilia.it (2012), *Foodies 2012: Gambero Rosso and Negroni's guide to Italian foods* available at http://www.agritourisme-sicile.com/blog.cfm?id=745

Episteme (2013), L'agroalimentare Italiano: centralità valoriale, strategicità economica, Presentation at Buying Tourism Online – 6th Edition, Florence (Italy), 4-6 December, 2013.

Gatti, S., & Incerti, F. (1998), The Wine Routes as an instrument for the valorisation of typical products and rural areas, typical and traditional products: rural effects and agro-industrial problems. 52nd Seminar of the European Association of Agricultural Economists, Parma, Italy, June 19-21, 1997, Parma, Italy

Mark-Up (2009), Foodies, esercito che avanza, 9 October 2009. Available at: http://www.mark-up.it/articoli/0,1254,41_ART_3646,00.html

Santini, C., Cavicchi, A., & Belletti, E. (2013), Preserving the authenticity of food and wine festivals: the case of Italy. Il Capitale Culturale. *Studies on the Value of Cultural Heritage*, (8), 251-271.

Santini, C., Cavicchi, A., & Canavari, M. (2011), The Risk™ strategic game of rural tourism: how sensory analysis can help in achieving a sustainable competitive advantage. In *Food, Agri-Culture and Tourism* (pp. 161-179). Springer Berlin Heidelberg.

Tardi, A. (2007), Spacious Food Bazaar in Turin Plans Manhattan Branch, New York Times, October 24, 2007, http://www.nytimes.com/2007/10/24/dining/24eata.html?pagewanted=print&_r=0

Unioncamere (2013), Impresa Turismo 2013, Istituto Nazionale Ricerche Turistiche. Available at: http://www.ontit.it/opencms/opencms/ont/it/documenti/02970

World Tourism Organization (2012), *Global Report on Food Tourism*, UNWTO, Madrid

Websites: http://www.italia.it/en/travel-ideas/gastronomy.html,

   http//www.italiaatavola.net,

   http://www.eataly.it

Specific products and experiences

■ Food trails and tours

Although wine trails appear to be more common, food trails have emerged as an important destination feature. Food and wine trails, according to Mason and O'Mahony (2007), and the businesses along them, can construct narratives in order to improve 'meaningful experiences' for contemporary culinary tourists. There is also plenty of scope for specializations, or theme trails (from food/restaurant streets to cheese trails), and they can be urban or rural.

6

Research note: food routes in Argentina

Schluter, R. (2011). Anthropological roots of rural development: A culinary tourism case study in Argentina. *Tourismos: An International Multidisciplinary Journal of Tourism*, **6**(3), 77-91.

Many attempts have been made to develop tourism in rural areas through the creation of food routes. Based on European experience, almost every country in Latin America, from Mexico to Chile and Argentina, has organised its rural tourist offering around itineraries centred on a food type or typical dish....which group together both gastronomic activities and other activities based on history and culture, ecology and sport. As a result of such complexity, food routes end up being perceived as a complete product that satisfies both different types of tourist and the widest range of tourist requirements, thus increasing the chances of a positive experience... Today, the Tomas Jofre Gastronomic Centre has fifteen restaurants spread over nine of the twenty-two existing blocks of the town. The old traditional eating-houses mingle with modern-built restaurants. Since the mid-90s the town has become a huge centre of attraction. Restaurants vie to gain the attention of the visitor with different typical delicacies.

New Zealand's Premium Food and Wine Tourism Experiences is the title of a manual produced for international agents and wholesalers who can sell product to clients (www.newzealand.com/travel/library/n99406_23.pdf; accessed Nov. 10, 2013). In other words, these are deemed to be 'export-ready', something you can count on, and not merely hope for. Featured are specific commercial services that provide a range of food and drink experiences. The NZ Food and Wine Tourism Network was formed in 2004 with the vision of providing world class experiences that will be a key driver of inbound tourists. It also works to enhance food and wine offerings at the regional and local-operator levels.

The Classic New Zealand Wine Trail (http://www.wellingtonnz.com/wine-trail) links three North Island wine producing regions, a capital city, rural towns and coastal waterways - a journey that takes the visitor through regions accounting for more than 80% of New Zealand's wine production. In the Hawke's Bay region tourists can follow the designated food trail: "Spend a half or full day discovering the tastes of Hawke's Bay Wine Country by following a self guided Food Trail. Visit farm gates, artisan food producers and food-destination outlets for fruit, honey, cheese, olives, wine, chocolate and much more. All Food Trail stops prominently display a sign at the gate or entrance. Collect a copy of the Food Trail map from any Hawke's Bay i-SITE Visitor Centre."

Biscardi et al. (2014) have provided advice on establishing a food tour business, starting with the admonition to define your target market. They determined that the growing popularity of food tourism had given rise to a new set of opportunities with a lot of possible specializations, including a focus on particular areas, demographics, products or services. Food and beverage tours can be combined, and tours plus cooking or agritourism.

In their chapter, Biscardi et al. (2014: 153) profiled three broad categories of potential customers. Food and drink professionals often want technical visits and meetings with owners, winemakers, or chefs. They can be very demanding of their hosts, and have high expectations. 'Food and drink epicureans' want to understand the host culture but seek a more relaxed itinerary and often combine their tastings with other cultural or natural attractions. 'Food and drink enthusiasts' appreciate insider tips and seek authentic experiences. This segment might include club members on group tours.

An insightful piece of advice offered by Biscardi et al. (2014, 153) is called 'nanodemography', based on the premise that all customers are individuals who can change their behaviours multiple times every day. Therefore service providers and experience designers should not stereotype people on the basis of a demographic profile.

This is equivalent to advocating activity or experience-based segmentation, rather than the typical demographics. It also argues for more psychographic information, such as values and attitudes.

Gourmet On Tour (http://www.gourmetontour.com/) is a company that offers experiences based on either a specific area or a style of travel, such as solo, private tour or group tours. The combinations seem endless, including Yorkshire Dales in England (cook with our guest celebrity chef; stay in a 17th century castle; pick fresh herbs from the kitchen garden; go for stunning country walks) to Taste of Sichuan, China (learn about Sichuanese food, one of the four great Chinese cuisines; visit adorable pandas at the world-renowned panda research centre; hike on the Happy Mountain, UNESCO site of the largest carved Buddha; join our professional food photographer for a night market photo tour).

Restaurants and cooking schools

Restaurants and cooking schools can play a supporting role in food tourism or become star attractions. A destination restaurant or cooking school will add great value to any food tourism cluster. But what is it?

A destination restaurant or cooking school is one that has a strong enough appeal to draw tourists. Its reputation is generally linked to a celebrity chef, or to its high standing within some regional, national or international ranking system.

■ The idea of a destination restaurant supposedly originated with the *Michelin Guide*, which rated restaurants as to whether they were worth a special trip or a detour while one travelled by car in France. Now there are many guides and online sources, so ratings and rankings can be confusing. One of the world's best restaurants, Noma, in Copenhagen, has been discussed earlier in this chapter in the context of New Nordic Cuisine.

According to Bennett and Freemantle (2014: 171) "Culinary schools and classes have always been driven by media." Movies about food and destinations, celebrity chefs and cooking channels all contribute to rising demand. Using the example of a Sonoma California culinary school, called Ramekins, these authors determine that the success of such an enterprise depends on utilizing the region's many culinary experts, artisans, farms and wineries to stay booked all year round. Ramekins is also popular for weddings, reunions and corporate events. Local products are promoted and tours of the region offered.

The Italian region of Tuscany inspires pilgrimages from both wine and food lovers the world over. It's no wonder that it is home to many destination cooking schools, often hosted by celebrity chefs. Here is one example:

6

"What do we offer on the cooking school Tuscany (tuscookany.com/ Cooking-School-Tuscany)

You will be cooking, dining, wining, relaxing, having fun and stay at a luxurious villas in Tuscany. During a week or three days' at the cooking school Tuscany you will not only learn some great new cooking techniques, you'll also make friends for life. It's the perfect way of learn cooking great food while discovering the regional culture and cuisine on our cooking school Tuscany.

- *Fun and relaxing atmosphere*
- *Professional hands-on lessons at our cooking school Tuscany in small groups*
- *Organic ingredients used in our cooking school*
- *Environmentally friendly villas in Tuscany*
- *Plenty of time to explore Tuscany*
- *Full day culinary Excursion*
- *English speaking Native chefs from Tuscany*
- *No commuting between the cooking school and accommodation"*

Destination restaurant: The Walnut Tree, Abergavenny, Monmouthshire, Wales

Contributed by Dr. Liz Sharples

The Walnut Tree is an award winning, one Michelin starred restaurant and Inn situated on the edge of the Brecon Beacons National Park close to the English/Welsh border (The Walnut Tree, 2014).

This famous establishment has been in operation since the early 1960s when Franco Taruschio OBE bought the pub and transformed it into one of the best loved restaurants in the UK. The Walnut Tree struggled when Taruschio retired and sold the restaurant in 2001 but recovered when one of the UKs most 'enduringly successful' (Great British Chefs, 2014) chefs, Shaun Hill, picked up the reins in 2008.

Hill began his career in 1966 working for Robert Carrier and Brian Turner at their top London restaurants, won a Michelin star for Gidleigh Park in Devon in the 1980s but is best known for the part that he played in putting the Shropshire town of Ludlow (about 50 miles from the Walnut Tree) on the gastronomic map. His ownership of the 24-seated Michelin starred Merchant House in Ludlow between 1994 and 2005 helped to pave the way for other world class chefs who have subsequently opened excellent restaurants in the town. He continues to be a loyal supporter of the Ludlow Marches Food and Drink Festival, arguably the most successful major food event in the UK. (Ludlow Food and Drink Festival, 2014)

The menu at the Walnut Tree changes daily according to the availability of high quality ingredients including local fish, shellfish, meat and game. Diners have to be sufficiently flexible to choose from the selection of food on offer at the time of their visit but special diets and children's portions are catered for. Hill has been at the forefront of the development of modern British Cuisine for over 30 years and the Walnut Tree menus reflects this trend promoting the use of seasonal, local foodstuffs cooked and presented with a high level of skill and creativity.

An additional part of the restaurant's product offer is the availability of two charming holiday cottages on site; the Old Post Office (which can sleep four) and the adjacent Ivy Cottage (which can sleep six) which are situated in the garden a short walk from the restaurant. Both of these cottages can be booked for one or two nights, so are designed to fit around a meal experience. There are also rooms available at the Angel Hotel in Abergavenny, which is a sister property to the Walnut Tree, a short taxi ride from the restaurant. This former 19th century coaching Inn with 35 guest rooms has been refurbished to a high standard and provides visitors with an opportunity to enjoy a longer stay in the town to fully experience the local attractions and outstanding Welsh scenery.

The key to the Walnut Tree's success lies in its strong connection with the locality, the excellent food that is produced in the region and the undeniable expertise of Shaun Hill who continues to demand respect from visitors far and wide. This destination restaurant is promoted through the restaurant's attractive website but also through its listings in many of the Welsh Tourist Guides (for example, Visit Wales, 2014) and a number of food guides (for example, The Good Food Guide, 2014). Gift Vouchers are available through the restaurant website.

References

Great British Chefs (2014) at http://www.greatbritishchefs.com/recipes/search?type=chef, last visited on 1/5/2014

Ludlow Food and Drink Festival (2014) at http://www.foodfestival.co.uk, last visited on 12/5/2014

The Good Food Guide (2014) at http://www.thegoodfoodguide.co.uk/, last visited 5/5/2014

The Walnut Tree (2014) at http://www.thewalnuttreeinn.com/, last visited 7/5/2014

Visit Wales (2014) at http://www.visitwales.com/things-to-do/attractions/food-and-drink, last visited on 5/15/2014

■   Markets

According to Zittlau and Gorman (2012), farmers' markets in Dublin offer authentic food experiences and the opportunity to meet local people. They identified the need to enhance the cultural experience and promote markets to food tourists. Research on farmers' or fishers' markets in the context of food tourism has been minimal, yet our research has demonstrated how important they are to foodies. Markets can exemplify fresh and local, cultural authenticity, and quality - all highly valued by foodies. They should be central features in both urban and rural food tourism clusters, and they can be considered special events in many different settings. If tourist cannot get to the markets, bring them to the places where tourists congregate.

To make experiences truly unique and memorable for foodies will probably require interpretation through the services of expert guides. Small market tours can incorporate learning, tasting, even shopping and cooking. These can be stand-alone products, export ready, or elements in larger packages. They can be add-ons to meetings, exhibitions and other events.

Food tourism in Niagara, Ontario, Canada

By David J. Telfer and Atsuko Hashimoto, Department of Tourism Management, Brock University, St Catharines, Ontario

Introduction to the Niagara Region

The Niagara Region in Ontario, Canada has been the site of a culinary revolution based on the abundance of locally available agricultural products and a rapidly growing wine route. Having the same latitude as southern France, the Niagara Peninsula in Ontario is surrounded by water on three sides with Lake Erie in the south linked by the Niagara River to Lake Ontario in the north. Along the Niagara River, the water traverses Niagara Falls, one of Canada's most recognisable tourist attractions. Soil in the Niagara region is predominantly Gleyed Luvisols of glacial origin that is characterised by relatively better drainage (Dagasse, 2013). Along with these favourable soil conditions for agriculture, a microclimate exists between the Niagara Escarpment and Lake Ontario resulting in the Niagara Region being home to one of the few tender fruit production areas in Canada. Soft fruit such as peaches, plums and grapes all can be harvested. As part of the Greenbelt, efforts are underway to protect Niagara's agricultural land. The Region has been rebranded as a food and wine destination, home to a culinary trail and a wine trail with over 80 wineries. Niagara cuisine, as part of multicultural Canada, combines cultural traditions and local products creating new styles of cooking (Hashimoto and Telfer 2006). With food and wine festivals, cooking schools, winery restaurants, celebrity chefs, farmers' markets, and U-pick farms the Region is highlighted in Ontario's Four-Year Culinary Tourism Strategy and Action Plan (2011-2015). The Region is known for its signature product of Icewine, produced after the grapes have been frozen on the vine. The evolving tradition of 'farm to table' cuisine is highlighted in many area restaurants such as Treadwell Farm to Table Cuisine and AG Inspired Cuisine. Tour operators are packaging hotels, or bed and breakfasts, with wine tastings and tours, stops at local restaurants featuring local cuisine and tickets to the Shaw Festival Theatre or other events. Festivals include the Niagara Wine Festival, Niagara Food Festival, Niagara Food and Wine Expo, Niagara New Vintage Festival, Niagara Icewine Festival and Springlicious.

Speciality tour companies such as Niagara Culinary Tours and Taste the Town Tours offer walking tours to locally owned restaurants featuring Niagara cuisine in locations such as St Catharines and Niagara-on-the-Lake. One suggested itinerary for independent tourists is the 'Brix and Bricks' with stops at wineries for tasting and to appreciate the architectural features of wineries. Elaborate tasting rooms have been built at many wineries, ranging from a French chateau at Château des Charmes to the very modern Jackson-Triggs, while Stratus Vineyards was the first to obtain LEED certification (Leadership in Energy and Environmental Design). Southbrook Vineyards won the 2009 International Architecture Award and also was the first Canadian winery to have LEED gold level certification. Their 150-acre vineyard is also certified as organic. Colaneri Estate Winery has been built in the design of an Italian village. Several wineries including Ravine Vineyard, Trius Winery at Hillebrand, Vineland Estates, and Peller Estates also offer high-end restaurants. Cave Springs winey is adjacent to On-the-Twenty restaurant in the tourist shopping village of Jordan. Celebrity chefs are based in area restaurants such as Massimo Capra at The Rainbow Room, Jamie Kennedy at Windows and Jason Parsons at Peller Estates. Anna Olsen has been the host of several food television programs broadcast in several countries. The Niagara Parks Commission also hosts the 'Niagara Showcase of Chefs' featuring 11 executive chefs paring food with local wine. The Niagara Region has several cooking schools including The Good Earth Food and Wine Company and the Wine Country Cooking School at Strewn Winery. The local food and wine trend is supported by links to Niagara College's Canadian Food & Wine Institute with its Benchmark restaurant with meals prepared by culinary students using local ingredients. Brock University has the Cool Climate Oenology and Viticulture Institute, a farmers' market on campus during summer and has recently opened the Guernsey market restaurant featuring local food (Telfer and Hashimoto 2003, 2013).

There are eleven farmers' markets and numerous specialty farms such as White Meadows, which produces maple syrup and offers pancake breakfasts in the spring, and the Tree and Twig farm, which focuses on heirloom vegetables. There is a community shared agriculture program where locals can purchase membership in the produce from a farm as well as a range of U-pick farms growing produce such as strawberries and cherries. There are microbreweries such as Taps Brewhouse & Grill, Niagara College Teaching Brewery and the Syndicate Restaurant and Brewery as well as cheese production at the Upper Canada Cheese Company in Jordan.

While Niagara Culinary Tourism has seen tremendous growth, it is not however, without controversies. The edited volume on Niagara wine by Ripmeester, Mackintosh and Fullerton (2013) does raise some controversial issues with agriculture and wine in Niagara including conflict over land use, authenticity, migrant workers, and the use of public space by the wine industry as wine is linked with municipal and regional political-economic aspirations. The success of Niagara as an emerging culinary destination is not only the result of an excellent agricultural base and growing wine industry, but it is also due to partnerships, innovation, entrepreneurship and marketing. While industry and government websites are important, in this era of social media, blogs and individual websites such as Eating Niagara, a website "devoted to local eating and agriculture in Niagara" (http://www.eatingniagara.com/) all play a role in the promotion of Niagara as a culinary destination.

References

Dagesse, D. (2013) Wine Producing Soils of Niagara. In M. Ripmeester, P. Mackintosh and C. Fullerton (eds.) *The World of Niagara Wine* (pp.165-184). Waterloo: Wilfrid Laurier University Press.

Hashimoto, A. and Telfer, D.J. (2006) Selling Canadian Culinary Tourism: Branding the Global and the Regional Product. *Tourism Geographies.* **8**(1), 31-55.

Ripmeester, M., Mackintosh, P. and Fullerton, C (eds.) (2013) *The World of Niagara Wine.* Waterloo: Wilfrid Laurier University Press.

Telfer, D. J. and Hashimoto, A. (2013) Wine and Culinary Tourism in Niagara. In M. Ripmeester, P. Mackintosh and C. Fullerton (eds.) *The World of Niagara Wine* (pp.281-300). Waterloo: Wilfrid Laurier University Press.

Telfer, D. J. and Hashimoto, A. (2003) Food Tourism in the Niagara Region: the development of a nouvelle cuisine. In C. M. Hall, L. Sharples, R. Mitchell, N. Macionis and B. Cambourne (eds.) *Food Tourism Around the World Development, Management and Markets* (pp. 158-177). London: Butterworth Heinemann.

Summary

This chapter provides the examples of a number of destinations that are aggressively pursuing food tourism development and marketing. As a starting point it is wise to consider that comparative and competitive advantages accrue both from resources or endowments from the past (what you have to work with) and from deliberate actions to achieve advantages, especially investments. When comparing destinations it is also important to consider their stage of development in tourism and food tourism.

New Nordic Cuisine is an example of how several countries have been working together to establish a brand and move forward their food culture. Cities like Gothenburg and Copenhagen have been positioning themselves as food tourist destinations, while famous chefs and world-class restaurants add considerably to the region's appeal. Many of the aims of New Nordic Cuisine are a clarion call to foodies and their passions, including: to express the purity, freshness, simplicity and ethics we wish to associate with our region; to reflect the changing of the seasons in the meals we make; to base our cooking on ingredients and produce whose characteristics are particularly excellent in our climates, landscapes and waters; to combine the demand for good taste with modern knowledge of health and well-being; to combine local self-sufficiency with regional sharing of high-quality products.

Ireland and Scotland share similar challenges when it comes to food culture and developing food tourism, and each one has taken great steps to change their image, cultivate a distinctive brand, and foster innovation. A Taste for Events is a guide from EventScotland to promote better food at planned events, and to encourage food events. Ireland's strategy rests on four pillars:

1 Brand development and promotion to communicate a clear message to the consumer;

2 Quality and value which are the cornerstones of visitor satisfaction;

3 Business and sector supports to enhance skill capability and encourage innovation;

4 Research and benchmarking to ensure the group have up to date and accurate information on which decisions can be based.

Italy usually ranks at the top of every foodie's list of preferred destinations, given its rich history, great wines, and distinctive, popular cuisine. Alessio Cavicchi provided a profile and analysis of Italy's advantages and food tourism initiatives. An important fact to remember is that, according to Unioncamere (2013), international tourists who travel to Italy with food and wine as their main motivation are 9% of arrivals - but this proportion has almost doubled during the last 10 years.

6

Specific products and experiences required by destinations were examined last in this chapter: restaurants and cooking schools, food trails and tours, and markets. Two contributed sections feature a destination restaurant in Wales (The Walnut Tree) and various aspects of food tourism development in the Niagara region of Canada.

Study questions

1   How does the New Nordic Cuisine movement relate to branding and positioning? What are its aims and how do they appeal to foodies?

2   What lessons can be learned from the examples of Italy, Scotland and Ireland that can be applied to the development and marketing of food tourism elsewhere?

3   In what ways can food trails and tours be considered an "experiencescape"?

4   Define 'destination' restaurants and cooking schools and explain what makes them attractive to foodies.

5   What is the appeal of farmers' and fishers' markets to foodies? Consider authenticity, provenance, and the other benefits sought by food tourists.

6   Discuss the roles of chefs in developing and marketing food tourism.

Online resources pertaining to food tourism destinations

Discover Italy: Gastronomy (www.italia.it/en/travel-ideas/gastronomy.html)

EventScotland: A Taste for Events (www.eventscotland.org/.../ event-planning-resources/a-taste-for-events)

Fáilte Ireland (2010). National Food Tourism Implementation Framework (www.failteireland.ie/FailteIreland/media/WebsiteStructure/Documents/3_ Research_Insights/1_Sectoral_SurveysReports/Food_Tourism_Implementation_ Framework-1-19-07-2012.pdf?ext=.pdf)

New Nordic Cuisine Manifesto (www.clausmeyer.dk/en/the_new_nordic_cuisine_/ manifesto_.html)

UNWTO (2012). Global Report on Food Tourism. Madrid: World Tourism Organization. (http://dtxtq4w60xqpw.cloudfront.net/sites/all/files/pdf/ food_tourism_ok.pdf)

Cornwall Food and Drink (2014) at www.cornwallfoodanddrink.co.uk/

Noosa International Food & Wine Festival (www.noosafoodandwine.com.au/)

Slow Food: www.slowfood.com/international/2/our-philosophy).

7 Food Events for Foodies

Learning objectives

Readers are expected to learn the following from this chapter:

- The critical importance of planned events in food tourism
- Designing events for foodies; experiences sought and how to co-create them
- The appeal to foodies of festivals, trade fairs, markets, degustations and tastings

The critical importance of planned events in food tourism

Food events are so important in food tourism that they deserve a separate chapter. Our research determined that markets and food festivals have universal appeal among food lovers, and that highly-involved foodies can be singled out by the number and scope of food events they attend. The most sought-after food tourists are those who also prefer the most specialized events including degustations, trade fairs, and cooking classes.

This chapter begins with a discussion of the critical importance of planned events in food tourism, including documentation from the research literature. Data from large-scale surveys in North America is presented. The specific benefits provided by planned events are both generic, satisfying normal interest in novelty, entertainment, consumption and socializing, and benefits specific to food lovers. Segmentation based on event attendance is documented, resulting in the identification of a cluster called 'dynamic foodies'. These are the most highly involved and well travelled for food experiences, and they are the ones most interested in all the planned events and especially the more specialized, tactile ones.

Based on our research, a model has been created for guiding the design of events targeted at foodies. Hallmark and iconic events are considered as to their special place in destinations and food tourism clusters.

A case study from Australia forms an important part of this chapter. David Gration lives and works in the Sunshine Coast of Queensland and he has documented the local food events that help position this resort area as a foodie haven.

The popularity and growth of food-themed events has been well documented, including many cases in a recent book edited by Cavicchi and Santini (2014) entitled *Food and Wine Events in Europe: A Stakeholder Approach*. Cavicchi and Santini (2014:8) said "The number of food and wine festivals throughout the world has grown impressively..." and this type of event has proliferated in some European countries. Hall and Sharples (2008), in their book on food and wine festivals around the world, also provided cases and examples of events that cater to wine and food tourists.

Festivals have attracted the most attention, and according to the 2011 *Restaurant, Food & Beverage Market Research Handbook* (Richard K. Miller & Associates: 231-233) there are more than 1,000 food and wine festivals held annually across the United States. In addition, one has to include a variety of other food events including markets, fairs, shows, congresses, and competitions, although few researchers have studied them. One example is by Brown and Chappel (2008) who examined 'Tasting Australia and the World Food Media Awards' in Adelaide, South Australia.

Motivation to attend food events is the one topic in which an ample body of research evidence exists. Nicholson and Pearce (2001) studied motivations of people attending four New Zealand festivals, one featuring wine and food, and one themed on wild food. Dominant motivations were generic, related to socializing, novelty-seeking, family, entertainment and escapism, but the two non-food related events attracted higher proportions of attendees holding specific interests, i.e. guitars and airplanes. Lilleheim et al (2005), in the context of examining motives of suppliers and exhibitors at the Miami South Beach Food and Wine Festival, concluded that fun and atmosphere were important overall motivators. Park et al. (2008) identified the major factors that motivated visitors to attend the South Beach Wine and Food Festival: the desire to taste new wine and food; enjoy the event; enhance social status; escape from routine life; meet new people; spend time with family, and get to know the celebrity chefs and wine experts.

Cela et al. (2007) surveyed visitors to local food festivals in Northeast Iowa who were found to be typically middle aged; were college graduates and affluent; were predominantly repeat visitors and not part of an organized group. Festivals attendees were mainly day trippers, primarily motivated to specifically attend the festivals, closely followed by the motivation to support, taste and purchase local food. Two food events in Tasmania were profiled by Crispin and Reiser (2008), with the emphasis appearing to be on food and wine consumption plus entertainment.

Hu (2010) studied visitors to a food festival with a focus on their expenditures. Most respondents were young, with more females than males, and predominantly locals in groups, so they do not constitute a real tourism sample. Their main motivations were generic (social and family related) rather than food-specific. They were, however, judged to be somewhat more highly involved with food than general food consumers, with special interests in cooking and taste judging. A study by Kim et al. (2010) employed an on-site survey with 335 visitors attending the Gwangju Kimchi (local food) Festival in South Korea showed that food neophobia had a negative effect on satisfaction and loyalty while food involvement had a positive relationship with loyalty, and satisfaction and loyalty showed a significant positive relationship.

Smith et al. (2010) concluded that food, event novelty, and socialization were push motivations for attending a culinary event, while food product, support services, and essential services were pull motivations. Chang and Yuan (2011) reviewed food-festival attendee studies, beginning with Uysal et al. (1993). Their conclusion was that festival motivations in general study confirm the Getz and Cheyne (2002) framework of combinations of intrinsic, generic, and extrinsic motives.

Conscious efforts to appeal to food lovers are noteworthy. Melbourne's Food and Wine Festival incorporates ticketed master classes and meetings (Hede, 2008), while the Ludlow Marches Food and Drink Festival features (beyond providing 'something for everyone') demonstrations and talks, and chefs who judge competitions. Sharples and Lyons (2008: 101) suggested it is "arguably the longest running and most popular food festival of its type in the UK", and the educational components "add value to the event in providing both entertainment and education and differentiate the festival from a regular farmer's market" (p. 110). And two unique food events were discussed by Hall and Sharples (2008: 331-348), with the international Salone del Gusto being a slow-food exhibition in Turin that showcases artisan products, plus demonstrations and workshops; the Terre Madre event was added as a closed meeting for producers and other 'food communities'.

Clearly there are generic reasons for attending any festival, particularly escapism, novelty-seeking, socializing, and being entertained, with food and beverage events offering a universally popular consumption element. But research has also demonstrated the importance of learning to attract more highly-involved food lovers. Kim et al. (2009) used factor analysis to identify factors behind food-event participation and suggested 'knowledge and learning' as a strong factor together

7

with 'enjoyment'. Smith, Costello and Muenchen (2010) came to similar conclusions with the dominant factor related to both 'enjoyment' and 'learning'. Park et al. (2008) identified 'enjoyment' as an important motive for visitors to a wine and food festival in Florida together with 'social status' describing the importance of how friends and other people recognized the value of attending the food event.

Smith and Costello (2009b) used cluster analysis to dichotomize a sample of visitors to a food event into 'food focusers' and 'event seekers' and found that food focusers are more interested in enjoyment and food tasting but less interested in event novelty and travel with friends and family compared to event seekers. Horng et al. (2012) studied visitors to the Macau Food Festival and Taiwan Culinary Exhibition. Structural equation modelling demonstrated that visitors with different lifestyles exhibited different behavioural patterns.

■ Data from America

The TAMS research (*Travel Attitudes and Motivations Study; A Profile Report*, July 4, 2007) generated data on "Visiting Fairs and Festivals While on Trips of One or More Nights". These are relevant highlights:

■ Over the previous two years (i.e., before 2006), 31.7% (69,847,152) of adult Americans visited fairs and festivals while on an out-of-town, overnight trip of one or more nights. A farmers' market or country fair (14.4%) was the most popular, followed by a fireworks display (12.3%), a free outdoor performance such as a play or concert (10.8%), an exhibition or fair (8.3%), a food or drink festival (7.7%), a carnival (6.9%), an ethnic festival (4.2%) and a circus (3.1%).

■ Those who visited fairs and festivals on trips exhibit particular interest in food-related activities. They were more likely than the average U.S. Pleasure Traveller to go fine dining and to visit spas, to have stayed at a country inn or resort with a gourmet restaurant or a cooking or wine tasting school and to have taken a winery tour. They seek vacation destinations that offer novelty, intellectual stimulation and opportunities to learn (e.g. gain knowledge of history and other cultures or places).

■ The majority in this segment have used the Internet to plan (75.6%) and book travel (54.8%) in the past two years. They are avid consumers of travel-related media (including websites, newspapers, magazines, television). Home and garden-related programming is also an effective method to reach this segment (e.g. house & home websites, home & garden and cooking TV shows, craft, antique & collectible magazines).

A related report from TAMS called *U.S. Festival Tourism Enthusiasts* (2004) (Prepared by Research Resolutions & Consulting Ltd. for The Canadian Tourism Commission) concluded that Festival Tourism Enthusiasts are equally as likely to be women or men. They span the age spectrum, averaging between 46 and 47 year of age. Most Festival Tourism Enthusiasts live in adult-only households – those with no members under the age of eighteen. These enthusiasts span the income and education spectrums. They are less likely to fall into the lowest education groups and are more likely have at least some post-secondary education.

- Because Festival Tourism Enthusiasts also go to other types of attractions when they travel, those who are packaging tourism products for this market might consider adding local arts and crafts studios and/or history or heritage museums to the package. Approximately three out of four members of this U.S.A. market segment go to these types of events on their leisure trips. Two out of three claim to visit zoos, farmers' fairs or markets, aquariums and art galleries on their travels.

- There is an appreciably higher level of participation in many performing arts and wine/culinary activities among tourists in the festival segment.

- Three-fifths of Festival Tourism Enthusiasts are in the market for dining at internationally acclaimed restaurants when they travel and almost one-half spend some of their time on trips touring wineries. These rates of participation in wine and culinary activities are noticeably higher than those evident for American travellers as a whole, suggesting that festivals might benefit from co-packaging with these experiences to lure the festival crowd. Almost three out of four share interests with Heritage Enthusiasts; two-thirds are also Museum & Related Cultural Institution Enthusiasts; and over a half are also Performing Arts and/or Visual Arts Enthusiasts. Two-fifths share the interests of Wine/Culinary and/or Soft Outdoor Adventure Enthusiasts. These overlaps suggest opportunities for cross-market packaging and promotion within cultural tourism products and between festivals and outdoor experiences for the American Festival Tourism Enthusiast market.

Multi-country research findings

In our research, we paid particular attention to the attractiveness and experiences associated with food events in our multi-country, online survey.

■ Attendance at food-related events

Respondents were asked to indicate which events they had attended in the previous 12 months (not necessarily while travelling), from a list of nine types. The choices were 'have not attended', 'a few times', and 'many times', so this is a simple categorization of popularity (see Table 7.1). They are listed in descending order in the 'have not attended' column.

Food/fish markets were the most frequented, and they are typically permanent features in European cities and many other countries. There was a high level of attendance at food festivals and ethnic/cultural festivals including food. Special gastronomic events at restaurants attracted a fairly high level of attendance, as did trade fairs for food producers, and this might reflect the high proportion of respondents who had some current or past work affiliation with the food and hospitality sectors. The very specialized events were the least attended: cooking classes, lessons, competitions and seminars.

Table 7.1: Frequency of attendance at food-related events in the previous 12 months

Food- Related Events	Have NOT attended in the last 12 months	A few times in the last 12 months (1-5 times)	Many times in the last 12 months (6+ times)
A food market where local farmers/ fishers sell their fresh food	18.6%	49.2%	32.2%
Food festival	56.8%	39.3%	3.8%
Special gastronomic events at restaurants	57.5%	34.4%	8.2%
An ethnic or cultural festival, including their food	59.3%	37.3%	3.4%
A trade fair for food producers	60.6%	32.6%	6.8%
Attending a food competition	74.4%	19.3%	6.2%
Lessons on what wine to drink with different foods	75.4%	20.8%	3.8%
Cooking classes offered by professionals	80.4%	16.5%	3.1%
Seminar or conference on food cuisine or gastronomy	82.4%	14.3%	3.3%

The widespread availability of festivals is reflected in these data, both food-themed and those in which food is a potential attraction because of ethnic or cultural uniqueness. However, festivals can attract people for multiple reasons, both generic (e.g. fun, family togetherness, novelty) and targeted (e.g. they include programming for special interests), and it cannot be assumed that any given festival has a strong appeal to food lovers.

As with any leisure/travel pursuit, a higher level of involvement or specialization can be correlated with certain desired experiences and activities that appeal mostly, and sometimes exclusively, to the most highly involved. Therefore it is not surprising to learn from these data that food competitions, seminars, lessons and cooking classes offered by experts generate the smallest frequencies of attendance. These behavioural measures can be used to separate respondents in terms of levels of involvement with food.

Italians and the 'Other' category were more highly involved with food and therefore attended events more frequently. Norwegians stood out for their low, overall involvement - except when it comes to food competitions and a food market where local farmers/fishers sell their fresh food.

Segmentation and target marketing

In marketing the general purpose of segmentation is to profile customers or potential customers in a way that enables effective marketing. In other words, you do not want to waste time and money with communications that fail to reach your primary targets. In the case of food tourism we are arguing that only certain foodies, the highly involved and those who have already traveled for food-related experiences, constitute primary targets for international food tourism. If these experienced food tourists and highly-involved foodies can be attracted to Sweden, for example, then others might follow - either because there is a long-term reputational impact (via word of mouth, social-world interactions and social media coverage) or because lesser-involved foodies and cultural tourists might evolve into higher levels of involvement over time.

Segmentation usually incorporates socio-demographic data, and our research shows that this is only a starting point. Food tourists can be male or female of any age, but are more likely to be female, younger to middle-aged, and travelling as couples. Probabilities are given by the analysis, not absolute divisions based on age, gender or marital/family status.

In looking for other analytical ways to segment the potential market, we tried to correlate past travel for food-related experiences with the involvement scale, but this did not work well - largely because our entire sample consisted of food lovers. It turned out that clustering (single-stage cluster analysis as provided by the software SPSS) based on respondents' participation in food-related events worked well to generate three target segments: dynamic foodies, active foodies, and passive foodies. Each segment is summarised below.

Segment 1 : Dynamic Foodies (n = 350)

Their past participation in food-related events, combined with the finding that highly-involved foodies love food events and have travelled the most, makes them 'dynamic foodies'. They tend to be younger, better educated and with higher incomes.

Segment 2: Active Foodies (n = 1,040)

The 'Active Foodies' segment are people who do not travel as much, and food is not as important in their decision-making and trip satisfaction. They value regional cuisine in a local restaurant, enjoy a farmers' market to look for and buy fresh food, tend to be older and have fewer children at home. They are likely to do all their travel and accommodation bookings online.

Segment 3: Passive Foodies (n= 1,430)

Although they are food lovers, few of this segment are food tourists. Almost 79% in this segment had not travelled for food experiences in the previous 12 months. They prefer farmers' markets, presumably close to home. They tend to rely on word of mouth from friends and relatives for information, but they will consult destination websites. They will demand value for money and use low-cost air flights and accommodation. We can assume they will want a good food experience when they do travel.

There is a fuller discussion of these segments in Chapter 8.

■ Learning events and enjoyment events

The above analysis makes it clear that foodies all love to attend food events, but not all types of events are equally attractive. Segmentation on the basis of attending events can be used in another way, to reveal the categorically different experiences desired by foodies. In addition to food markets, which have great universal appeal to all foodies, the most-attended events are those that cater to hedonism, usually a combination of consumption and entertainment in the form of festivals. The least attended are those that feature learning opportunities (including competitions) or are trade-related.

The nine types of events used in the questionnaire can be divided into two categories: 'Learning events' and 'Enjoyment events'. Correlations between the frequency of visits indicate two clusters of events with three types of events in the 'Enjoyment' cluster (i.e. food festival; an ethnic or cultural festival, including their food; a food market where local farmers/fishers sell their fresh food) and six events in the 'Learning' cluster (i.e. cooking classes offered by professionals; lessons on what wine to drink with different foods; attending a food competition; special gastronomic events at restaurants; seminar or conference on food cuisine or gastronomy; a trade fair for food producers).

All respondents who on average had visited the three Enjoyment events at least once during the last 12 months were classified as 'Enjoyment event visitors' and correspondingly 'Learning event visitors' includes respondents who on average had visited the six 'Learning events' at least once during the last 12 months. There were four times more visitors to Enjoyment events than visitors to Learning events (1143 versus 286). There is a strong correlation between the two types of event visitors (Chi-square= 293, d.f.=1; p= 0.01), however while most (83%) of the visitors to Learning Events are also visitors to Enjoyment Events, only 21% of the visitors to Enjoyment Events are also visitors to Learning Events. We believe that this distinction reflects the more specialized interests of the most highly involved foodies.

Table 7.2: The relationship between food tourism and event preferences

How many times have you travelled internationally in the last 12 months with food as the main reason?	Enjoyment event visitors	Learning event visitors	Total average
No time	48%	18%	41%
1 to 3 times	46%	60%	49%
4 or more times	6%	22%	10%
Total	100%	100%	100%

There are other significant behavioral differences (Chi-square=114; d.f=2; p=0.01) between the foodies who prefer Enjoyment Events and those who prefer Learning Events. Those more highly involved foodies that attend learning events also had travelled internationally much more with food as the main reason in the previous twelve months. This included a significantly higher importance assigned to food in both travel decisions and satisfaction with trips. Also of note are the following differences, with Learning Event visitors being more inclined towards:

■ Luxury hotels and business hotels and spa

■ Using travel agencies and package tours

■ Having visited and planning to visit Sweden

■ Using loyalty (air, hotel) programs

Other comparisons revealed that Enjoyment Event respondents were more inclined towards city breaks and shopping tourism, as well as activities in nature, whereas Learning Event visitors seem to prefer touring by car, visiting farmers' markets and meals at country inns. Socio-demographic variables indicate no significant differences regarding gender or relationship status, but weak (p=0.05) significance regarding personal income and education. Learning Event visitors were on average two years younger (p=0.10) and had higher personal income and education levels. Learning Event visitors also had significantly more children under the age of 15 living at home (p=0.01), presumably as a function of their younger average age, and had travelled significantly (p=0.01) more both for business and for leisure purposes. Italians were significantly more frequent visitors to Learning Events than other nationalities (Germans, Norwegians and UK residents significantly less), which of course could indicate a higher level of involvement with food and/or a greater availability of food events that meet their needs.

7

Table 7.3: Travel preferences and behavior related to enjoyment and learning events

(1= Strongly disagree; 7= Strongly agree) related to event preferences	Enjoyment event visitors	Learning event visitors	Total	ANOVA
	Mean	Mean	Mean	Sign.
How important was food when you last decided where to go for a holiday?	5.31	5.82	5.43	p=0.01
When you were on your last holiday trip, how important was the food experience for your total satisfaction?	5.65	5.90	5.71	p=0.01
Stay in a business hotel (4 star)	4.03	4.65	4.18	p=0.01
Stay in a luxury hotel (5 star)	3.56	4.24	3.72	p=0.01
Camping	2.43	3.05	2.58	p=0.01
Stay in a spa resort	3.57	4.20	3.72	p=0.01
Take the train when travelling between destinations	4.15	4.50	4.23	p=0.01
Take a sightseeing tour in a new destination	4.29	4.62	4.37	p=0.01
Book a package tour online	3.29	4.17	3.50	p=0.01
Use a travel agent for booking	3.09	4.11	3.33	p=0.01
Book my travel ticket using my loyalty frequent-flyer program	3.11	4.30	3.40	p=0.01
Book my hotel using my hotel loyalty program	3.00	4.22	3.29	p=0.01
Have you previously visited Sweden?	45%	73%	51%	p=0.01
Do you plan to travel to Sweden within the next two years?	2.14	2.28	2.17	p=0.01

'Dynamic foodies' had a significantly higher preference for Learning Events. Learning Event visitors were all in the segment 'dynamic foodies', and most Enjoyment Event visitors were in the segment called 'active foodies'.

Development and marketing of food tourism has become a globally competitive phenomenon, so it is crucial to know what really attracts dedicated food tourists. However, the literature on food events has been unclear, if not confusing, on differences between generic and specific motivators and the kinds of experiences desired by food-event tourists. This has arisen largely because of the paucity of research specific to foodies and a reliance on data from actual event attendees.

Learning events appear to be more important as primary travel motives/attractions whereas Enjoyment events are likely to be more useful in a supplementary role. Highly involved foodies and food tourists want tactile learning experiences, although this does not preclude an interest in enjoyment or consumption. Events designed for the dedicated food tourist must provide experiences that meet higher-order, self-development needs. These should include opportunities for learning (e.g. seminars and demonstrations from chefs; tours featuring terroir;

exposure to authentic cuisine), doing (e.g. picking produce, preparing food, cooking), and sharing with other foodies. Creating memorable, unique experiences is a primary goal of festivals and events catering to food tourists. And because many food tourists have professional interest in food, or a background in food-related production and services, technical and career development opportunities are also desired.

Designing food events for foodies

There are clear implications arising from our literature review and empirical research for the design of food events, at least insofar as attracting and satisfying food tourists is concerned. Even so, cultural differences must be taken into account.

Charters and Mitchell (2014:25), in a comparison of European and New World food and wine events, suggested that the New World events are much more consumer-oriented. "Having said this, it is also the case that food and wine more naturally correspond in Europe than in the New World. The link between the two is accepted without having to be reinforced or made overt. In part this stems from the natural evolution of food and wine relationships in a region (something which has not yet occurred in much of the New World), in part this also results from the fact that wine has been seen as a foodstuff rather than as just another alcoholic drink which needs to mark out its own territory and image vis-a-vis other drinks." As argued by Hjalager and Corigliano (2000) and Che, Veeck and Veeck (2005), food festivals may become strongly related to a sense of place and pride since they relate to local products and culinary arts consumption.

■   ## Hallmark and iconic events

Many destinations hold periodic events of great symbolic meaning to residents and visitors alike, but few are food-themed. Here is a definition specific to food tourism:

Hallmark food event: A major food-themed event held periodically, co-branded with the destination, strongly appealing to foodies, and considered to be a permanent institution and valued tradition by residents.

Hallmark events themed with food might have to be developed over many years or created specifically to implement a food tourism strategy. An alternative is to start adding substantial food components to existing major festivals or annual sport events, but here the risk is that foodies will not see the more sophisticated benefits they desire.

Also needed are iconic events:

Iconic food event: Events with strong symbolic appeal to foodies with special
interests.

Every food-related interest, whether it be a food type, traditional cuisine, cooking method, or beverage, can be translated into events for special foodie interests.
As well, highly-specialized events can gain a strong reputation within social
worlds or special- interest communities through social media, so that only those
already linked will find out about it. Reputation can be based on one or more of
these characteristics: size, quality, setting, authenticity or celebrity status. Finding
other forms of distinction can be an interesting challenge for event designers and
marketers.

A planned event can be placed on a spectrum from completely place dependent to completely footloose. By definition, a food festival as an institution must be
positioned as a local or regional event that is by and for locals, and preferably as
a hallmark event that also appeals to tourists. A closely-related alternative is to
be an iconic event that appeals to food tourists in a symbolic way, but otherwise
lacks the size or local interest to be a hallmark. The danger with this category
is that residents will not find it worthy of support should problems occur, and
therefore it requires the support of tourism and other interest groups.

While 'biddable events' are often desired to fill a gap in a destination's event
portfolio, or to achieve goals that can only be met through attracting major, one-
time events, bidding can also be employed to initiate a local event. The one-time
event is in this way introduced as the precursor of a planned, permanent event,
and its reception provides a test of both demand and political/stakeholder support for the concept. The idea behind place dependence is that an event cannot be
moved, or even replicated elsewhere, as it will lose its authenticity and potentially
its very reason for being if it is not tied to a specific place. Indeed, this combination of food-related traditions and uniqueness of place is particularly significant
for food festivals because the cuisine, terroir and setting are integral elements of
the attraction for food tourists.

Any number of well-established food and wine events can be seen to offer
both generic and specialist benefits, thereby combining elements of both hallmark
and iconic events. Here are two descriptions from the website vacationhomes.net
(http://www.vacationhomes.net/blog/2012/04/03/top-10-food-festivals-around-
the-world/) which feature elements intended for foodies and food tourists:

Melbourne Food and Wine Festival

*"At the beginning of March, head for Victoria in the very south of Australia to its
capital Melbourne, which proudly declares itself the food and wine capital of the
continent. For 20 years, this celebration of the vintners and chefs has been going*

strong. It celebrates the very best produce and preparation in Victoria and attracts over 350,000 visitors each year. The festival actually lasts for 20 days with events all over the state. Over 100 local and international chefs come and give master classes, demonstrations and there are gala dinners. Now famous is the World's Longest Lunch and the Langham Masterclass.

The World Gourmet Summit, Singapore

At the end of April and beginning of May, head to one of Asia's most exciting destinations: Singapore. Here there is a conference, masterclasses and workshops by Michelin level chefs and vintners from all over the globe –from Norway to Australia. The Summit focuses on both the best in food and wine and has a great program of events that includes golf, themed and celebrity dinners and invitational parties. This is a high-class, epicurean celebration for the true connoisseur and those working in the industry. Over 140,000 people come here, and the summit has been running for fifteen years."

Design and marketing principles

The first principle to keep in mind is that there are usually going to be two categories of food tourists to consider, the first being attracted primarily to the event (these are the most desirable as they would not necessarily visit the destination otherwise), and the other being those who are interested in food events while travelling but have different trip motivations (events can be attractive add-ons to business trips, conventions, etc..). Most cities and regions want a range of events appealing to different target segments, at different times of the year, and food/beverage events have great potential to generate off-peak, dedicated event tourists.

Second, the design of all events also has to consider local target markets and other stakeholders. Few events can succeed if they are unappealing to locals, and indeed the dedicated event-tourist segment might be a small minority, but a high-yield one. Sometimes this will require a separation of tourists and locals in time and space because they have different interests and price sensitivities (tourists generally will pay more for unique experiences), but getting hosts and guests together in a celebratory environment is also a valued experience for those seeking authenticity.

Third, a wide range of food-themed events exists, even though festivals have occupied most attention in the literature and popular media. Our research considered a full range of event types and the analysis clearly demonstrates that learning events (including trade fairs and competitions) have more specialized appeal to the highly involved. But they can be combined with more hedonistic consumption events.

The fourth principle is that interpretation is essential for the dedicated food tourist. As long as food/beverage events are positioned largely within the hedonistic (including consumption and entertainment) dimensions their value in generating cultural, educational and aesthetic experiences will be minimized. Because so many foodies and beverage lovers want to learn and value authentic cultural experiences, the challenge is to shift such events into those dimensions, and hence the need for active interpretation. The hedonistic/consumptive aspects of food-related events do not have to be sacrificed in order to shift their appeal; it is more a matter of what is added to the program and the designer's skills in shaping experiences. Then, marketers have to communicate the right images and messages, targeted in a manner that reaches foodies.

The most important concept in need of interpretation is cultural authenticity, which in a food-event context can pertain to the following:

- Connection to the land and sea; local supply; how food is grown/caught and distributed; stories and legends can be appealing interpretive tools

- Intangible heritage: ways of preparing food; the nature of meals; recipes; chefs and ordinary people can share their cuisine

- Symbolic value of food, and rituals pertaining to meals/consumption; this needs an expert, perhaps trained guides

- Uniqueness: flavours; aesthetic appreciation of food and how it is prepared and served; also requires an expert interpreter, but with tactile participation by foodies.

The fifth principle is that as far as possible, experiential learning will enhance both the educational and transforming power of the food-event experience, and this presents opportunities for a wide range of programming:

- Direct involvement in the harvesting and preparation of beverages and foods

- Participating in cooking demonstrations, classes and competitions

- Dining, but with professional commentary (e.g. chefs and winemakers)

- Learning through interpretive stories and themes attached to food tourism experiences

- Entry to the behind-the scenes of farms and fisheries, restaurants, food-preparation factories and even local residents' kitchens.

Personally relevant experiences should be co-created with various suppliers, leading to higher levels of emotional engagement and celebration of things valued by the foodie and local communities.

In addition, three forms of mastery will be appealing to foodies:

- Technical mastery through cooking, planting, harvesting, tasting, smelling, etc.

- Creative mastery through menu and serving design, design of meals or consumption settings, etc.
- Physical mastery through exertion, endurance or applied motor skills (e.g. picking fresh produce, preparing, cooking, and serving a meal)

A design model

Figure 7.1 illustrates the multi-dimensionality of an event targeted at foodies. In contrast to a typical event which emphasizes hedonism in the forms of consumption and entertainment (perhaps with some family fun activities provided), the food tourist event must co-create benefits that can be described as learning and mastery, aesthetic appreciation and creativity, and cultural authenticity through celebration, ritual and heritage interpretation. This is a positioning model in that the location of the central box suggests that the event is only in part oriented towards hedonism, but it encompasses strong elements of the other three dimensions. In reality, any given event could provide all these elements at different times and places.

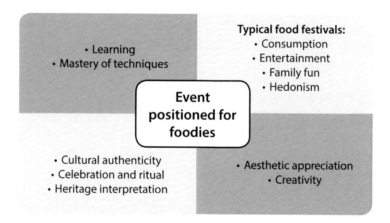

Figure 7.1: Design model for events targeted at foodies

■ Food events and food tourism clusters

Every food tourism cluster will require a portfolio of planned food events of various kinds, at different times of the year, and appealing to a number of segments. Both residents and dedicated food tourists are targets, but one or more events aimed specifically at foodies should be a top development priority. In Figure 7.2 we illustrate how the food tourism cluster should plan to create or develop four categories of events, each of which is targeted in whole or part at foodies.

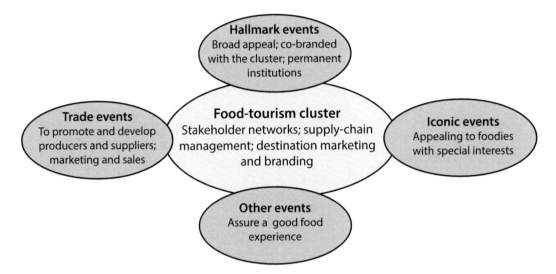

Figure 7.2: Events and food tourism clusters

The terms 'hallmark' and 'iconic' are functional, pertaining to the roles these events play, and any form of event can serve in these capacities. Typically hallmark events will be periodic festivals, while iconic events with special meaning to the target market can be anything. In terms of costs and risks, permanent events will generally yield more benefits than one-time events, but that should not prevent destinations from experimenting and bidding on events that fit into their event portofolios.

Trade events

Not every cluster will have the potential to attract international audiences to its trade fairs, conventions, competitions or seminars, but there can nevertheless be potential for regional and national appeal. These events can be as simple as fairs aimed at connecting producers with buyers in nearby cities (e.g. fostering a 100 mile marketplace), or as specialized as international competitions for chefs featuring local fish or agricultural specialties. Anything intended to attract the food industry and food-service professionals can also have appeal to highly-involved amateur foodies.

Other events, including sports and conventions should provide a taste of the cluster's produce and food-service abilities. Compared to food, no other tangible aspect of travel presents a better opportunity for authentic cultural experiences, and every visitor should have a quality food experience. This can only be accomplished when all the stakeholders are working with common purpose, and a formal cluster strategy will help ensure this goal is realized.

Food events in the Sunshine Coast, Australia: Paddock to Patisserie and Back

By: David Gration (University of the Sunshine Coast, Queensland, Australia)

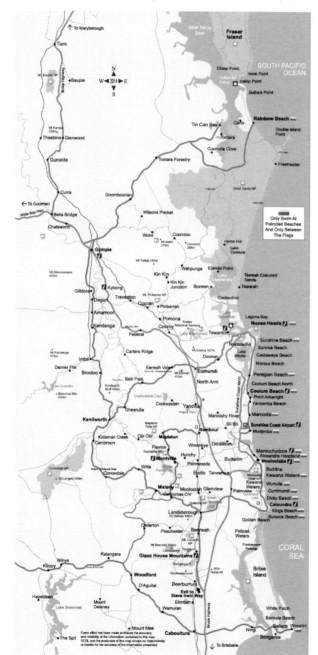

The Sunshine Coast. Source: Sunshine Coast Destination Ltd (http://scdl.com.au/)

The Sunshine Coast Region of Queensland, Australia has long been a strong tourism destination, with its beautiful beaches and lush hinterland mountain settings. Since the mid 1970s individual restaurants throughout the region have achieved great recognition amongst both locals and visitors. Likewise food-based attractions such as the Buderim Ginger Factory, The Big Pineapple, The Macadamia Factory, Maleny Cheese Factory and Kenilworth Country Foods have developed strong food based attractions and associated events. Seafood, and in particular the Mooloolaba Prawn, has also established a strong brand in the marketplace.

Glasshouse Mountains, Pumicestone Passage. Source: Sunshine Coast Destination Ltd

Despite the benefits of these strong individual products and services it was not until the 1990s that individual townships such as beach-side Noosa, at the northern end of the Sunshine Coast region, started to appear on the food tourist's radar.

Source: Photographs courtesy of Sunshine Coast Destination Ltd.

The driving forces behind this gradual development of the Sunshine Coast as a food destination have been a relatively small group of founding stakeholders who have had both the energy and vision to create something new and unique that appealed to both the local community and tourists. This case study examines how two of these regional food events, the Sunshine Coast Real Food Festival and the Noosa International Food and Wine Festival, are building a regional food tourism brand and food culture.

Source: Courtesy of Sunshine Coast Real Food Festival (http://realfoodfestivals.com.au/)

Born out of the paddocks and farms of the Sunshine Coast hinterland township of Maleny, the Sunshine Coast Real Food Festival was established in 2011 by passionate local food grower and food champion Julie Shelton, and Event and Market expert Lena Smeaton. According to founder Julie "the Festival came out of a series of stakeholder conversations, visions, passions and ideas.., related to how to gain recognition for local produce, what we didn't have was event management expertise…just having the passion and vision and good intentions was not enough…It was hard to know who would come in the first year…I didn't consider it a tourist event. It was a one day event that was there to service our food producers, for me it was more an industry event…going to 2 days was the key". This change saw the range of stakeholders grow with a "…much stronger representation from tourism stakeholders as the festival matured" (Shelton, 2014). In 2013 Lena left the festival which is now run by Julie Shelton as sole Festival Director.

The Festival's aim is to promote 'authentic' food experiences, which in their interpretation means enjoying nourishing healthy food that is grown and prepared by passionate food enthusiasts who live in the region. This is in part assured through the process of vetting exhibitors to weed out 'truck farmers' and re-sellers, and promote produce that is slow food - 'good, clean and fair' (http://www.slowfood.com/international/2/our-philosophy). This helps to build trust in both exhibitors and visitors, eliminating any perception of façade. According to Julie "In terms of the name Real Food, I was concerned to bring into the whole conversation some discussion about quality and our food system in Australia… not just about price and convenience but also about quality, diet, health and nutrition. Making that connection between has opened both opportunities for funding and new stakeholder connections." Each new stakeholder cluster that the Festival has connected

7

with are groups of individuals that are seeking to have conversations with those who have like interests, for example in terms of health and well-being "there's probably not one representative group, it doesn't really have even a real umbrella term that fits what these people are talking about… food intolerance and allergies, illness prevention and health enhancement – one of the challenges is how do we aggregate that and how do we service that?" (Shelton, 2014).

For the casual visitor the festival provides a relaxed lifestyle experience where visitors can immerse themselves in an environment that is an escape from urban busy-ness. For the serious food grower, manufacturer and retailer, the festival provides a celebratory and networking place where members of the food supply chain can meet. Held in September each year the festival has grown rapidly. In 2011 the inaugural festival was a one day event attracting 4038 attendances and 84 exhibitors ranging from iconic regional primary produce to organic foods to speciality foods and other food related products and services. The following year (2012) the festival moved to two days to meet demand and to position itself as a tourism event. While there was concern at the time that this move might split the attendance over two days this proved to be wrong. The 2012 festival attracted 8035 attendances (+99%) and exhibitors increased to 119 (+ 42%). On-site surveys provided strong support for the move to two days and evidence of the tourism related benefits from the events (see Figures 1 to 3 below)

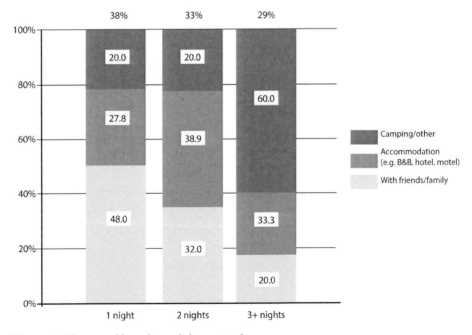

Figure 1: Where and how long did you stay?

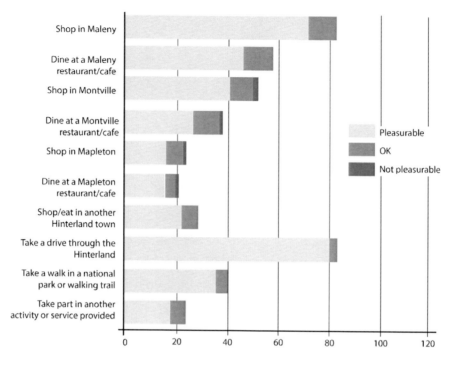

Figure 2: Which of the following did you undertake and how was the experience?

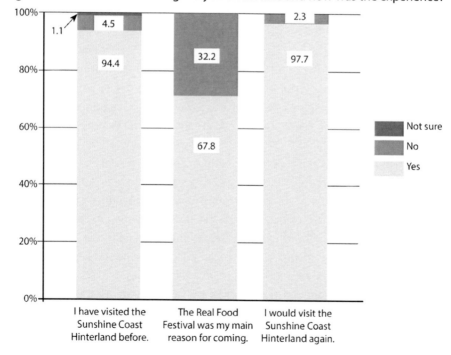

Figure 3: Responses to questions about visiting the Subshine Coast.

7

Source: Courtesy of Sunshine Coast Real Food Festival

In 2013 the festival stabilised with 8,108 attendances and 113 exhibitors. Approx. 31% of respondents to the visitor survey in that year lived outside the region and of those approx. 40% were overnight stayers, as opposed to day trippers, creating approx. 2,700 bed-nights. While the type of visitor changed by the third festival so too had the type of exhibitor. The 2011 festival exhibitor list was generally evenly spread between growers, restaurants, manufacturers, retailers (with a slight accent on growers and restaurants) and service providers, by 2013 manufacturers (29%) overtook growers (approx. 26%) and service providers (14.5%) with restaurants and retail participation reduced to approx.13% each. According to festival director Julie Shelton this shift to the manufacturer exhibitors has meant that this stakeholder group now plays a more prominent role in the shaping of the festival experience. This growth has also resulted in the Real Food Festival assisting exhibiting enterprises to improve their capacity in areas such as marketing, packaging, presentation of stalls and digital presence. "All of those things are as important for the Festival and our growth and success and giving our visitors a good experience as it is for our other stakeholders" (Shelton, 2014).

Source: Courtesy of Sunshine Coast Real Food Festival

Projections for the 2014 Festival are for between 8 and 10 thousand attendances, and more than 120 Sunshine Coast based exhibitors. Cooking classes, films, seminars, children's activities, and for the first time social activities will be incorporated. "The Sunshine Coast is a lifestyle area and the festival's demographic fits as it is around food and foodies, as well as families where there is a strong push to know more about what to feed their kids. It is about providing a soft entry point for people who have questions and concerns and want to find out more but don't know how to go about it, they can come to this event which is a festival, a great day out, a joyful experience and while they are there they can sit in at a couple of talks and maybe gather a few pamphlets, that's often the start of their journey" (Shelton, 2014).

How then does this event fit into the concept of regional branding of the Sunshine Coast as a food and foodies destination? According to Shelton (2014) "... we need a 5 to 10 year vision where we look at a strategic approach to building the capacity with the enterprises that are going to do the delivery ... at the moment we have this gap between the policy makers and marketers and the ones who are actually doing the delivery in those food tourism and agritourism areas."

7

Source: Noosa International Food & Wine Festival (www.noosafoodandwine.com.au/)

In contrast to the Real Food Festival, the Noosa International Food and Wine Festival has its foundations in the work of restaurateurs Jim Berardo and Greg O'Brien who saw the growing trend to culinary tourism and believed that Noosa, with its modern regional cooking style and high quality chefs promoting innovative fusion style dining utilising quality produce, was perfectly positioned to ride this upwards trend. Starting in the 1990s as the Noosa Hot and Spicy Festival the event reached a pivotal moment in 2003 when 150 key players in the Australian Food and Wine Industry came together to celebrate the industry and discuss its future. This event which included chefs, restaurateurs, wine makers and culinary critics, was the genesis for the Celebration of Australian Food and Wine Noosa Style. "Initially it was a way to say thank you to all the wonderful local producers and growers who supplied the restaurant and to celebrate the culinary reputation of Noosa and the many world class chefs who made Noosa their home"(Berardo, 2013, http://chubbyhubby.net/).

Ten years later the Noosa International Food and Wine Festival attracts over 25,000 attendees from Australia and overseas. In 2013 the festival attracted 62% of its attendees from Interstate and 5% from overseas. A major marketing campaign into the Asia Pacific region is focused on increasing international visitation rates. In 2014 Jim Berardo and Greg O'Brien undertook a six week road trip to promote the Festival. From Hong Kong, Singapore, Shanghai, Hangzhou and New Zealand, then to Perth, Adelaide, Hobart, Melbourne, Sydney, and finally Brisbane, Jim and Greg took the Noosa International Food & Wine Festival out to hundreds of chefs, restaurateurs, media and foodies. According to Jim Berardo, "Social media went mad. We promoted the festival in these countries in restaurants operated by the chefs who are coming to Noosa for our festival. Obviously the chefs in those countries have their own followings so that led to fans and friends of theirs promoting and pushing the event. We love showing off Noosa to the rest of the world. Food and wine is at the top of everyone's agenda no matter what country you live in so we were all on the same page. There was such strong interest in Noosa especially in China. There isn't much greenery there and when you show imagery of Noosa and the Sunshine Coast it is like a dream for them to think of coming here, to our fresh air, our fresh produce." (Berardo, 2014, (http://www.noosanews.com.au/news/festivals-the-word-on-lips-across-globe/2190356/)

In addressing his recipe for the Festival's success Jim Berardo is quoted as saying, "'One of the key elements of the event's success was to keep it fresh and evolving, so we started with a local focus and moved onto regional, then State, then national and naturally next to international. Also, Noosa and the Sunshine Coast have evolved into an amazing international destination and it was naturally fitting to take this Festival to that level. We made the name change to 'International' 2 years ago. Planning for the 2014 event is well underway and will have a much larger international component to it." (Berardo, 2013, http://chubbyhubby.net/). In 2014, 180 leading international, national and local chefs, iconic winemakers and food and wine media joined with restaurateurs, serious foodies and a swathe of other attendees to enjoy four days of food and wine related events from May 15th to 18th.

Source: Photographs courtesy of Noosa International Food and Wine Festival

Initially the stakeholders of this festival were the restaurateurs and chefs of the township of Noosa, and their key local suppliers. This expanded to include other chefs, winemakers and food growers, wholesalers and small boutique product retailers. While the festival now embraces a wide target market, its heart still lies in its foundation of exciting chefs and restaurateurs with the public being the invited guests. Some 156 events and packages offer a wide range of food and wine experiences that are accessible by all. With ticket prices ranging from $20 to $495 for individual events the festival, while accessible to most, is still unashamedly aimed at delivering quality culinary experiences to patrons who appreciate their worth. "…the Festival has become a 'chefs' festival in that every chef that comes to Noosa goes back to their roots of cooking… every chef that attends, whether celebrity chef or local chef, rolls up their sleeves and cook. We bring the chefs to the people and they are all accessible. But most of all the NIFW is a party for the contributors and patrons alike … it's hard not to smile when you're having fun!" (Berardo, 2013, http://chubbyhubby.net/).

The role of festivals as food destination attractors has been of increasing interest to researchers and industry (Che, Veeck a & Veeck, 2005; Cohen & Avieli, 2004; Hall & Sharples, 2008; Hede, 2008; Hjalager & Corigliano, 2000; Ren & Liburd, 2012; Rotherham, 2008; Telfer & Hashimoto, 2003). As can as seen above these two food festivals can be interpreted as celebrations of a local community (Alonso & Bressan, 2013; Getz, 1997, Quan & Wang, 2004), promoters of local products and services (Einarsen & Mykletun, 2009) and food destination identity building activities (Lin, Pearson & Cai, 2009; Du Rand, Heath & Alberts, 2003).

The 'co-producer' stakeholders (Getz, Andersson & Larson, 2007) involved in these two food festivals played a driving role in the creation and programming of the festivals. The ethos of the Noosa International Food & Wine Festival is firmly based in the beliefs and aspirations of local chefs and restaurateurs, while the Sunshine Coast Real Food Festival is still strongly linked to local food growers and boutique manufacturers. Both diverse food festivals are grounded by the place in which they are held. Quality produce, local landscape aesthetics and local communities are pivotal to their success. Both festivals have become substantial drawcards for visiting the region. The challenge for the Sunshine Coast region is how to turn the food tourism branding success of individual food related festivals and events, such as those mentioned, into a regional food destination brand. In the words of Julie Shelton (2014) "…we have to care about our food before we can even think about being a food destination… that parochial pride and valuing of not just the produce but the people behind the produce, to me that's the foundation of a food destination."

At its core, the Sunshine Coast region is well positioned with assets of mild climate, good soil, pollution free oceans and scenic beauty. Dedicated stakeholders, such as local food growers, culinary manufacturers, chefs and restaurateurs are working together with government, the tourism industry, the health/well-being sector and a band of dedicated event organisers to create the level of synergy necessary to grow a great food and foodies destination. From paddock to patisserie and back, the story of this developing food destination, is moving towards its next evolutionary, rather than revolutionary, course.

Summary

This chapter emphasizes the importance of food-related events in food tourism development and marketing. The critical importance of events to foodies, and to our segmentation, was revealed through research. There is a very high correlation between being a highly-involved foodie (using our scales), having traveled previously for food experiences, and attending planned food-related events.

Almost all food lovers attend farmers' and fishers' markets, seeking the fresh and local, quality produce that foodies crave. While these are often permanent fixtures, they can also be designed as special events in addition to or incorporated within festivals and other planned food events. Food festivals are probably the most widespread in terms of appeal and availability, and food is generally a feature of beverage festivals as well. But they are often not targeted with the benefits foodies want, such as tactile, learning experiences.

Design principles for food events have been drawn from the research findings. While typical food festivals are based on consumption (food and drink) and hedonism (entertainment, having fun, socializing), foodies want much more. The foodie-targeted food event should feature a combination of learning, cultural authenticity, aesthetic appreciation, and tactile, hands-on experiences like creative cooking. Interpretation is essential if authenticity and learning are goals.

Events can be co-branded with clusters and destinations, and form the centrepiece of food tourism development. Hallmark events are firmly attached to a specific place, permamnent institutions with multiple values to residents and attractiveness for tourists. Every food tourism destination needs a food-specific hallmark event, but this is a function and not a type of event - it could be a festival, exhibition, competition or convention. Iconic events holding high symbolic value to target segments can also be of any type, but in the food tourism context should be aimed directly at the benefits sought by foodies with special interests.

A case study from the Sunshine Coast, Australia, written by David Gration, illustrates the power of events in enhancing destination branding and attractiveness. This case also reflects a number of other important themes, including the importance of fresh and local produce, the necessity for bringing key stakeholders together, and the critical roles of chefs and restaurateurs.

Study questions

1 Explain why foodies want much more than consumption and entertainment from the events they attend; what are the elements they desire?

2 Define these terms in the context of food tourism and cluster development: hallmark and iconic events; co-branding; destination event; interpretation

3 What are the relative advantages of periodic and one-time events in food tourism?

4 Are farmers' and fishers' markets special events? Why are they so important to foodies?

7

Further reading

Cavicchi, A., and Santini, C. (Eds.) (2014). *Food and Wine Events in Europe: A Stakeholder Approach*. London: Routledge.

Getz, D. (2013). *Event Tourism*. New York: Cognizant

Hall, C.M., Sharples, L. (Eds.) (2008). *Food And Wine Festivals And Events Around The World*. Oxford: Butterworth Heinemann.

8   Experience Marketing

Learning objectives

Readers are expected to learn the following from this chapter:

- The nature of experience marketing and why it is crucial in food tourism
- Service dominant logic and the co-creation of food experiences
- Visitor engagement
- The inter-relationships among image, brand, positioning, and reputation
- Branding strategies specific to food and food tourism
- The formulation and uses of segmentation
- A decision-making process for food and travel experiences
- Media and communication channels to reach foodies
- How to use various mass and social media to reach foodies with the right images and messages
- Packaging for and selling export-ready product to foodies
- Conducting marketing campaigns aimed at foodies

Introduction to experience marketing

Foodies will be motivated to travel to any given restaurant or destination by the promise (i.e. a value proposition) of a great food + destination experience. Our research has clearly demonstrated what the components of these experiences must be, and how they should be packaged, promoted and communicated. Therefore, this chapter concentrates on experiential marketing to foodies, including the need for targeted messages and images through appropriate communications channels.

Experience marketing is quite different from selling products, and by now the reader should be fully aware that foodies are not merely purchasing food or a travel package. They are looking for rewarding and often novel experiences in which their interaction with the combination of food, culture, and terroir helps create and reinforce their personal and group identities, facilitate personal development (through learning, mastery, aesthetic appreciation), and gives them a great story to talk about later.

Tressider and Hirst (2012: 14) said that experience marketing: "...utilises a set of conventions and approaches that represents events, tourism, hospitality and food in a particular way that has heightened significance within the rootlessness of the post-industrial/modern world ... by elevating the represented experience to that of the 'extraordinary' and is in direct opposition to everyday reality." The profane, or everyday, is contrasted with the extraordinary, or sacred experience that consumers really must enjoy for themselves. While this sacred/profane dichotomy has been used many times to describe the touristic experience in general, it has special meaning for those in pursuit of authenticity.

When it comes to practical applications of experience marketing, Canada's Province of Nova Scotia has the right idea: (http://www.novascotia.ca/econ/tourism/marketing-business/experiences/) access Nov. 26, 2013.

Experiential Tourism: Delivering Tourism Experiences

Travel is not just about where you've been anymore – it's about what you did while you were there, how it made you feel, the people you met while you were there, and the memories you took home. A product is what you buy; an experience is what you remember. Through crafted experiential tourism opportunities, experiences provide our visitors unique, entertaining, and/or educational activities that make it possible for them to have a personal connection to Nova Scotia and its people. It is about visitors becoming an active participant where they can try a new skill, learn about who we are or how we live, or challenge themselves. It is about meeting the locals – the fishermen, farmers, chefs, artisans, guides, musicians, storytellers, and all of those people in our communities across the province that have a special skill to share or an interesting story to tell and which make Nova Scotia a great place to live and visit.

Just to be clear, what is being sold is a food-related experience, and the style of marketing called experience marketing is how it should be communicated. Experience marketing has a number of inter-dependent elements with overlapping terms:

■ *Relationship marketing:* establishing and maintain rewarding relationships with foodies and food tourists; for destinations and food brands, this includes developing brand communities wherein loyal followers feel a special affinity to the brand.

■ *Engagement marketing:* involving consumers actively in the production and co-creation of marketing programs.

■ *Co-creation of experiences:* highly-involved foodies want to be able to create or participate in the creation of their experiences through: hands-on learning and cooking; choosing from attractive options; customized trip packaging, starting with their own internet searches and bookings; sharing experiences live, through social networking.

- *Live communications* (or event marketing): the use of planned events to make a brand 'real' to the consumer; direct experience of a food destination builds and/or reinforces the overall food brand of the nation.

■ Service-dominant logic

Service-dominant (SD) logic (see: www.sdlogic.net), as articulated by Vargo and Lusch (2004) and Lusch and Vargo (2006), provides a set of principles that can guide all marketing. It starts with the premise that the traditional distinctions between goods and services are invalid, and that all marketing is concerned with the exchange of service.

Here are the key principles (adapted from Lusch and Vargo), with our interpretation of implications for food tourism.

- *Service is the fundamental basis of exchange; goods derive their value from the service they provide to users.* Food and food-service value is defined by the users. Restaurants and other venues exist to provide service (as benefits or measured value) to specific user groups.

- *Service is the application of knowledge and skills; these are the source of competitive advantage.* Not venues or natural resources, but knowledge and skill lead to success in food tourism.

- *Complex combinations of goods, money and institutions provide service, which can make the nature of service difficult to perceive.* Food tourism as a system is complex, involving many stakeholders and interactions, but the entire process is intended to provide valued service to customers.

- *Service is exchanged for service; all markets exist for the exchange of service; a customer-centered view is essential.* The foodie is at the core of food tourism - not resources, supply, restaurants or chefs.

- *Co-creation: the customer is always a co-creator of value; it is an interactional process; firms and destinations offer value propositions, they do not deliver value on their own.* Destinations and food-service venues and events offer the potential to satisfy customer needs and give event-tourists rewarding experiences; it is the job of suppliers to work with customers to ensure the experience is rewarding, even memorable; close and on-going relationships are essential.

- *Value is determined by beneficiaries; it is idiosyncratic, experiential, contextual and meaning-laden.* This principle of SD logic is identical to the core phenomenon of event tourism and event management, as explained in *Event Studies* (Getz, 2007; 2012). This is why interdisciplinary theory is essential.

8

- *The context of value creation is networks of networks, or resource integrators.* Food tourism as a system requires that resources are devoted to venues, events, infrastructure, marketing, skill development and knowledge creation. DMOs know this is their job – to be team leaders in getting the resources and applying the knowledge. The cluster concept is directly related to this proposition.

Factors (Source: Moscardo, 2010)	Applications to food tourism (Source: the authors)
Theme: strong, clear and consistent, supported by design and 'servicescape'	Themed food trails; theme years built around cuisine; themed food districts/restaurant streets; themed markets; slow food in slow towns; settings designed to facilitate particular styles of meal (e.g. fine dining, casual and authentic, self-catered)
Story or narrative: allows customers to play a desirable role or create their own stories to tell others	Myths and legends involving food; story telling by chefs, farmers, fishers, expert guides
Perceived authenticity	Access to objects, places and people (i.e. objective authenticity) associated with cuisine; genuine interactions with chefs; pick-your-own experiences; and opportunities for activities that reflect one's true self such as cooking, fishing, collecting; authenticity markers (as in communications about food that are intended to convey cultural authenticity, such as the specific provenance of food and beverages)
Interactive, participatory and engaging: customers as co-creators of the experience	(Help) cook your own meal; self-guided food trails with access to producers; customized packages; hands-on cooking classes; buying fresh and local at markets
Uniqueness, rarity, novelty, and surprise	Celebrity appearances; sampling from the best supplies (e.g. vintage wine, aged cheese, very expensive fish); adding surprise extras to meals
Easy to access: easy to get to, move around and understand (i.e. legibility)	Guides and trails available; online information; servicescapes designed for food tourists
Multi-sensory	For foodies this means touch, taste, smell and even listening; can be augmented by expert advice
Emotive	Genuinely friendly host-guest contacts; inspirational stories about food or cooking; communitas (i.e. belonging and sharing) with other food lovers; celebrating culture and cuisine with residents; the inspiration provided by celebritiy chefs
Opportunities to be social	Shared meals and cooking experiences; communitas with other foodies; hosts and guests interacting; co-created family/friend experiences
Personal relevance: making connections to personal history	Stressing ethnicity or roots in cuisine; stories about professional chefs and their history
Total immersion in the setting	Hotels, resorts, cities/towns offering complete foodie experiences; staying in cooking schools with other foodies; connecting intimately to foodscapes
Learning opportunities	Classes, seminars, guides; thematic interpretation at events; mentors

Figure 8.1: Factors associated with effective and rewarding customer and tourist experiences, applied to food tourism

■   ## Visitor engagement

The idea of engaging visitors, that is getting them really involved as co-producers of experiences, is not at all new to those in tourism and hospitality. Moscardo (2010) summarized the literature on effective and rewarding customer and tourist experiences, and this body of knowledge is easily adaptable to designing and marketing food-tourism experiences. Her discussion was in the context of the importance of story-telling and themes for tourist experiences. In Figure 8.1 we adapt Moscardo's framework to food tourism.

Decision-making by foodies and food tourists

In Figure 8.2 we present a simple process illustrating how consumers make decisions about food and travel experiences. It might logically begin with needs and motives, but these are influenced by previous experiences, so the process is circular and never-ending. Understanding the elements and process of consumer decision making is necessary if the various aspects of marketing and communications are to be effective.

■   ## Needs and motives

Refer back to our discussions of identity, lifestyle, and involvement, and to our presentation of data on food-tourism motivations. You might ask, do people need to travel or travel for food experiences? The answer is no, but people do need to enjoy rewarding, memorable experiences that provide meaning to their lives. In this sense, people 'need' leisure and social experiences, and to a certain extent travel provides the means. And the more involved people become with a special interest or social world, the more events and travel become important in their lifestyle.

Intrinsic motivation is what we are mostly talking about, that is doing things because we want to. That is the essence of leisure travel. Sometimes extrinsic motivation is relevant, as when foodies travel to learn in order to develop their professional skills, or some reward is offered, or their 'significant others' make decisions for them! But we feel the evidence is clear that most food tourism is intrinsically motivated, including by couples and families who realize somewhat different benefits from their collective experiences.

The 'motive' for any particular trip is a slightly different concept, as every trip might offer different opportunities. So while foodies in general seek learning and novel, high-quality, authentic food experiences, their next trip could be motivated by the desire to participate in a food event with other foodies (i.e. communitas) or enjoy a famous destination restaurant. They might even be motivated to travel

8

to a specific city in order to make purchases at a special market, or to visit the countryside in order to pick their produce. For any given trip it is necessary to question the underlying needs and motivational forces and not simply look at a single reason given by survey respondents.

■ Benefits sought

We already know what benefits foodies want in general, but every trip offers something new. It might be a dedicated food-motivated trip, or food might be an adjunct to other benefits sought. There can be a package of benefits delivered through an event or destination from which foodies make selections, as from a menu, or the benefits can be co-created through interactions of suppliers and consumers. When co-created they are most likely to be unique and highly valued.

It always pays to ask if the product, experience, event or destination offers benefits that are easily substitutable. Generic benefits are those that can be obtained anywhere, through many outlets, and are therefore highly substitutable. This includes entertainment, socializing with friends and families, being part of a group, eating and drinking. Those are the typical elements in food and beverage events, and therefore they are weak attractions for foodies.

Highly targeted benefits are required for food tourists, and the more the foodie is involved the more specific the benefits must be. Remember that suppliers and marketers are (according to service-dominant logic) merely making a service proposition. It requires the active engagement of foodies to make it a rewarding, memorable experience. Uniqueness is always an important factor, so if the competition is also doing it, what value can be added?

■ Information search

All the previous knowledge and experiences of foodies can influence their decisions, which is why loyalty is hard to obtain, and why so much marketing emphasis is placed on branding and image-making. Later in this chapter we examine the information sources used by food tourists and which ones they trust the most, including social media, word of mouth recommendations and various online sources.

■ Decision made

There are many constraints to negotiate before an actual decision is made to travel and a booking is paid for. While all visitors to an area might be induced to purchase a food-related experience, getting dedicated food tourists to plan and take a trip to a particular place is challenging. Those who have already sought information, formed an intent to travel and overcome the inherent costs and time constraints to make such a trip are to be highly appreciated and not taken for granted. They are also to be encouraged to make a repeat visit and spread positive word-of-mouth recommendations.

There is a big difference between routine decisions, like which store to shop at, and unique decisions like going on a food or beverage tour. While marketers aim to generate loyal customers, this might not be possible for most food tourists given that many special-interest tourists are novelty seekers and want new experiences all the time. Nevertheless, every tourist should at least take away positive, memorable experiences to share with others and thereby contribute to image boosting and future demand. And for those who do make repeat trips, it makes sense to reward them.

The experience

Experiences cannot be fully designed as they are co-creations of suppliers and consumers, with many environmental factors intervening. Engaging in a specific activity, like going on an oyster safari, could have quite different meanings depending on what visitors expect, their level of involvement with food, and their social setting. This all makes experience evaluations difficult, but every consumer can at least be asked if they were satisfied, and if they would return or recommend it. Clearly, dissatisfied food tourists are likely to convey a negative image and make it more difficult to attract future food tourists.

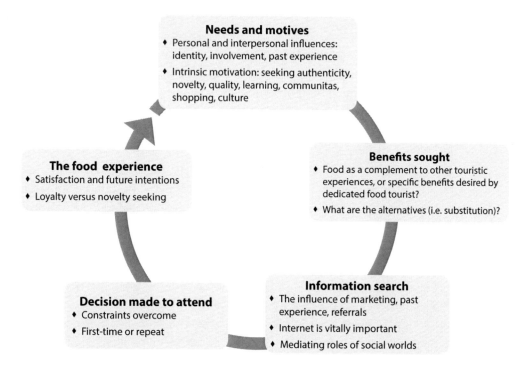

Figure 8.2: Consumer decision-making process for food tourism

Image, reputation, positioning and branding

As depicted in Figure 8.3, branding is closely related to image, positioning, and reputation. Co-branding enters the picture especially when events are expected to develop and reinforce a destination or cluster brand.

■ Image

Consumers and target markets might hold a positive or negative image of a destination or its food, or none at all. This was tested in our multi-country research, and the Swedish example tells us that image is vital, beginning with overcoming stereotypes and simultaneously fostering positive images of a foodie destination. If potential food tourists hold an image of Sweden that is more about IKEA and meatballs than about the wonderful food experiences you can find there, then we have a failure to communicate.

Sweden has been working on this, and the whole New Nordic Cuisine movement aims to change the worlds' perceptions and image, but much more remains to be done. Information comes first, then a multitude of factors influence image, and many of these are beyond the control of marketers. As well, every city and destination is making a lot of noise about food and everything else to attract tourists, so getting the message across is extremely difficult and normally very time consuming.

Ling et al. (2010) surveyed departing tourists at the Kuala Lumpur airport to measure their image of Malaysian food and the connection to trip satisfaction and future intentions. Food price, rich flavours, high availability, good services and variety were ranked highly. Food added value to their experiences, but more could be done to ensure that visitors learn about Malaysian food culture. Positive image did correlate with overall satisfaction and future intentions (word of mouth and repeat visits).

In a study of the food image of France, Italy and Thailand, Karim and Chi (2010) sought to determine the relationship between a destination's food image and travellers' visit intention, as well as the relationships between information sources and purchase decisions. The results revealed positive relationships between food image and visit intentions. In general, Italy had the most favourable food image and the highest potential to be visited in the future.

The diagram (Figure 8.3) provides another interpretation of image – this one from the marketer's perspective. In this context image is something to cultivate and control. Through various messages, images, and media management, the marketer seeks to create and sustain a certain viewpoint of food and cuisine which will be attractive to foodies and other visitors. This viewpoint must accord with the destination brand and the city's or country's food brand in particular.

■ Reputation

Reputation can be defined as a social evaluation (i.e. by potential food tourists) of a destination's food and cuisine on specific criteria. Those criteria might change over time, and some might be more important than others given the comparison group. If you want to be compared favourably with Italy as a foodie destination, the criteria will be different than if one city wants to compare its reputation against its neighbour. Reputation and image can be monitored through research and direct customer feedback, but that intelligence is best when one's own image and reputation are compared to competitors.

Monitoring of the social and mass media can reveal both the criteria by which foodies select destinations or experiences and how they compare one destination to another. A lot of the material in this book provides a starting point. See the later analysis of Sweden's food image for ideas, such as the favourable image of Sweden in terms of organic and ecological food. Uniqueness is another important criterion.

Probably most marketers have had to deal with damaged reputations, and in the world of food tourism this could easily arise from unfavourable reviews of meals, events, or other experiences. The internet is full of customer reviews, so it's possible to gain a sense of trends or major problems that have to be countered.

■ Positioning

Unique selling or value propositions define positioning, and it's always a matter of positioning relative to competitors. If Italy cannot be beaten on cultural authenticity and uniqueness, than why not stress organic and ecological? The attributes or brand values being positioned require careful thought, because the aim is to acquire and sustain competitive advantages among your target segments.

■ Branding

Branding is somewhat hierarchical, with sub-brands all supposed to reflect and support the parent brand. Hence, events and food should help build and protect the country brand. In a perfect marketing world, that is. The reality is that it is not exactly clear how a food brand should relate upwards to a country brand, and downwards to the myriad individual components of food tourism. This issue relates both to brand values and to the more visual aspects of branding like design and logos. Can they all work together in harmony?

FutureBrand creates an annual Country Brand Index (CBI), taking into account a number of 'image attributions'. The top three factors were culture, identity and people. The top five country brands (2011-2012) according to FutureBrand, were Switzerland, Canada, Japan, Sweden and New Zealand, yet these are not exactly the top food-tourism nations of the world. Just how important food is in this index is questionable, but at least those canvassed should think it to be edible and safe! Food was ranked highest in (surprise!) Italy then France, with Sweden in 12th spot. In the tourism dimension, Sweden also ranked well down the list, yet is among the highest in environmental and value dimensions.

Most important are the values that give a unique, positive identity to food in the destination. Identity in this case implies cultural authenticity or uniqueness, including the food that is produced/available and distinctive, appealing cuisine. Our research tested several dimensions or values that should contribute to a country food brand. For Sweden, despite its reputation among foodies having suffered by stereotyping (i.e. IKEA and meatballs), and its positioning relative to other food destinations being rather weak, there was revealed a relatively high reputation for organic and ecological food. Focus groups also revealed that some foodies had a favourable impression of Swedish seafood. Given Sweden's consistently high rankings in country brand comparisons, and especially in sustainability initiatives, there is a clear and important co-branding baseline: Swedish food is to be trusted, and consuming it will enhance foodie identification with all things clean, green, (and by implication) fresh and local. With this in mind, work remains to effectively communicate the right image through media management, and in profitable co-branding with events, restaurants, cities and regions, and other experience providers.

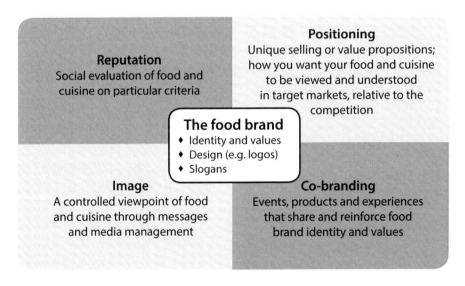

Figure 8.3: The food brand in the context of image, reputation, positioning and co-branding

■   ## Branding Ireland

The Irish Food Tourism Strategy (Failte Ireland 2010) stresses 'Unique and Distinctive' as its first guiding principle, with this elaboration: "Promoting locally produced Irish food which is reflective of our image as a natural, unspoilt destination." Its vision is: "Ireland will be recognised by visitors for the availability, quality and value of our local and regional food experiences which evokes a unique sense of place, culture and hospitality."

The strategy identified a number of priority tasks, including:

■ Develop a consistent, clear message about Ireland's food offering to domestic and international markets.

■ Integrate branding and relevant food imagery into all international promotions.

■ Develop the 'Place in a Plate' concept to deliver memorable food experiences.

Commenting on the Place on a Plate concept, Mossberg et al. (2014: 339) described it as an "...industry focused initiative to encourage all food and hospitality providers to offer fresh, locally sourced, seasonal food on their menu and just as importantly, make sure they are telling their customers about it".

■   ## Multi-country research on Sweden's food image

It takes a long time to change or create a destination image, and this also applies to a country's food image. Branding is only part of the process. Our research concerning Sweden's food image provides a lesson to all marketers.

As part of the multi-country survey on foodies and food tourism, respondents were asked about their image of Swedish food. The question was:

"Please tell us your general image of food from the following countries regardless if you have experience of the food in the countries or not. For each of these following six categories please pick the BEST (1), SECOND BEST (2) and the THIRD BEST (3). Do not rank your own country. You can only pick three countries, and score them 1, 2 and 3.

Six dimensions of food were included in this question: ecological and organic; good taste; value for money; trendy; unique, and fresh and local. These could be considered as brand values for destination or country food brands, or as attributes of images formed by potential customers.

To make a numerical comparison we assigned 3 points if the respondent ranked the country as best, 2 for second best, and 1 for third best. Overall, Sweden did not rank highly against the other countries - in terms of five of the dimensions combined it got the fewest points (see Figure 8.4). Sweden did do fairly well in one category: ecological and organic. It shared fifth place with Norway and compared quite favourably with the top-ranked Denmark and Italy. Since this accords with

8

Sweden's general reputation as a country practicing sustainable development, alongside clean and green, it suggests a strong position to be developed among foodies.

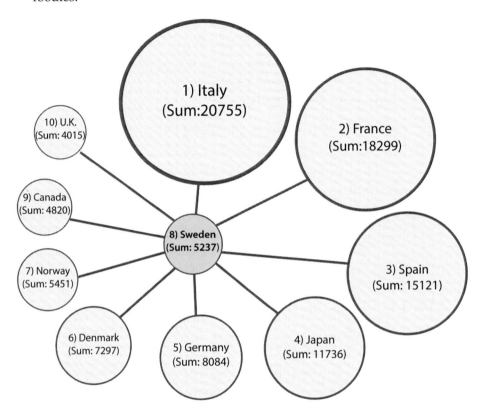

Figure 8.4: Image of Swedish food compared to nine other countries on six different dimensions. (Good taste, value for money, trendy and exiting, uniqueness, fresh and local, ecological and organic). Source: Vujicic et al (2013).

Note: In calculating the sum: 3 points awarded if the respondent ranked the country as best; 2 points for second best, and 1 for third best.

To gain insights on how image is formed, participants in all focus groups were asked to discuss Sweden as a food-tourism destination. Below are some quotes from these discussions:

"I know very little about Swedish food, and that is why I wouldn't go on a food trip to Sweden." (Barbara, 49, Germany)

"I think that Sweden has some really good Guide Michelin restaurants. Sweden does not really have an image of being a food nation...I have experienced bad food in Sweden." (Rita, 62, U.K.)

"Never considered Sweden as a place for gastronomic tourism." (Pierluigi, 35, Italy)

"...it might be so that the image of Sweden is basic, fresh food like fresh fruit...I think

that Sweden has a great tradition of pastry and bread, but many people probably do not know about this." (Rita, 62, U.K.)

"If I think about Sweden I guess good fish, but there are negative impressions about the harmony of food; let's say I could find food pairings of something very salty with something very sweet." (Lucia, 46, Italy)

"Sweden has fantastic seafood. I have been there fishing". (Haakon, 65, Norway)

"I personally just know some like IKEA stuff dishes." (Toby, 23, Germany)

"Looking on it from the outside, people know about cafes and IKEA, and the food provided there." (John, 26, U.K.)

"Even if the idea about food can be of heavy foods with terrible mix of flavours and taste (something that you can experience at IKEA), probably my prejudice could be disconfirmed; fascinated by these places." (Francesco, 38, Italy)

"Indeed, Sweden is associated with IKEA, but they have lots of other good food like fish, moose, and good pastry". (Signe, 60, Norway)

The comments above reflect a mix of positives and negatives, but also indicate varying degrees of ignorance about Swedish cuisine. The challenge is difficult for any country, and especially difficult if there is lots of competition - as is the case in Europe.

Awareness comes first, and awareness/image-building campaigns have to target their messages to those foodies who travel and might be receptive to a country's or city's particular appeal. That cannot be done without sound market intelligence and including knowledge of the benefits to be offered and the channels to reach the target segments.

Segmentation of food tourists

Describing segments is a common marketing-research outcome. Applied to food tourism we have classifications from Ignatov and Smith (2006), Smith and Costello (2009), and Bitsani and Kavoura (2012) as examples. A classification (or typology, or categorization) can be based on many variables, and the researcher or marketer has to determine which ones are important and useful. Scientists first explore a phenomenon like food tourism by noting its existence, then describing the phenomenon through available data, followed by more refined research. If there are observable patterns, or differences, then a classification might be useful.

Segmentation is a traditional marketing technique that aims to assist the marketer in reaching their existing or potential customers with the right images and messages. It is an optimization process in that the marketer ends up with one or more target segments to which resources can be allocated.

Several approaches to classifying food tourists have already been mentioned (e.g. see psychographics). Some have been intuitive, drawing from wine tourism or other special-interest travel, and a few have been research based. Similar to pioneering research on wine tourists, it is easiest to identify and sample tourists when they actually travel, namely at visitor centres, wineries, resorts, hotels, restaurants, food festivals, or pick-your-own places. In this way it is possible to ask who is a tourist, why they travelled here, and what they are doing and spending money on. In this way it is quite easy to determine that for any given gastronomic experience there are visitors who came specifically for an attraction (i.e. the dedicated food tourist), those who primarily travelled for other reasons but nevertheless wanted, or were induced to do some culinary tourism (often called incidental or accidental food tourists), and those who couldn't care less, but they had to eat! The problem is that researchers only reach those who made the decision to travel to a specific place at a particular time; this method reveals little about the potential market. It is also a classification process, but could be the initial step in developing target segments.

The other research approach has been to sample people at home and select actual travellers who did specific things related to wine and food (e.g. the large-scale surveys discussed earlier, including the article by Ignatov and Smith (2011), or (rarely) to sample the population at large and estimate what the potential market is. In this approach to gaining market intelligence, respondents can be sorted by reference to their attitudes and interests, previous travel experience, future desires and preferences, images held of specific destinations, and even the likelihood that they might visit a particular place. This yields good data for both classifications and segmentation.

Some interesting classifications can be cited. Paolini (2000) distinguished between 'gastronauts' and 'foodtrotters', in this way referencing a popular description of certain foodies. At www.gastronauts.net, for example, we find "the club for adventurous eaters" who seek out unusual, even bizarre things to eat.

Croce and Perri (2010) classified the food (and wine) tourist by reference to three variables (thereby creating a pyramid in which degrees of overlap were illustrated): awareness of the food and wine sectors; specialization of interests and knowledge, and the integration between cultural experiences and other tourism. They claimed this to be the result of considerable observations and surveys. At the apex of the pyramid are the 'novices', and these contrast with 'experts' and 'multi-interest visitors'. Experts are likely to be dedicated food or wine tourists with a great deal of past experience. We can link this category to the highly-involved foodie identified in our own research in Australia and through the multi-country survey.

A problem with this approach, and all segmentation that places people into homogeneous categories in which everyone is believed to be the same, is that people change. They change from trip to trip, and over time, through experience and because of their life stage. So today's expert food tourist might be tomorrow's multi-interest traveller. Furthermore, the expert or highly-involved foodie might take a food-specific trip to Tuscany this month, and take his/her family to Disneyworld a month later. One always has to be cautious of stereotyping and of static classification or segmentation systems.

Croce and Perri also noted other categories of food and wine tourists that will be of interest to marketers, and potentially become target segments. Some are 'technicians' who have a professional or business interest motivating their travel. There are also clubs and specialist associations with very specific interests, such as chefs and amateur cooking clubs. Students of hospitality, cooking, tourism, etc. can make good visitors because of their need to learn. Also of potential value: the media, including bloggers; tour groups, even if they are novices, and VIPs who might generate publicity.

■ Segmentation in the multi-country research

Market segments are those groups of people with similar-enough characteristics to justify becoming specific targets. A good target market is one that will respond positively to messages and images - in this case, to get them to visit Sweden for food experiences- is large enough to warrant special communications, and has all the characteristics of being a high-yield group. Segmentation can be based on any number of variables, with the object being to maximise between-group differences and to generate one or more target groups.

We employed the technique called cluster analysis, and based the segmentation on respondents' participation in food-related events. This yielded three distinct segments:

1 Dynamic foodies (n=350 respondents)

2 Active foodies (n=1040)

3 Passive foodies (n=1430).

Cluster analysis on the basis of event attendance works very well to create three target segments in which the first one is clearly preferred for future marketing campaigns. Their past participation in food-related events, combined with the finding that highly-involved foodies love food events and have travelled the most, makes them 'dynamic foodies'.

The 'dynamic foodies' segment is not identical to the 'Highly involved foodies' (HiFs), as that analysis employed the involvement scale. However, there is a considerable overlap with this cluster-based segmentation, as the 'dynamic foodies' are, for the most part, in the highly-involved category, and are very-well travelled.

8

The next step in this segmentation process is to correlate a number of other variables with each of the three segments to obtain a detailed profile of who is included and what they do and prefer.

Segment 1: Dynamic foodies (n = 350)

This is the obvious prime target segment for food tourism marketing. Experiences, images and messages should be aimed at this niche market, with the expectation that potential food tourists for Sweden will be reached. They hold the following characteristics, relative to the other two segments:

- They have the highest propensity to attend food events of all kinds.
- They are younger, on average.
- They have higher incomes and are better educated.
- 49% are females, and they have more children living at home.
- They have already travelled the most for food-tourism experiences (80% have done so, and 20% have done so four or more times).
- Food is a more important factor in deciding where to go for a holiday, and is more important in their reported satisfaction with holidays.
- From the photo elicitation, this segment is the highest in preferring to meet and learn from chefs, attend food festivals and farmers' markets; they are willing to pay most money for many of the preferred activities.
- There are a disproportionate number of Italians and 'Other' in this segment (i.e. the two groups with the highest percentage of Highly Involved foodies)
- They have a higher likelihood of visiting Sweden, and have done so more in the past.
- They are the most frequent travellers, are most likely to stay in 4 and 5-star accommodation, spas, or self-catering.
- Of the three segments they are most likely to book a package online, take the train, and employ hotel loyalty or frequent-flyer programs.
- In terms of media use, they are internet savvy and reliant on online bookings and information.

In summary, the 'dynamic foodies' are experienced, up-market travellers. It makes sense to reach them through both food-specific media and promotions and regular loyalty programs for accommodation and air. They will seek out destination-specific information about food online, but they will have to be motivated more in the future to look for Swedish destinations. Regarding experiences, Sweden has to offer more and better food events, and package food with city breaks and luxury opportunities. These are not your usual Swedish visitors engaged in outdoor activities, and they want tactile food experiences. The 'dynamic foodies' are often travelling in couples, or as families, which affects their decisions and opportunities.

Segment 2: Active foodies (n = 1,040)

The 'Active foodies' segment holds the following characteristics, relative to the other two segments:

- They do not travel as much, and food is not as important in their decision-making and trip satisfaction; we can view them as possible food tourists to Sweden, and a larger potential market in numbers.
- 52% travelled for food in the previous 12 months, but only 5.4% did so four or more times.
- This segment also attends events, but at a lower frequency; farmers' (or fishers') markets have the highest appeal among the events, followed by special gastronomic events at restaurants, a trade fair for food producers, food festivals and ethnic or cultural festivals.
- 51% are females; they are older and have fewer children at home.
- Active foodies prefer enjoying regional cuisine in a local restaurant, enjoy a farmer's market to look for and buy fresh food, take a trip to the islands and stay in a cottage and attend a food festival
- Travel preferences: they are very low on camping, likely owing to older age and fewer children; they seek the cheapest air fares
- Media preferences: more reliance on friends and family, but destination websites are also consulted; they are likely to do all their travel and accommodation bookings online
- There are disproportionately fewer Norwegians in this segment, mainly because they mostly show a lower level of food involvement.

Norwegians present a special challenge for Sweden. They are wealthier, closer, and already have a high propensity to travel to Sweden – but not for food. Indeed, this country displayed the lowest level of foodie involvement. Presumably Norwegians will require good food experiences, and can pay for them, but are much less likely to be lured by fine dining and food events. Packaging therefore becomes essential, including food with activities desired by Norwegians, such as yachting and skiing. Business travellers should also be considered, given the close economic ties between the countries. Other special events, such as sports and cultural festivals, might be good vehicles for pleasing Norwegian food tastes.

Segment 3: Passive foodies (n= 1,430)

Although they are foodies, few of them are food tourists. Almost 79% in this segment had not travelled for food experiences in the previous 12 months. They prefer farmers' markets, presumably close to home. They tend to reply on word of mouth from friends and relatives for information, but they will consult destination websites. Some of them can be motivated to travel to Sweden but they are much less likely to seek the same experiences as the more involved and active foodies. They will demand value for money and use low-cost air and accommodation. We can assume they will want a good food experience, but are unlikely to be lured to Sweden by food events and fine dining.

Media

A wide range of communication tools must be used in the marketing of food tourism, from traditional mass media to blogging, and the internet (all online sources) is usually found to be the most popular source of information (Karim & Leong, 2008). However, these researchers also found that the type of information sources used depended on demographics.

Social media offers considerable potential. Chawla et al. (2014: 74) emphasized that well-defined communities of interest, such as dedicated food tourists, can be reached effectively through social media. They did a scan of Flickr and found over 500 groups linked to the term 'culinary' and over 29,000 groups linked to 'food'.

Fandos-Herrera and Shah (2014: 379) outlined the new paradigm for marketing to special-interest groups like foodies: "In a hyper-connected culture, it is the customer who should be at the center of a successful marketing strategy, with all communication channels and touch points being personalized and tailored to impact the customer journey of the food tourist in a positive way." Those authors stressed the need for marketers to provide all the information their targets want, when they want it, and in the desired media.

Social and other online media offer new ways to connect directly with foodies in an apparent and sometimes real one-to-one manner. Fandos-Herrera and Shah (2014) commented on the use of a number of popular media: Foursquare, which is a location-based, check-in site; Foodspotting, which shares images and integrates with Facebook, Foursquare and Twitter; OpenTable, a leading online restaurant reservation system facilitating customer reviews; TripAdvisor, a leading customer review site, and Groupon and other daily deal sites.

Countless apps have flooded the market, including those targeted at foodies and food tourists. "Adventures in Taste: Nova Scotia" is an app that promotes local food through, for example, the Chowder Trail. Specific experiences can be searched by the intrepid food adventurer. The point is to both enhance information availability and to permit co-creation of the experience as users can effectively make decisions about where to go, what to do, and how to interact with the opportunities available in the destination.

Word-of-mouth is still important in marketing, and according to Bussell and Roberts (2014) it can make or break a food-tourism business or destination. This makes it essential to monitor and manage reputation. But the form of word-of-mouth recommendations, or condemnations, has certainly changed through the rise of the internet and social media. Bussell and Roberts (2014: 423) noted that "digitally connected consumers simply log into their Twitter, Facebook, Foodspotting, Vine, or Yelp accounts and share their experiences in real-time – the good, the bad and the mediocre – before their bill has even been presented. The net result is a significant increase in the 'power of the people', and their collective social influence over food-related planning and purchasing decisions."

As a consequence, we can expect to see continuing development of businesses and brands actively seeking advocates and recommendations, as well as consumers gaining access to many more platforms upon which they can express their desires, needs and reactions. This reinforces the roles of special events as platforms for live communications between brands and consumers, and helps establish brand communities in which consumers strongly identity with particular places or companies.

■ Research findings: information sources for food tourists

From our Australian survey we determined that over a third, or 34% (n=182), of the sample indicated they regularly purchased or subscribed to a food magazine. Comments indicated some of these magazines were the coffee table 'glossies' like *Gourmet Traveller*, but several e-magazine titles were also listed. Additionally, 19% (n=105) participated in food blogs or other food-related online communities and 6% (n=30) belonged to a food club and 11% (n=58) belonged to a wine club.

In the international survey respondents were asked about their consultation of various media channels when making decisions to travel. The respondents had the option to answer 'never' (score 1), 'sometimes' (score 2) or 'always' (score 3). The top five media channels consulted by all respondents, in descending order, were:

1 My friends and relatives

2 Guide books

3 The official city/destination webpage

4 Travel magazine

5 The national tourist organization's webpage

Foodies to a large extent consult friends and relatives. There is only a small difference between guide books and the official city/destination webpage. It is a close tie between travel magazines and the national tourist organization's webpage. It can also be said that foodies much prefer to consult the official city/destination webpage rather than the national tourist organization's webpage. One explanation to this can be that foodies primarily have consulted friends and relatives who likely have recommended a specific city/destination, then they go directly to the official city/destination webpage.

Social media were being consulted, but less frequently (those named were TripAdvisor, Twitter, and Facebook). Food and travel blogs, and food magazines were popular with many respondents, notably among the 'other' category which we found to consist of more highly-involved foodies from outside the four target countries. Media use is therefore correlated to some degree with involvement.

Again, there were country-specific differences in media use. Norwegians ranked friends and relatives highest, and this might reflect a higher average age. British respondents were the only nationality to include ranking sites like TripAdvisor in their top five preferences.

Equally important is the level of trust placed in sources by foodies, and results of our international survey show the following to be most trusted when booking a holiday:

1   My friends and relatives (21.5% of respondents)

2   The official city/destination webpage (19.2%)

3   Guide books (13.8%)

4   Social ranking sites or services like TripAdvisor (12.2%).

Perhaps surprisingly, social media and blogs were mostly not trusted! Perhaps that is attributable to the impersonal nature of the sources, but this discrepancy should be studied in greater detail.

Trip planning and packaging

While there are independent, luxury-only foodies, most are not in that category. In a time of discount airlines, charters, and online booking choices, most prefer to do their own planning and save money on the essentials, leaving more to spend on the really desired experiences.

The top six preferences for accommodation and transportation among all respondents in our international survey were:

1   Do all the accommodation and travel booking myself online (mean=5.07 out of 7)

2   Find the cheapest air fares (4.95)

3   Take a car to explore the destination (4.49)

4   Take a sightseeing tour in a new destination (4.30)

5   Stay in a budget accommodation (2-3 stars) (4.10)

6   Stay in a bed and breakfast (4.03).

There was a lot of variation by country or origin (see Figure 8.5). For example, Germans ranked taking a car highest and were more likely to stay in a 4-star business hotel. These are important differences when it comes to target marketing and there is no validity in making sweeping generalizations about food-tourist preferences.

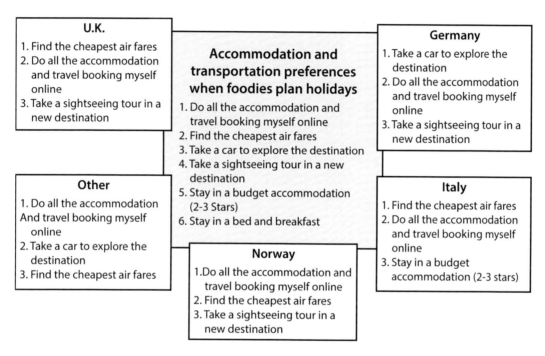

U.K.
1. Find the cheapest air fares
2. Do all the accommodation and travel booking myself online
3. Take a sightseeing tour in a new destination

Accommodation and transportation preferences when foodies plan holidays
1. Do all the accommodation and travel booking myself online
2. Find the cheapest air fares
3. Take a car to explore the destination
4. Take a sightseeing tour in a new destination
5. Stay in a budget accommodation (2-3 Stars)
6. Stay in a bed and breakfast

Germany
1. Take a car to explore the destination
2. Do all the accommodation and travel booking myself online
3. Take a sightseeing tour in a new destination

Other
1. Do all the accommodation And travel booking myself online
2. Take a car to explore the destination
3. Find the cheapest air fares

Italy
1. Find the cheapest air fares
2. Do all the accommodation and travel booking myself online
3. Stay in a budget accommodation (2-3 stars)

Norway
1. Do all the accommodation and travel booking myself online
2. Find the cheapest air fares
3. Take a sightseeing tour in a new destination

Figure 8.5: Accommodation and transportation preferences when foodies plan holidays. Source: Vujicic et al (2013).

Summary

Traditional marketing will not work to attract food tourists. They are not buying products, but co-creating experiences with destinations and suppliers. That is why this chapter is called 'Experience Marketing to Foodies', and we started with an explanation of what this approach means and what it requires. Service-dominant logic is part of the approach, and various ways to engage the foodie arise from this philosophy.

A consumer decision-making model was presented and discussed. Marketers have to understand consumer needs and motivation, and other antecedents to food tourism such as cultural influences and, of course, income levels. Those with experience are likely to behave differently from novice food tourists, as experience shapes trip motives and preferences. The specific benefits sought by foodies and food tourists have been elucidated in our research, but they will vary a lot, and evolve with experience. Information search by experienced food tourists will also differ from that of the novice, and the experienced can certainly influence decisions of others through positive world of mouth recommendations.

Even if consumers hold a strong, positive image of a food destination that does not mean they will overcome the various cost, time and other barriers to enable a trip - that is why it is useful to focus on people who have previously visited, and those who express an intention to travel. Understanding the barriers, real and perceived, can greatly help in the marketing and packaging process.

The interrelationships among image, reputation, positioning, branding and co-branding have been explored. Image and reputation have to be managed, not allowed to evolve without monitoring and direction. Events and other products or experiences should help build and reinforce the destination's food brand, although the exact methods are only weakly understood. The example of Ireland was examined, as that country has being working hard to develop its food brand domestically and internationally.

Sweden's image as a food destination was tested in our multi-country research, and it really only compared well on one dimension out of six. While being perceived as having ecological and organic food is good, and offers some positioning advantage, the results show just how difficult it is to overcome stereotypes and develop a strong brand.

Segmentation is of considerable value to marketers, and in the context of experience marketing, it is essential to find out who exactly can be attracted, what they want, and specifically how to communicate with, and engage them. Three segments from our multi-country research were profiled, with the Dynamic Foodies offering the greatest potential for Sweden (and presumably other destinations). The Dynamic Foodies were generally the highest in involvement, had travelled the most for food experiences, and were most likely to attend food events; they prefer hands on or tactile experiences and are more inclined to the specialist food events like cooking classes, trade fairs and degustations.

How to reach foodies with the right messages and images is a crucial issue in food-tourism development and marketing. An informative online presence is essential, while mass and social media must also be utilized. Many foodies can be reached through travel and food/beverage magazines or clubs, yet they all tend to place the most trust in personal recommendations from friends and relatives.

The final section dealt with trip planning and packaging, revealing a widespread preference among foodies for planning their own food-related trips. This requires easy, online access to all the information desired by foodies. Many food tourists will want cheap airfares and prefer to spend their money on experiences. There are up-market foodies who want spas and luxury, and those who want a quick city break on a budget. It is unwise to generalize, especially as we found substantial country-specific differences.

Study questions

1   What is service-dominant logic and how is it related to experience marketing?

2   What methods exist for engaging food lovers in food tourism experiences?

3   Show how to apply the principles of experience co-creation to the design of a foodie event

4   Define image, brand, reputation and positioning; explain how they are inter-related

5   What is needed to change the image or reputation of a destination for food lovers?

6   Discuss the relative value of mass and social media for communicating with foodies

7   Why are some media trusted more than others?

Additional reading

Moscardo, G. (2010). The shaping of tourist experience: The importance of stories and themes. In, M. Morgan, P. Lugosi and J.R.B. Ritchie (eds), *The Tourism and Leisure Experience: Consumer and Managerial Perspectives*, 43-58. Bristol: Channel View.

Mossberg, L., Mulcahy, J., Shah, N., and Svensson, I. (2014). Best practices in destination food tourism branding. In, E. Wolf (ed.), *Have Fork Will Travel: A Practical Handbook for Food and Drink Professionals*, pp. 337-352. Portland OR: World Food Travel Association.

Tresidder, R., and Hirst, C. (2012). *Marketing in Food, Hospitality, Tourism and Events: A Critical Approach*. Oxford: Goodfellow.

8

9 Summary and Conclusions

In this concluding chapter we thematically summarize the main ideas and conclusions of this book, with emphasis on how our improved understanding of foodies contributes theoretically and aids food tourism development and marketing. In this way the various theories, ideas, facts and research findings are integrated in a way that should be conducive to discussion, idea-generation, and action, both for students and practitioners. The chapter concludes with a discussion of research needs and some thoughts on future prospects for food tourism and foodies.

The phenomenon of food tourism

Food tourism is a recent global phenomenon of considerable importance to cities and destinations, and its prospects for continued growth are strong. Food tourism and foodies are integral parts of the experience economy. Forces of globalisation, especially economic growth and the influence of mass and social media, will continue to cause growth in food tourism for some time - but constraining forces, and ever-expanding competition, must always be considered. To be competitive, marketers must understand the foodie and the experiential benefits they will travel for - this requires demand-side research and planning. Market intelligence on foodies that can be effectively employed in food tourism planning, development and marketing has been slow to develop, and this book provides the first and most comprehensive effort to fill the gap.

Food and beverages are essential services, at the very core of hospitality and inseparable from tourism. Food quality has always been recognized as a 'hygiene' factor in the sense that bad food experiences can ruin a trip and generate negative publicity. But food quality has become an important issue, alongside food security and health matters, and it is now understood that food helps define a culture and often motivates travel.

Food tourism is now being promoted globally, as made clear in the World Tourist Organization's report on food tourism, and its great potential to generate profits and create jobs has been firmly recognized. Many cities and countries are investing heavily in the planning, development and marketing of food tourism, with a number of associations and marketing consortia, like Good Food Cities and Slow Food, leading the way.

Examples provided in this book include Cornwall, England (contributed by Liz Sharples), where the organization Cornwall Food and Drink is a successful regional initiative. Sharples also provided the case of a destination restaurant in Wales, the Walnut Tree, and highlighted the importance of the innovative chef and local/fresh food in attracting food tourists. Developments in the Niagara Region of Canada were reported by Atsuko Hashimoto and David Telfer, and in that region it is a combination of food and wine tourism that has made it popular. Alessio Cavicchi's profile of Italy makes it clear why that country always ranks at the top of food and wine-lovers' preferred destinations. We have outlined New Nordic Cuisine as a branding and cultural development scheme, with specific examples of food tourism development in Gothenburg (Goteborg), Sweden, and Copenhagen, Denmark. Data from large-scale, North American surveys enabled us to profile the scale, significance and nature of culinary tourism, plus we presented visitor-survey data from Charleston, South Carolina - a top foodie destination - to demonstrate economic impacts. David Gration's case study of food events in the Sunshine Coast region of Queensland, Australia illustrates both the region's use of food as an attraction and the crucial roles played by events. As well, we have referred to Scotland and Ireland as examples of countries aggressively pursuing food tourism, and especially have noted the branding efforts of Ireland.

Forces shaping food tourism were considered in Chapter 2. While the forces propelling growth have been, and will likely remain dominant for some time, it is always wise to consider constraining forces affecting food tourism (and tourism in general). A general evolutionary process can be seen, with food being elevated over time (but only in privileged, wealthier parts of the world) from a necessity in meeting basic human needs to a product and service satisfying diverse preferences in a consumer society, and most recently becoming a defining element of lifestyle and identity – hence the emergence of foodies and food tourism. Within the context of the experience economy, food experiences, or food plus beverage, are now seemingly on par with all other leisure and travel experiences in terms of the food-lovers' willingness to pay for novelty, excellence and authenticity.

As an important social and economic phenomenon, food tourism has to be examined from both supply and demand sides. We have placed the demand-side first, as research and theory development on the foodie and food tourist have lagged behind supply-side studies. It is a complex phenomenon, not quickly summarized in a few statements about the attractiveness of food. Foodies are not all the same in their personalities, interests, level of involvement and travel propensities. Food destinations offer quite different experiences and are at varying stages of development and sophistication in catering to food tourists.

Motivation to travel for food experiences does not automatically arise from a love of food, although high involvement is definitely correlated with high travel propensity. There have to be present additional motivations (both seeking and escaping, or push and pull factors) to attract foodies to travel to specific destinations, events or restaurants. Research makes it clear that food tourists seek authenticity, novelty, learning opportunities, socializing and communitas with fellow foodies. They are willing to pay for the memorable experience, the ones that lead to story telling and yield life-long pleasure. In these pursuits they are influenced by personal recommendations from friends and relatives, and their social-world links.

What it means to be a foodie

The term 'foodie' is open to interpretation, and it is not always used in a flattering way. Some people think being a foodie is good, reflecting progressive social, cultural and environmental values, while others associate it with snobbery or elitism. We have taken a rather neutral perspective, exploring all the points of view and related terminology, and often we have simply refered to 'food lovers'. The bottom line is that being a foodie is a matter of self-identification. It is whatever you want it to be, and probably its various connotations are constantly evolving.

We defined foodie this way: a food lover, one whose personal and social identity encompasses food quality, cooking, sharing meals and food experiences. Foodies incorporate all aspects of food into their lifestyle, which often leads them to travel for new and authentic food experiences.

Foodies can be examined in different ways, related to their cooking and eating behaviour, self and social identities, values and attitudes, lifestyle and travel, and these are all themes developed throughout the book, particularly through research findings. Our analyses have revealed that being a foodie is much more than eating or a love of food. The key dimensions of being a foodie are found to be identity (i.e. self identification in which a love of cooking and learning about food are central), a concern for quality of produce and meals, social bonding (as in sharing meals and other food-related experience) and conscientiousness (including care with the purchase, preparation and disposal of food). We have not found evidence that healthy eating is of paramount concern, but we suspect that is the case for many foodies. Many foodies are also novelty-seekers, looking for new experiences and tastes. And of course many foodies are motivated to travel by all these factors.

9

Psychological and social theory was brought to bear in examining the personal and social identities of foodies, and this reflection is essential to understand any leisure or lifestyle pursuit. Only individuals can decide if they are foodies, because they identify with what it means; it cannot be determined solely by appearances or behaviour. And what it means to them is always in part a reflection of social considerations including the possibility that foodies are part of a social world consisting of many other like-minded people. Whether the bonds are local, national or global in scale, foodies and other special-interest groups can connect easily and frequently through social and mass media.

The social-psychological construct called ego-involvement was very important in our research and theorizing about foodies and food tourists. Scales were developed and refined, first in Australia and then through the multi-country online survey that generated over 3,000 respondents - all self-declared food lovers. It was clear, through analysis, that involvement with food is a flexible and evolving thing, but most people are readily categorized into high versus lesser involvement. We used the top 11% of means on our involvement scale to classify and analyse the 'highly involved foodies' or HiFs in our Swedish study.

Highly involved foodies make food a central part of their lifestyle and take all food-related activities very seriously. This is where the connection to serious leisure theory is important. It is now clear that a high level of involvement with food is closely associated with food tourism and with certain preferences that are important to destination developers and marketers. This does not imply, however, that foodies will always get more involved over time, nor that all highly-involved foodies will become food tourists. It does mean that marketers should seek, and now have the tools to identify, the highly-involved foodies who are most likely to visit their destination for food-related experiences.

Food lovers can elect to become involved with others who share their passion, and these 'social worlds' are increasingly found through social networking. Evidence exists to support the contention that online social networking through blogs and other websites influences foodies as to their preferences and habits and encourages food-related travel. Celebrities and experts can influence the decision-making process, attracting foodies to specific areas and getting them interested in particular foods and experiences. For marketers, this means that traditional mass media are now less important, and very precise targeting of communications is essential.

If you believe you are a foodie, it does not necessarily brand you as being the same as all the others. There are numerous ways in which food-loving can be manifested, through an interest in styles and processes of cooking, specific foods and beverages, authentic culture-based cuisines, or visiting particular destinations associated with food. That means careful attention is required by marketers to all the nuances of self and social identity, and to the many possible outlets for self expression.

There are a number of inter-connected concepts and terms that we have used that have particular significance for foodies: fresh and local (see also localvores and omnivores), authenticity, provenance, terroir, interpretation, learning, creativity, tactile experiences, co-creation, and engagement. Suppliers of experiences and destination marketers need an understanding of the significance of all these concepts to foodies, and particularly to the central idea that food tourism is all about experiences, not consumption.

The study of foodies and food tourists

The study of foodies and food tourism is not only important to academics, as practitioners too should be concerned about the creation and dissemination of knowledge that can be helpful in development and marketing. Most work to date has been on the supply side, while knowledge of foodies and food tourists has lagged far behind.

Figure 2.1 (on page 18) is a framework for understanding and creating knowledge about foodies and food tourism that can serve as a guide for future research and evaluations with both theoretical and practical implications. Our research has focused on antecedents to food tourism and the nature and meanings of the experience. The book has also included very practical consideration of planning and marketing by destination marketing organizations and suppliers, and outcomes at the personal, social, economic and environmental levels. Some insights have also been provided on policy related to food tourism, and to its geography and history, although those are largely topics for others to pursue in greater detail.

We looked at where and how the study of foodies and food tourism forms part of food, tourism and hospitality studies. At the nexus of these three fields, food tourism can be viewed as both an essential service and an attraction. Key related terms have been scrutinized, with the cultural significance of 'cuisine' being of particular importance to foodies and 'culinary tourism' being a common substitute for food tourism. Other terms like gastronomy and gastronomic tourism are considered to be value-laden, at least in the minds and definitions of some, so we prefer 'food tourism'.

Food studies as a field incorporates the issues of food supplies, sustainable production and security, including the trend towards favouring local foods. In hospitality studies the emphasis is placed on food service, meals, chefs and cooking in the settings of restaurants, hotels, resorts or event venues. Dining out is an experience, usual social, that requires careful design to attract and satisfy foodies.

Hospitality is also concerned with host and guest interactions, which relates to the authentic food tourist experience.

Tourism studies naturally focus on the travel experiences, both for business and pleasure, but also on destination planning, development and place marketing. Many individual suppliers and packagers/wholesalers of food tourism experiences are also important. Food tourism is both a rural and urban phenomenon of great importance around the world, with links to agri-tourism. As with many other special interest forms of tourism, there is a direct connection between higher levels of involvement and travel. Our research makes it clear that highly involved foodies are the most travelled for food experiences, attend the most food-related events, and have specific benefits in mind when being food tourists.

Dr. Roger Haden contributed a piece on degree programmes for gastronomy and gastronomic tourism, with reflections on why these subjects have become popular, and their connection to culture studies in general.

In the social sciences and humanities the study of food, foodies and food tourism is widespread. A good place to start is with cultural anthropology, which concentrates on the importance of food within culture and introduces the concept of cultural authenticity. From this perspective we can speak of foodways and food culture, and their roles in establishing or reinforcing identity. While the emphasis on this book has been on the foodie's perspective, as in searching for authentic food experiences, it is equally important to consider how the hosts can benefit from or be harmed by attracting and catering to visitors.

From a sociological point of view it is important to look at the social settings for food tourism, and the social worlds that influence foodies in their preferences and choices. Many of the meanings attached to food and food tourism experiences are culturally and socially derived, which makes it necessary to always consider host and guest backgrounds. Social identity for foodies is connected to the sharing of meals and stories about food tourism experiences, and to the communitas that is facilitated by attending planned events.

Psychological theory is important in understanding needs, motivation, benefits sought – especially personal development – and the nature of experience and how reality is perceived. Research has shown that personality is important when considering the degree to which foodies might be neophiles looking for new tastes and novelty-seekers when it comes to travel decisions. The ego-involvement construct has been instrumental in our research as it permits the identification of highly-involved foodies. We constructed involvement scales, and found that the short version employed in the multi-country research worked very well in enabling us to identify and describe the highly-involved foodies as well as the most important elements of being a self-identified foodie.

The important contributions of leisure studies were acknowledged, particularly with regard to the nature of leisure experiences and serious leisure. Highly involved foodies are, in lifestyle, similar to people who engage in lifelong, serious leisure pursuits like sports or hobbies. When it comes to engaging foodies fully in events or other food tourism experiences, it is wise to draw on what is known about leisure experiences as activity, cognitive processes, and emotions.

Geography was found to be important in providing insights for various places having special attractiveness to foodies, and this connects to the concept of terroir. The history of food and food tourism is of interest, and some references have been provided. From economics and business studies we get the concepts of supply chains and value chains, which are critical for developing the full economic potential of food tourism. We also looked at how food tourism generates economic benefits, and how to measure them.

A number of concepts and terms have been employed which are useful in understanding the phenomena of foodies and food tourists. Readers should be able to inter-relate these for a full understanding. Here are the most important:

- Identity
- Ego-involvement
- Serious leisure
- Psychographic segmentation
- Social worlds
- Social bonding
- Communitas
- Neophilia
- Novelty seeking
- Lifestyle.

There are stay-at-home foodies, and globetrotting foodies. It is not the travel that defines them.

9

Implications for destinations, events, suppliers, and marketers

Many implications arise for those wishing to develop product, co-create experiences, heighten their destination's competitiveness, or market to foodies. It all starts with demand-side thinking, requiring market intelligence that can only be gained through original research. Too much effort and money is commonly wasted because of the dominance of supply-side approaches, typically taking the form of: "Here is what we have, our chefs, restaurants and food are great, so why not visit us?" Some cities and suppliers are doing well, that is obvious, but as the marketplace gets more and more competitive the only advantages are going to come from carefully targeting the foodies who travel the most because of their passion.

■ Destinations

Food tourism destinations can be cities, countries, resorts, restaurants or events. The key is to attract visitors who are dedicated food tourists and who are motivated by food. This is not to say that other visitors should be neglected in food tourism development and marketing, because every visitor consumes food and beverages and should be assured of both quality and having a cultural experience through food. Some cities and countries are already highly developed as food destinations, while others are still considering how to get started. The stage of development and current reputation will greatly affect strategy and marketing. We provided a tool for destination diagnostics and suggested many key performance indicators that can be used to evaluate current conditions and help in formulating strategy for food tourism.

Key principles for food tourism planning were derived from a discussion of supply and value chains, namely that benefits will likely be maximized when food tourism is dispersed (i.e. both urban and rural clusters are desirable), and value is added through an emphasis on utilizing local produce, place-specific food branding, and fostering innovation by experience suppliers.

With foodies at the core, a planning and development model for food tourism was presented. Our whole approach stresses the necessity of demand-side research and thinking, starting with an understanding of the foodie and food tourism motivation, which is usually referred to as market intelligence. One could also start planning with a competitive analysis, as it is always important to monitor trends and to know what the alternatives are for your target markets. Developing and testing new products should logically follow from market intelligence and the evaluation of actual food tourism experiences, but usually it is left to entrepreneurs and suppliers to take action and see if they can make a profit. This is an area in which destinations should intervene to foster innovation. As well, the marketing mix has to be constantly evaluated (e.g. with regard to getting the right messages to the intended target segments).

Several food tourism development concepts emerged from our research. Australian food lovers looking for a domestic experience placed learning, socializing, and consuming authentic food together with fine dining at the core. These experiences can be packaged with shopping, touring, cultural and heritage experiences (events are valued), and indulgence and luxury (e.g. spas and other high-end accommodation). From the multi-country research another model emerged, this one focused on implications for developing Sweden as a food tourism destination. At its core were four experiences: farmers' and fishers' markets, food festivals, regional cuisine and romantic meals. These can be packaged with urban culture, or with resort, nature and spa experiences. In addition, for the highly involved or 'dynamic foodies' segment, a range of specialized, tactile experiences and learning events are to be featured. A third model looked at the urban or resort-based package in which accommodation was the core and several brand values are communicated to the consumer: exclusivity, quality, authenticity and co-creation.

Cluster development for food tourism is a logical strategy for destinations to pursue, although few real-world examples are evident. The basic idea is that in cities and areas with potential, all the stakeholders (representing the entire supply chain from farmers and fishers to tourism marketers) need to develop a common vision and strategy for developing and marketing food tourism. Within the cluster, planning thought must be given to creating and sustaining value for all the participants so that the entire economy and society can prosper. This will inevitably tie in with concerns for food security, health, sustainable development, and cultural authenticity - it is a complex matter, not to be taken lightly. Catering services and restaurants are essential, but events and markets should also figure prominently in food tourism clusters. It might very well be that creation or development of a hallmark event can be both the catalyst for action and the cluster brand leader.

■ Events

An entire chapter has been devoted to food-related events, as they have been found to be essential elements in food tourism attractiveness. Principles for event design were advanced, essentially to ensure that it is not all about food and beverage consumption or other hedonistic activities and entertainment. Events for foodies should be positioned quite differently, stressing learning, authenticity, aesthetic appreciation, celebration, communitas, creativity, and tactile experiences. Interpretation will be necessary.

The concepts of hallmark and iconic events were discussed, especially as to their roles in food tourism clusters. Hallmark events are conceived as permanent institutions fulfilling many important roles in the community and destination, with major implications for branding and for attracting both residents and food tourists. They are often festivals. Iconic events can be of any type, but they must hold special symbolic significance for the target segments. Within the food tourism cluster concept, it is less about the types of event than their functions that matters. Events are needed to help build the brand and attract specific target segments.

9

David Gration's profiling of food events in the Sunshine Coast of Australia pointed out the importance of chefs and other stakeholders in getting events started and growing them into tourist attractions. Building a food tourism brand for the region is closely related to two successful events aimed at foodies.

Specific products and experiences

While not being our focus, many specific ideas are found in this book for product development and experience design. Some of them come from the examples and cases featured, and some are derived from the research. We looked at farms, markets, trails, tours, destination events, restaurants, and cooking schools. The roles of chefs and restaurateurs were highlighted. Because the emphasis has to be placed on creating memorable, satisfying experiences for foodies, the various methods of visitor engagement and co-creation must be implemented. And it has to be remembered that highly involved foodies want tactile, learning experiences that manifest cultural authenticity.

A key conclusion for destinations and experiences is that they must be 'export ready'. While it can be expected that some food tourists following food/ beverage routes or visiting cities and resorts will find food-related experiences through locally-provided information, the development of food tourism requires that products and experiences be saleable, online, globally. Tour companies and travel agents can organise appropriate platforms, but it will be the job of tourist organizations and cluster organizers to get suppliers into this mode of business planning and marketing.

Marketing and communications

Experience marketing is required for food tourism, and all lifestyle pursuits. This approach recognizes that the foodie-consumer is looking for memorable, authentic, educational, unique and engaging experiences that build and reinforce identity. Experiences are co-created, with service-dominant logic instructing marketers that they are making service propositions rather than simply selling an experience. Co-creation is based on engaging the consumer, and a set of ideas for food tourism engagement has been provided, modified from the work of Moscardo. Interpretation is always needed, but can be delivered in different ways from story-telling to the instructions of chefs and details from expert guides.

There are many important implications to be derived for food tourism marketing and communications. Image, reputation, positioning, branding and co-branding must be managed by suppliers and destinations. The food brand of countries and destinations has not been studied much, but the examples of Ireland and New Nordic Cuisine suggest appropriate strategies and actions. Changing a stereotyped image is a long and probably difficult process, as evidence by our testing of Sweden's food image relative to other countries. That exercise did reveal that positioning with organic and ecological food should provide competitive advantages for Sweden, in concert with its global reputation for sustainability initiatives. Food tourism clusters also need specific branding, and in that setting hallmark and iconic events can be crucial.

Segmentation is a necessary analytic tool in food tourism marketing. Psychographic segmentation has been referred to, and our approach utilizing ego-involvement is closely related in theory as it incorporates personal and social identity and attitudes. In our research we found such a strong correlation between high involvement, previous food-related travel, and event attendance that we used events in cluster analysis to segment and profile the dynamic foodies. Note that this approach requires original research among the target markets, focused on food lovers (not the general population) and differs greatly from traditional segmentation with its focus on socio-demographic variables (like age, gender, income, marital status). Having said that, perhaps the most useful finding from our segmentation analyses is likely to be the fact that couples form a dominant segment of food tourists. There are others who travel with family and groups of friends, and so it is necessary to avoid generalizations.

Communications and media use were explored. Foodies want all the necessary information to be readily available on line when it comes to travel, but they are most likely to trust the recommendations of friends and relatives. Accordingly, ensuring positive word of mouth from food tourists is a key, so every visitor must have a good food experience.

Communicating the right messages and images to foodies is critical. Far too many marketing efforts are wasted in trying to convey a nice image, attractive to everyone, or in boasting about what wonderful chefs and restaurants are available. That is supply-side thinking. The foodie wants to be part of the process, involved in co-creating their own experiences, and they need assurances that what is available in any place are the experiential benefits valued by food lovers. To truly communicate with foodies it is necessary to understand their passion and motivations for travel.

Research needs

■ Demand

Our research confirms some aspects of what has already been reported about foodies and food tourists, and adds considerably to the available knowledge in several important ways. Findings from the Australian and multi-country research described in this book make it clear what self-identification as a foodie or food lover means, both in personal and social identity terms. We now have a sound basis for understanding food tourism motivation by the highly involved foodie, and this has very important marketing and development implications.

If we look at what is readily available to international tourists, most products and events do not go far enough in catering to the specific needs of food lovers, and instead make assumptions about what is desired. The frequent absence of interpretation, which is essential to providing learning and culturally-authentic experiences, is a major omission from events and other food-related experiences.

The food tourists we identified can be reached through produce markets, good restaurants, and gourmet clubs. Messages that will appeal to them should focus on unique and authentic cultural experiences aimed at gourmets, but probably should also stress experiences for couples and families. The kinds of experiences desired will fuel many after-trip stories and long-lasting memories. But how exactly do foodies react to branding, packaging, and various communications? Are the messages and images generating awareness, interest, and a decision to travel for food-related reasons?

A remaining challenge is to gain greater understanding of actual food tourism experiences, requiring participant observation and other phenomenological methods that investigate the cognitive, affective and conative (behavioural) dimensions of experience. Experience research can easily be connected back to product development and marketing, but as yet we know little (in theoretical terms) about what separates food tourism experiences from other travel or leisure experiences, and how food combined with wine, culture, adventure or nature creates unique, desirable experiences. This line of research will also pay dividends in generating greater understanding of authenticity from the consumer perspective, which can be translated into branding and marketing implications for suppliers and destinations.

How people become involved as food lovers in the first place is an unanswered question. Several logical hypotheses can be suggested, related to the influence of family, culture, and the media, but they have yet to be researched. Cooking appears to be an essential and defining attribute of foodies, and this requires some degree of training or participation in the home - or perhaps professional development. A related question is how a food lover might develop a specialized travel career, and its evolution through all the person's life stages. Will food lovers who have not travelled start with domestic trips to nearby wine and food regions and will they eventually progress to international food tourism? Are there essential pre-conditions pertaining to age and income? Are couples more likely to travel than singles?

■   ## Supply

Most of what has been reported in the literature is related to the existence, nature, planning, development and marketing of food tourism - in other words the supply side. Most destinations start with supply-side approaches, trying to brand and sell what they have. We advocate a demand-side approach based on better understanding of foodies and food tourists, but there is still work to be done in researching the supply side.

Of great practical value would be comparative evaluations of the effectiveness of development strategies and specific food products and experiences, but theoretical development can also benefit from this line of research. For example, how do entrepreneurs innovate and evaluate the products they sell to food tourists - are they learning valuable lessons about co-creating experiences? Which destinations have been most successful and why?

Cluster development for food and food tourism needs to be encouraged and evaluated. What are the best methods for getting stakeholders across the entire supply and value chain to network and co-operate in enhancing both their food brand and food tourism outcomes? How can sustainable food production and food tourism be fostered?

Also of great importance is the effectiveness of marketing aimed at foodies. How do target segments respond to promotions, messages, images, packaging, and the range of offered experiences? How exactly does co-creation work before, during and after food tourism?

Future perspectives

For destinations and suppliers seeking to capitalize on the foodie and food tourism phenomena, the prospects look good. But competition is increasing, and so nothing should be taken for granted. Comparative advantages must now be augmented through market intelligence and capital investments.

Current trends of importance (to be monitored) include:

■ Trading up, or constantly seeking higher quality in food, and in food tourism experiences.

■ Health concerns, and related emphasis on slow, fresh and local, provenance, organic and ecological, sustainable production and distribution.

■ Omnivorism and novelty-seeking, or the desire to try new things or everything; related in part to the spread of ethnic and culturally authentic cuisines.

■ Learning opportunities and the desire to learn even more, including more cooking classes and schools; food-related resorts and retreats.

9

- Food plus! there should be continued packaging quality and authentic food experiences with nature-based, cultural and both urban/rural experiences.

- The popularity and branding roles of celebrity chefs and food-related entertainment.

- Couples on short breaks should continue to dominate food tourism; cities dominate.

- Families with foodie lifestyles; accordingly, family food tourist units should grow in number and importance.

- Both luxury and budget food tourism markets should grow.

- Destination choices should broaden, both in response to competition and to demand for novelty.

- Social worlds centred on food (and related online and social media) will grow in diversity and influence; everyone with a special interest can find fellow devotees.

Looking ahead, emerging trends were identified by Bussell, Tomei and Wolf (2014) in the book Have Fork Will Travel. Here are the highlights:

- Growing outbound tourism from Asia, and especially China, will bring with it many new opportunities but also different culture -based expectations regarding food and drink. We acknowledge the focus of our book has been on Europe and the English-speaking world. As such Asia, as well as South America and Africa are open-books in terms of future research efforts.

- Rapidly changing technology makes it difficult to predict what will have a major impact on marketing, communications, or consumerism in general, but it is apparent that consumers will continue to benefit from more choices and more information and that consumer content will grow.

- More local cooperation will be needed for small businesses to remain competitive.

- Food services and food tourism will likely have to react more to scarcity, rising costs, the threat of disease, allergies and food-preference concerns and become more sustainable and less wasteful.

While predicting the future is risky, by applying some of the principles of future studies to the study of foodies and food tourism it is possible for the authors of this book to state a number of research-based propositions with implications:

- Food tourism will likely continue to grow, but as a reflection of wealth and materialism it has to be considered a luxury market, and one that will inevitably face serious constraints such as food scarcity and rising costs; sustaining a competitive position will therefore require constant attention to the underlying forces and trends.

- Foodies exist in a special marketplace wherein their interests can be satisfied because they have great purchasing power; this makes them a viable and desirable target market, but they are a highly varied one (consider levels of involvement, a myriad of possible food and travel-related interests, and changing fashion) which makes investment in market intelligence crucial.

- Diversification should be expected in the range of experiences supplied and valued by foodies and food tourists; this will come about as more businesses and destinations develop and market food tourism; innovation will follow in part from intelligence gained from social media, as it is the fastest.

- Since being a foodie is a matter of self identification, its meanings and related social status might very well shift; it is possible that 'foodie' could take on mostly negative connotations, and that is something to worry about.

Food and culture are intertwined, therefore as global and country-specific cultures change in response to economic trends, resource scarcities, migration, technology, tourism, and climate change, food preferences and the nature of being a foodie and food tourist will inevitably evolve; food might become a key factor in cultural and sub-group differentiation, but it can also be a source of conflict.

For now, consider the words of celebrity-chef Jamie Oliver (http://www. brainyquote.com/quotes/authors/j/jamie_oliver.html):

What I've enjoyed most, though, is meeting people who have a real interest in food and sharing ideas with them. Good food is a global thing and I find that there is always something new and amazing to learn - I love it!

9

References

Abarca, M. (2004). Authentic or not, it's original. *Food & Foodways*, **12**, 1–25.

Agriturismo-Sicilia.it (2012), FOODIES 2012: Gambero Rosso and Negroni's guide to Italian foods now available, http://www.agritourisme-sicile.com/blog.cfm?id=745

Alonso, A. & Bressan, A. (2013). Stakeholders' perspectives on the evolution and benefits of a traditional wine festival: The case of the Grape Festival ('Festa dell' Uva') in Impruneta, Italy. *Journal of Convention and Exhibition Management*, **14**(4), 309-330.

Alonso, A. & Northcote, J. (2010). The development of olive tourism in Western Australia: A case study of an emerging tourism industry. *International Journal of Tourism Research*, **12,** 696-708.

Andersson, T., & Mossberg, L. (2004). The dining experience: Do restaurants satisfy customer needs? *Food Service Technology*, **4**(4), 171-177.

Arnould, E., & Thompson, C. (2005). Consumer culture theory (Cct): Twenty years of research. *Journal of Consumer Research*, **31**(4), 868-882.

Barbieri, C. & Mahoney, E. (2009). Why is diversification an attractive farm adjustment strategy? Insights from Texas farmers and ranchers. *Journal of Rural Studies*, **25,** 58-66.

Barcelona Field Studies Centre (2013) (online source: *ontarioculinary.com/uncategorized/ tasty-tidbits-consumer-trends*; accessed Nov. 9, 2013).

Barr, A., & Levy, P. (1984). *The Official Foodie Handbook*. London: Ebury Press.

Barrera, E. & Alvarado, O. (2008). Food trails. Tourist architectures built on food identity. *Gastronomic Sciences*, **3** (8), 36-43.

Barrows, C. (2008). Food and beverage management. In B. Brotherton and R. Wood (Eds.), *The Sage Handbook of Hospitality Management*, pp. 421-442. London: Sage.

Beer, S. (2008). Authenticity and food experience: Commercial and academic perspectives. *Journal of Foodservice*, **19,** 153-163.

Bell, R., & Marshall, D. (2003). The construct of food involvement in behavioral research: Scale development and validation. *Appetite*, **40**(3), 235-244.

Benckendorff, P., & Pearce., P. (2012). The psychology of events. In, S. Page & J. Connell (Eds.), *The Routledge Handbook of Events*, pp. 165-185. London: Routledge.

Bennett, L., and Freemantle, J. (2014). Cooking schools and classes. In, E. Wolf (ed.), *Have Fork Will Travel: A Practical Handbook for Food and Drink Professionals*, pp. 171-179. Portland OR: World Food Travel Association.

Bertella, G. (2011). A knowledge-based model for the development of food tourism. In, M. Romano (Ed.), *Proceedings: The First European Conference on Wine and Food Tourism*. Pisa: Edizioni ETS

Bessiere, J. (1998). Local development and heritage: Traditional food and cuisine as tourist attractions in rural areas. *Sociologia Ruralis, 38* (1), 21-34.

Biscardi, N., Casciola, C., Hrabec, M., Partain, H., and Wolf, E. (2014). Culinary Tours, Guides, Packages and Agents. In, E. Wolf (Ed.), *Have Fork Will Travel: A Practical Handbook for Food and Drink Professionals*, pp. 145-155. Portland OR: World Food Travel Association.

Bitner, M. (1992). Servicescapes: The impact of physical surroundings on customers and employees. *The Journal of Marketing, 56* (2), 57-71.

Bitsani, E. & Kavoura, A. (2012). Connecting oenological and gastronomical tourisms at the wine roads, Veneto, Italy, for the promotion and development of agrotourism. *Journal of Vacation Marketing, 18,* 301-312.

Boniface, P. (2003). *Tasting Tourism: Travelling For Food And Drink*. Farnham, Surrey: Ashgate Publishing.

Bourdieu, P. (1979). *Distinction: A Social Critique of the Judgment of Taste*, trans. Richard Nice, 1984. Boston MA: Harvard University Press.

Boyne, S., Hall, D. & Williams, F. (2003). Policy, support and promotion for food-related tourism initiatives. *Journal of Travel & Tourism Marketing, 14,* 131-154.

Boyne, S., Williams, F., & Hall, D. (2002). On the trail of regional success: Tourism, food production and the Isle of Arran Taste Trail. *Tourism and gastronomy*, 91-114.

Branscombe, N., & Wann, D. (1992). Role of identification with a group, arousal, categorization processes, and self-esteem in sports spectator aggression. *Human Relations, 45*(10), 1013-1033.

Brillat-Savarin, J. (2000). *The Physiology of Taste, or Meditations on Transcendental Gastronomy*. Counterpoint (trans. by MFK Fisher; first published in French in 1825).

Brown, G., and Chappel, S. (2008). Tasting Australia: A celebration of cultural identity or an international event? In, J. Ali-Knight et al. (Eds.) *International Perspectives of Festivals and Events*, pp. 139-148. Oxford: Elsevier.

Brown, G., and Getz, D. (2005). Linking wine preferences to the choice of wine tourism destinations. *Journal of Travel Research, 43*(3): 266-276.

Brown, G., Havitz, M., & Getz, D. (2007). Relationships between wine involvement and wine-related tourism. *Journal of Travel and Tourism Marketing, 21*(1): 31-46.

Bruwer, J., & Lesschaeve, I. (2012). Wine tourists' destination region brand image perception and antecedents: Conceptualization of a winescape framework. *Journal of Travel & Tourism Marketing, 29*(7), 611-628.

Bryan, H. (1977). Leisure value systems and recreational specialization: The case of trout fishermen. *Journal of Leisure Research, 9*(3), 174-187.

Bussell, J., and Roberts, K. (2014). Power of the people: Word of mouth marketing in food tourism. In, E. Wolf (ed.), *Have Fork Will Travel: A Practical Handbook for Food and Drink Professionals*, pp. 423-431. Portland OR: World Food Travel Association.

Bussell, J., Tomei, A., & Wolf, E. (2014). Future of food tourism. In, E. Wolf (Ed.), *Have Fork Will Travel: A Practical Handbook for Food and Drink Professionals*, pp. 467-472. Portland OR: World Food Travel Association.

Byrkjeflot, H., Pedersen, J., & Svejenova, S. (2013). From label to practice: The process of creating new Nordic cuisine. *Journal of Culinary Science & Technology, 11*, 36–55.

Cairns, K., Johnston, J., & Baumann, S. (2010). Caring about food: Doing gender in the foodie kitchen. *Gender & Society, 24*(5), 591-615.

Carlsen, J., and Charters, S. (Eds.) (2006). *Global Wine Tourism: Research, Management and Marketing*. Wallingford, England: CABI.

Carlsen, J., & Edwards, D. (2008). Tasting Arizona, Arizona, USA. *Innovation for Sustainable Tourism: International Case Studies, 48*.

Carroll, G., & Torfason, M. (2011). Restaurant organizational forms and community in the US in 2005. *City & Community, 10*(1), 1-24.

Casciola, C., Laurin, U., & Wolf., E. (2014). Developing a food tourism destination. In, E. Wolf (Ed.), *Have Fork Will Travel: A Practical Handbook for Food and Drink Professionals*, pp. 221-232. Portland OR: World Food Travel Association.

Cavicchi, A., and Santini, C. (Eds.) (2014). *Food and Wine Events in Europe: A Stakeholder Approach*. London: Routledge.

Cela, A., Knowles-Lankford, J. & Lankford, S. (2007). Local food festivals in northeast Iowa communities. A visitor and economic impact study. *Managing Leisure, 12,* 171-186.

Chang, W., & Yuan, J. J. (2011). A taste of tourism: Visitors' motivations to attend a food festival. *Event Management, 15*(1), 13-23.

Charters, S., Mitchell, R. (2014) Food and wine events in Europe and the New World: A comparison, in Cavicchi, A., Santini, C., *Food and Wine Events in Europe. A Stakeholder Approach*, Oxford: Taylor & Francis.

Charters, S., & Pettigrew, S. (2006). Product involvement and the evaluation of wine quality. *Qualitative Market Research: An International Journal, 9*(2), 181-193.

Chawla, S., Elliot, S., Wansink, B., and Wolf, E. (2014). How foodies make decisions. In, E. Wolf (ed.), *Have Fork Will Travel: A Practical Handbook for Food and Drink Professionals*, pp. 71-81. Portland OR: World Food Travel Association.

Che, D. (2006). Select Michigan: Local food production, food safety, culinary heritage, and branding in Michigan agritourism. *Tourism Review International, 9*(4), 349-363.

Che, D., Veeck, A., & Veeck, G. (2005). Sustaining production and strengthening the agritourism product: Linkages among Michigan agritourism destinations. *Agriculture and Human Values, 22*, 225-234.

Cohen, E. & Avieli, N. (2004). Food in tourism: Attraction and impediment. *Annals of Tourism Research, 31,* 755-778.

R

Commonwealth Department of Tourism (Australia) (1994). *Australian Rural Tourism Strategy*. Canberra: Australian Government Publishing Service.

Correia, A., Moital, M., Ferreira Da Costa, C. & Peres, R. (2008). The determinants of gastronomic tourists' satisfaction: A second-order factor analysis. *Journal Of Foodservice, 19,* 164-176.

Crispin, S., & Reiser, D. (2008). Food and wine events in Tasmania, Australia. In, C.M. Hall and L. Sharples (Eds.), *Food and Wine Festivals and Events Around the World*, pp. 113-131. Oxford: Butterworth-Heinemann.

Croce, E., & Perri, G. (2010). *Food And Wine Tourism: Integrating Food, Travel and Territory*. Wallingford, England: Cabi.

Crotts, J., Pan, B., & Raschid, A. (2008). A survey method for identifying key drivers of guest delight. *International Journal of Contemporary Hospitality Management, 20,* 462-470.

Csikszentmihalyi, M. (1990). *Flow: The Psychology of Optimal Experience*. New York: Harper & Row.

Culinary (Gastronomic) Tourism (2011). Retrieved From www.onecaribbean.org/content/files/CulinaryCaribbeanNicheMarkets.Pdf).

Dagesse, D. (2013). Wine producing soils of Niagara. In, M. Ripmeester, P. Mackintosh and C. Fullerton (Eds.), *The World of Niagara Wine*, 165-184. Waterloo: Wilfrid Laurier University Press.

Delamont, S. (1994). *Appetites and identities: Introduction to the social anthropology of Western Europe*. London: Routledge.

Deloitte and Touism Industry Association of Canada (2012). *Navigate*, Vol. 4.

Demby, E. (1989). Psychographics revisited: The birth of a technique. *Marketing News*, January, p. 21.

Dodd, T. (1998). Influences on search behavior of industrial tourists. *Journal of Hospitality & Leisure Marketing*, 5(2-3), 77-94.

Du Rand, G., & Heath, E. (2009). Local food as a key element of sustainable tourism competitiveness. In, J. Saarinen, F. Becker, H. Manwa, & D. Wilson (Eds.) *Sustainable Tourism in Southern Africa. Local Communities and Natural Resources in Transition*. Bristol: Channel View Publications.

Du Rand, G., Heath, E. & Alberts, N. (2003). The role of local and regional food in destination Marketing. *Journal of Travel & Tourism Marketing, 14,* 97-112.

Dwyer, L., Forsyth, P. J., & Dwyer, W. (2010). *Tourism Economics and Policy*. Bristol: Channel View Publications.

Einarsen, K. & Mykletun, R. (2009). Exploring the success of the Gladmatfestival (The Stavanger Food Festival). *Scandinavian Journal of Hospitality and Tourism, 9,* 225-248.

Episteme (2013). L'agroalimentare Italiano: centralità valoriale, strategicità economica, Presentation at Buying Tourism Online – 6th Edition, Florence (Italy), 4-6 December, 2013.

Everett, S. (2012). Production places or consumption spaces? The place-making agency of food tourism in Ireland and Scotland. *Tourism Geographies*, **14**(4), 535-554.

Everett, S., & Aitchison, C. (2008). The role of food tourism in sustaining regional identity: A case study of Cornwall, South West England. *Journal of Sustainable Tourism*, **16,** 150-167.

Failte Ireland (2010). *National Food Tourism Implementation Framework 2011-2013.* Dublin: National Tourism Development Authority. Available from: http://www.failteireland.ie/FailteIreland/media/WebsiteStructure/Documents/3_Research_Insights/1_Sectoral_SurveysReports/Food_Tourism_Implementation_Framework-1-19-07-2012.pdf?ext=.pdf

Fandos-Herrera, C., and Shaw, N. (2014). New marketing tactics in food tourism. In, E. Wolf (Ed.), *Have Fork Will Travel: A Practical Handbook for Food and Drink Professionals*, pp. 379-387. Portland OR: World Food Travel Association.

Festinger, L. (1954). A theory of social comparison processes. *Human Relations*, **7**(2), 117-140.

Food and Agriculture Organization (FAO) of the United Nations (1996). *Rome Declaration on Food Security and World Food Summit Plan of Action.*

Fox, R. (2007). Reinventing the gastronomic identity of Croatian tourist destinations. *International Journal of Hospitality Management*, **26**(3), 546-559.

Frochot, I. (2003). An analysis of regional positioning and its associated food images in French tourism regional brochures. *Journal of Travel & Tourism Marketing*, **14**(3-4), 77-96.

Gale Encyclopedia of Food and Culture (2004). Gale Virtual Reference Library: www.gale.com/eBooks.

Galloway, G., Mitchell, R., Getz, D., Crouch, G., & Ong, B. (2008). Sensation seeking and the prediction of attitudes and behaviours of wine tourists. *Tourism Management*, **29,** 950-966.

Getz, D. (2000). *Explore Wine Tourism: Management, Development, Destinations.* New York: Cognizant Communication Corp.

Getz, D. (2007). *Event Studies: Theory, Research and Policy for Planned Events.* Oxford: Elsevier.

Getz, D. (2013). *Event Tourism.* New York: Cognizant.

Getz, D., T. Andersson, & M. Larson (2007). Festival stakeholder roles: Concepts and case studies. *Event Management*, **10** (2/3), 103-122.

Getz, D., & Cheyne, J. (2002). Special event motivations and behavior. In, C. Ryan (Ed.), *The Tourist Experience: A New Introduction* (2nd ed.), pp. 137–155. London: Cassell.

Getz, D. & Brown, G., (2006). Critical success factors for wine tourism destinations. *Tourism Management*, **27** (1): 146-158.

Getz, D., & McConnell, A. (2011). Serious sport tourism and event travel careers. *Journal of Sport Management*, **25**(4), 326-338.

Getz, D., & Patterson, I. (2013). Social worlds as a framework for event and travel careers. *Tourism Analysis*, **18**(5), 485-501.

Getz, D., & Robinson, R.N.S. Love Food, Will Travel: Foodies' propensity for travel. *Tourism Analysis* (forthcoming)

Getz, D., & Robinson, R.N.S. (2014). Foodies and Food Events, *Scandinavian Journal of Hospitality and Tourism*, **14**(3), 1-16.

Gilmore, J., & Pine, J. (2007). *What Consumers Really Want: Authenticity*. Harvard Business School Press: Boston.

Goody, J. (1982). *Cooking, cuisine and class: A study in comparative sociology*. Cambridge: Cambridge University Press.

Gössling, S., Garrod, B., Aall, C., Hille, J., & Peeters, P. (2011). Food management in tourism: Reducing tourism's carbon 'foodprint'. *Tourism Management*, **32**(3), 534-543.

Green, B.C., & Chalip, L. (1998). Sport tourism as the celebration of subculture. *Annals of Tourism Research*, **25**(2), 275-291.

Grimod de La Reynière (1803-1812). *Almanach des Gourmands*. Paris: Mercure de France (2003 edition).

Gross, M., & Brown, G. (2008). An empirical structural model of tourists and places: Progressing involvement and place attachment into tourism. *Tourism Management*, **29**(6), 1141-1151.

Groves, A. (2001). Authentic British food products: A review of consumer perceptions. *International Journal of Consumer Studies, *25** (3), 246-254.

Gyimóthy, S., and Mykletun, R. (2009). Scary food: Commodifying culinary heritage as meal adventures in tourism. *Journal of Vacation Marketing*, **15**(3): 259-273.

Hall, C.M., & Gossling, S. (2013). *Sustainable Culinary Systems: Local Foods, Innovation, Tourism and Hospitality*. Oxford: Routledge.

Hall, C. M., & Macionis, N. (1998). Wine tourism in Australia and New Zealand. In, R. Butler, C.M. Hall, & J. Jenkins (Eds.), *Tourism and Recreation In Rural Areas*, 197-224, New York: Wiley.

Hall, C.M., & Page, S. (2005). *The Geography of Tourism and Recreation*. Oxford: Routledge.

Hall, C.M., Sharples, L. (Eds.) (2008). *Food and Wine Festivals and Events Around The World*. Oxford: Butterworth Heinemann.

Hall, C.M., Sharples, L. Mitchell, R. Macionis, N., Cambourne, B. (2003). *Food Tourism Around The World. Development, Management and Markets*. Oxford: Butterworth-Heinemann.

Hashimoto, A., & Telfer, D. (2006). Selling Canadian culinary tourism: Branding the global and the regional product. *Tourism Geographies*, **8**(1), 31-55.

Havitz, M., & Dimanche, F. (1997). Leisure involvement revisited: conceptual conundrums and measurement advances. *Journal of Leisure Research*, **29**(3), 245-278.

Havitz, M., & Dimanche, F. (1999). Leisure involvement revisited: Drive properties and paradoxes. *Journal of Leisure Research,* **31**(2), 122-149.

Hede, A. (2008). Food and wine festivals: Stakeholders, long-term outcomes and strategies for success. In, C.M. Hall and L. Sharples (Eds.), *Food and wine festivals and events around the world,* pp.8 5-101. Oxford: Butterworth-Heinemann.

Heldke, L. (2003). *Exotic Appetites: Ruminations of a Food Adventurer.* London: Routledge.

Henderson, J. (2004). Food as a tourism resource: A view from Singapore. *Tourism Recreation Research,* **29** (3): 69-74.

Hjalager, A-M. (2002). A typology of gastronomy tourism. In, A-M Hjalager and G. Richards (Eds.), *Tourism and Gastronomy,* 21-35. London: Routledge.

Hjalager, A-M., & Corigliano, M. (2000). Food for tourists? Determinants of an image. *International Journal of Tourism Research,* **2**, 281-293.

Hjalager, A.-M., and Richards, G. (2002). *Tourism and Gastronomy.* London: Routledge.

Horng, J., Liu, C., Chou, H., & Tsai, C. (2012). Understanding the impact of culinary brand equity and destination familiarity on travel intentions. *Tourism Management,* **33**(4), 815-824.

Hu, Y. (2010). An exploration of the relationships between festival expenditures, motivations, and food involvement among food festival visitors. Thesis, The University of Waterloo. (uwspace.uwaterloo.ca).

Huang, R. & Hall, D. (2007). The New Tea Appreciation Festival: Marketing and socio-economic development in Hunan Province, China. In, L. Jolliffe (Ed.) *Tea And Tourism: Tourists, Traditions And Transformations.* Clevedon, Uk. : Channel View Publications.

Hughes, G. (1995). Authenticity in tourism. *Annals of tourism Research,* **22**(4), 781-803.

Ignatov, E., & Smith, S. (2006). Segmenting Canadian culinary tourists. *Current Issues In Tourism,* **9,** 235-255.

International Culinary Tourism Association (2010) *Culinary Tourism.* (www. culinarytourism.org, accessed 21 December 2010; now World Food Travel Association, see: www:worldfoodtravel.org)

Jacobsen, R (2010) *American Terroir: Savoring the Flavors of Our Woods, Waters, and Fields,* Bloomsbury

Johnston, J., & Baumann, S. (2007). Democracy versus distinction: A study of omnivorousness in gourmet food writing. *American Journal of Sociology,* **113**(1), 165-204.

Johnston, J., & Baumann, S. (2009). *Foodies: Democracy and Distinction In The Gourmet Foodscape.* London: Routledge.

Jolliffe, L. (Ed.). (2007). *Tea and Tourism: Tourists, Traditions and Transformations.* Bristol: Channel View Publications.

Joliffe, L. (Ed.). (2010). *Coffee Culture, Destinations and Tourism.* Bristol: Channel View Publications.

R

Karim, S., & Chi, C. (2010). Culinary tourism as a destination attraction: An empirical examination of destinations' food image. *Journal of Hospitality Marketing and Management*, **19** (6): 531-555.

Karim, S. & Leong, J. (2008). Information sources in culinary tourism for France, Italy and Thailand. *Anatolia, an International Journal of Tourism and Hospitality Research*, **19,** 161-171.

Khan, S. (2010). Foodies: Democracy and Distinction in the Gourmet Foodscape (book review). *Social Forces*, **89** (2), 731-732.

Kim, Y. G., Eves, A., & Scarles, C. (2009). Building a model of local food consumption on trips and holidays: A grounded theory approach. *International Journal of Hospitality Management*, **28**(3), 423-431.

Kim, Y-S., Raab, C., & Bergman, C. (2010). Restaurant selection preferences of mature tourists in Las Vegas: A pilot study. *International Journal of Hospitality & Tourism Administration*, **11,** 157-170.

Kim, Y. G., Suh, B., & Eves, A. (2010). The relationships between food-related personality traits, satisfaction, and loyalty among visitors attending food events and festivals. *International Journal of Hospitality Management*, **29**(2), 216-226.

Kivela, J., & Crotts, J. (2005). Gastronomy tourism: A meaningful travel market segment. *Journal of Culinary Science and Technology*, **4,** 39-55.

Kivela, J., & Crotts, J. (2006). Tourism and gastronomy: Gastronomy's influence on how tourists experience a destination. *Journal of Hospitality & Tourism Research*, **30,** 354-377.

Kivela, J., & Crotts, J. (2009). Understanding travelers' experiences of gastronomy through etymology and narration. *Journal of Hospitality & Tourism Research*, **33**(2), 161-192.

Kleidas, M., & Jolliffe, L. (2010). Coffee attraction experiences. A narrative study. *Tourism, An International Interdisciplinary Journal*, **58,** 61-73.

Knowd, I. (2006). Tourism as a mechanism for farm survival. *Journal of Sustainable Tourism*, **14,** 24-42.

Krešić, G., & Sučić, M. (2010). Organic food in Croatia: Production principles and outlook. *Tourism & Hospitality Management*, **16,** 63-74.

Kuznesof, S., Tregear, A., & Moxey, A. (1997). Regional foods: A consumer perspective. *British Food Journal*, **99** (6), 199-206.

Kyle, G., Absher, J., Norman, W., Hammitt, W., & Jodice, L. (2007). A modified involvement scale. *Leisure Studies*, **26**(4), 399-427.

Lang Research Inc. (2001). *TAMS (Travel Activities and Motivation Survey) (2001). Wine and Culinary*. Toronto. www.tourism.gov.on.ca/english/tourdiv/tams

Lashley, C., and Morrison, A. (Eds.) (2000). *In Search of Hospitality: Theoretical Perspectives and Debates*. Oxford: Butterworth-Heinemann.

Lashley, C., Lynch, P., & Morrison, A. (Eds.). (2007). *Hospitality: A Social Lens*. Oxford: Elsevier.

Leal, F., & Arellanoe, S. (2012). *Foodies: How Status Is Manifested In The Kitchen.* Thesis: Lund University School of Economics and Management.

Lepp, A., & Gibson, H. (2003). Tourist roles, perceived risk and international tourism. *Annals of Tourism Research,* **30**(3), 606-624.

Lilleheim, H., Mykletun, R., Quain, W., & Engstrom, C. (2005). South Beach Wine and Food Festival - why participate? *FIU Hospitality Review,* **23**(2), 9-18.

Lin, Y., Pearson, T., & Cai, L. (2011). Food as a form of destination identity: A tourism destination brand perspective. *Tourism and Hospitality Research,* **11**(1), 30-48.

Ling, L., Karim, M. & Othman, M. (2010). Relationships between Malaysian food image, tourist satisfaction and behavioural intention. *World Applied Sciences Journal,* **10,** 164-171.

Liu, B., Norman, W., Backman, S., Cuneo, K., & Condrasky, M. (2012). Shoot, taste and post: An exploratory study of food and tourism experiences in an online image-share community. *e-Review of Tourism Research,* **10**(3).

Long, L., (2003). *Culinary Tourism.* Lexington, KY: University of Kentucky Press.

Lu, S., & Fine, G. (1995). The presentation of ethnic authenticity: Chinese food as a social accomplishment. *The Sociological Quarterly,* **36**(3), 535-553.

Lusch, R., & Vargo, S. (2006). Service-dominant logic: reactions, reflections and refinements. *Marketing Theory,* **6**(3), 281-288.

Macionis, N., & Cambourne, B. (1998). Wine tourism: Just what is it all about? *Australian & New Zealand Wine Industry Journal,* **13**(1): 41-47.

MacKay, K., & Fesenmaier, D. (1997), Pictorial element of destination in image formation. *Annals of Tourism Research,* **24,** 537-565.

MacLaurin, T. (2001). Food safety in travel and tourism. *Journal of Travel Research,* **39,** 332-333.

McCall, G., & Simmons, J. (1966). *Identities & Interactions: An Examination of Human Associations in Everyday Life.* New York: The Free Press.

McMahon, R. (2005). A city of excess…in a good way. *Journal of Culinary Science & Technology,* **4,** 91-93.

Mandala Research (2013). *The American Culinary Traveler.* (summary posted by the Arizona Office of Tourism. (www.azot.gov/system/files/1051/original/The%20American%20Culinary) (accessed Jan. 13, 2014)

Mannell, R., & Iso-Ahola, S. (1987). Psychological nature of leisure and tourism experience. *Annals of tourism research,* **14**(3), 314-331.

Mannell, R., & Kleiber, D. (1997). *A Social Psychology of Leisure.* Venture Publishing Inc.

Mark-Up (2009). Foodies, esercito che avanza, 9 October 2009. Available at: http://www.mark-up.it/articoli/0,1254,41_ART_3646,00.html

Marshall, D., & Bell, R. (2004). Relating the food involvement scale to demographic variables, food choice and other constructs. *Food quality and preference,* **15**(7), 871-79.

R

Martin, A., & McBoyle, G. (2006). Scotland's Malt Whisky Trail: Management issues in a public–private tourism marketing partnership. *International Journal of Wine Marketing,* **18**(2), 98-111.

Maslow, A. (1954). *Motivation and Personality.* New York: Harper & Row.

Maslow, A. (1962). *Toward a Psychology of Being.* Princeton: Van Nostrand.

Mason, R., & O'Mahony, B. (2007). On the trail of food and wine: The tourist search for meaningful experience. *Annals of Leisure Research,* **10**(3-4), 498-517.

Moisio, R., Arnould, E., & Price, L. (2004). Between mothers and markets: Constructing family identity through homemade food. *Journal of Consumer Culture,* **4**(3), 361–384.

Molz, J. (2007). Eating difference: The cosmopolitan mobilities of culinary tourism. *Space And Culture,* **10,** 77-93.

Montanari, M. (2006). *Food Is Culture.* Translated from the Italian by Albert Sonnenfeld. New York: Columbia University Press.

Moscardo, G. (2010). The shaping of tourist experience: The importance of stories and themes. In, M. Morgan, P. Lugosi and J.R.B. Ritchie (Eds), *The Tourism and Leisure Experience: Consumer and Managerial Perspectives,* 43-58. Bristol: Channel View.

Mossberg, L., Mulcahy, J., Shah, N., and Svensson, I. (2014). Best practices in destination food tourism branding. In, E. Wolf (ed.), *Have Fork Will Travel: A Practical Handbook for Food and Drink Professionals,* pp. 337-352. Portland OR: World Food Travel Association.

Mykletun, R., & Gyimóthy, S. (2010). Beyond the renaissance of the traditional Voss Sheep's-Head Meal: Tradition, culinary art, scariness and entrepreneurship. *Tourism Management,* **31,** 434-446.

Natilli, M., Pavone, P., Romano, M. (2012), The language of tourists in a Wine and Food Blog, In, M. Natilli, & M. Romano (Eds.)(2012). *Wine And Food Tourism,* pp. 267-86. Pisa: Edizioni ETS.

Nicholson, R., & Pearce, D. (2000). Who goes to events?: A comparative analysis of the profile characteristics of visitors to four South Island events in New Zealand. *Journal of Vacation Marketing,* **6,** 236-253.

Nicholson, R. & Pearce, D. (2001). Why do people attend events?: A comparative analysis of visitor motivations at four South Island events. *Journal of Travel Research,* **39,** 449-460.

Nield, K., Kozak, M., & Legrys, G. (2000). The role of food service in tourist satisfaction. *International Journal of Hospitality Management,* **19,** 375-384.

O'Dell, T., & Billing, P. (Eds.). (2005). *Experiencescapes: Tourism, Culture and Economy.* CBS Press.

O'Donovan, I., Barry, T., and Quinlan, T. (2012). From farm to fork: An assessment of collaborative supply relationships to underpin food tourism. Paper presented at the Dublin Gastronomy Symposium, 2012, School of Culinary Arts & Food Technology, Dublin Institute of Technology (accessed March 3, 2014, at: *arrow.dit.ie/dgs).*

Okumus, B., Okumus, F., & Mckercher, B. (2007). Incorporating local and international cuisines in the marketing of tourism destinations: The cases of Hong Kong and Turkey. *Tourism Management*, **28**, 253-261.

Ollenburg, C., & Buckley, R. (2007). Stated economic and social motivations of farm tourism operators. *Journal Of Travel Research*, **45**, 444-452.

Ottenbacher, M., & Harrington, R. (2013). A case study of a culinary tourism campaign in Germany: Implications for strategy making and successful implementation. *Journal Of Hospitality & Tourism Research*, **37**(1), 3-28.

Page, S., and Getz, D. (Eds.) (1997). *The Business of Rural Tourism*. London and Boston: International Thomson Business Press.

Paolini, D. (2000). *I luoghi del gusto: Cibo e territorio come risorsa di marketing*. Milano: Baldini and Castoldi.

Park, K-S., Reisinger, Y., & Kang, H-J. (2008) Visitors' motivation for attending the South Beach Wine and Food Festival, Miami Beach, Florida. *Journal of Travel & Tourism Marketing*, **25** (2), 161-181.

Pechlaner, H., Raich, F., & Fischer, E. (2009). The role of tourism organizations in location management: the case of beer tourism in Bavaria. *Tourism Review*, **64**(2), 28-40.

Pendergast, D. (2006). Tourist gut reactions: Food safety and hygiene issues. In, J. Wilks, D. Pendergast, & P. Leggat (Eds.), *Tourism in Turbulent Times: Towards Safe Experiences For Visitors*, pp. 143–154. Amsterdam: Elsevier.

Peters, G. (1997). *American winescapes: The cultural landscapes of America's wine country*. Boulder CO: Westview Pres.

Pettigrew, S., and Charters, S. (2006). Consumers' expectations of food and alcohol pairing. *British Food Journal*, **108**(3), 169 - 180.

Pine, J., and Gilmore, J. (1999). *The Experience Economy*. Boston: Harvard Business School Press.

Plummer, R., Telfer, D., Hashimoto, A., & Summers, R. (2005). Beer tourism in Canada along the Waterloo–Wellington ale trail. *Tourism Management*, **26**(3), 447-458.

Plummer, R., Telfer, D., and Hashimoto, A. (2006). The rise and fall of the Waterloo-Wellington Ale Trail: A study of collaboration within the tourism industry. *Current Issues in Tourism*, **9** (3), 191-205.

Porter, M. (1990). *The Competitive Advantage of Nations*. New York: The Free Press.

Porter, M. (1998). Clusters and the new economics of competition. *Harvard Business Review*, **76** (6), 77-90.

Porter, M. (2000). Location, competition, and economic development: Local clusters in a global economy. *Economic Development Quarterly*, **14** (1), 15-34.

Quan, S., & Wang, N. (2004). Towards a structural model of the tourist experience: An illustration from food experiences in tourism. *Tourism Management*, **25**, 297-305.

Ren, C. B., & Liburd, J. J. (2012). Stakeholders, high stakes and high tides: Quality of life in a small island festival context. In K F Hyde, C Ryan & A G Woodside (eds) *Field Guide to Case Study Research in Tourism, Hospitality and Leisure*. (pp. 439-455)

R

Research Resolutions & Consulting Ltd. (2004). *TAMS (U.S. Festival Tourism Enthusiasts: A Special Analysis of the Travel Activities and Motivation Survey)* prepared for The Canadian Tourism Commission (CTC).

Richard K. Miller & Associates: *2011 Restaurant, Food & Beverage Market Research Handbook.*

Richards, G. (2002). Gastronomy: An essential ingredient in tourism production and consumption. In, A-M. Hjalager & G. Richards, (Eds.) *Tourism and Gastronomy.* London: Routledge.

Ripmeester, M., Mackintosh, P. and Fullerton, C. (Eds.) (2013). *The World of Niagara Wine.* Waterloo: Wilfrid Laurier University Press.

Ritchie, J. B., & Crouch, G. (2003). *The Competitive Destination: A Sustainable Tourism Perspective.* Wallingford UK: CABI.

Robinson, R.N.S. & Clifford, C. (2007). Primi, secondi, insalata: Augmenting authenticity at special events via foodservice experiences. *International Journal of Event Management Research,* **3**, 1-11.

Robinson, R.N.S. & Clifford, C. (2012), Authenticity and festival foodservice experiences, *Annals of Tourism Research,* **39**(2) 571-600

Robinson, R.N.S. & Getz, D. (2012). "Getting Involved: 'Foodies' and food tourism", Proceedings of CAUTHE Conference, Melbourne, Australia. 6th -9th February.

Robinson, R.N.S., & Getz, D. (2013). Food enthusiasts and tourism: Exploring food involvement dimensions. *Journal of Hospitality and Tourism Research.* doi:10.1177/1096348013503994

Robinson, R.N.S. & D. Getz (2014). Profiling potential food tourists: An Australian study. *British Food Journal,* **116** (4), 690 -706.

Rojek, C. (1995). *Decentring Leisure: Rethinking Leisure Theory.* London: Sage.

Rotherham, I. (2008). From haggis to high table: A selective history of festival and feast as mirrors of British landscape and culture. In, C.M. Hall & L.Sharples, (Eds.), *Food and Wine Festivals and Events Around The World,* pp. 47-62. Oxford: Butterworth Heinemann.

Ryu, K., & Jang, S. (2006). Intention to experience local cuisine in a travel destination: The modified theory of reasoned action. *Journal of Hospitality and Tourism Research,* **30**, 507-516.

Santich, B. (1996). *Looking for Flavour.* Kent Town, South Australia: Wakefield Press.

Santich, B. (2004). The study of gastronomy and its relevance to hospitality education and training. *International Journal of Hospitality Management,* **23**, 15-24

Schluter, R. (2011). Anthropological roots of rural development: A culinary tour ism case study in Argentina. *Tourismos: An International Multidisciplinary Journal of Tourism,* **6** (3), 77-91.

Scott, D., & Godbey, G. C. (1992). An analysis of adult play groups: Social versus serious participation in the contract bridge. *Leisure Sciences,* **14**, 47-67

Scottish Government (2010) Scotland's Food and Drink. Available at www.scotland.gov.uk/News/Releases/2010/05/26141519 (accessed 18 December 2010).

Sharples, L., & Lyons, H. (2008). Ludlow Marches Food and Drink Festival. In, C.M. Hall & L. Sharples (Eds.), *Food and Wine Festivals and Events Around the World: Development, Management and Markets*, pp. 101-112. Oxford: Butterworth Heinemann.

Shenoy, S. (2005). *Food tourism and the culinary tourist*. PhD dissertation, Clemson University.

Sidali, K., Kastenholz, E., & Bianchi, R. (2013). Food tourism, niche markets and products in rural tourism: Combining the intimacy model and the experience economy as a rural development strategy. *Journal of Sustainable Tourism*, DOI: 10.1080/09669582.2013.836210.

Sims, R. (2009). Food, place and authenticity: Local food and the sustainable tourism experience. *Journal of Sustainable Tourism*, **17,** 321-336.

Smith, S. & Costello, C. (2009a). Culinary tourism. Satisfaction with a culinary event utilizing importance-performance grid analysis. *Journal of Vacation Marketing,* **15,** 99-110.

Smith, S., & Costello, C. (2009b). Segmenting visitors to a culinary event: Motivations, travel behavior, and expenditures. *Journal of Hospitality Marketing and Management,* **18,** 44-67.

Smith, S., Costello, C., and Muenchen, R. (2010). Influence of push and pull motivations on satisfaction and behavioral intentions within a culinary tourism event. *Journal of Quality Assurance in Hospitality and Tourism,* **11** (1), 17-35.

Smith, S. L., & Godbey, G. (1991). Leisure, recreation and tourism. *Annals of Tourism Research*, **18**(1), 85-100.

Smith, S. L. & Xiao, H. (2008). Culinary tourism supply chains: A preliminary Examination. *Journal of Travel Research,* **46,** 289-299.

Sparks, B., Roberts, L., Deery, M., Davies, J., & Brown, L. (2005). *Good Living Tourism: Lifestyle Aspects of Food and Wine Tourism*. Gold Coast, Australia: Cooperative Research Centre for Sustainable Tourism.

Stebbins, R. A. (1992). *Amateurs, Professionals, And Serious Leisure*. Montreal: Mcgill-Queen's University. Press.

Stebbins, R. (1993). *The Barbershop Singer: Inside The Social World of a Musical Hobby*. Toronto: University of Toronto Press.

Telfer, D., & Hashimoto, A. (2003) Food tourism in the Niagara Region: The development of a nouvelle cuisine. In, C. M. Hall, L. Sharples, R. Mitchell, N. Macionis and B. Cambourne (Eds.), *Food Tourism Around the World: Development, Management and Markets*, pp. 158-177. London: Butterworth Heinemann.

Telfer, D., & Hashimoto, A. (2013) Wine and culinary tourism in Niagara. In, M. Ripmeester, P. Mackintosh and C. Fullerton (Eds.), *The World of Niagara Wine*, 281-300. Waterloo: Wilfrid Laurier University Press.

R

Tellstrom, R., Gustafsson, I., & Mossberg, L. (2006). Consuming heritage: The use of local food culture in branding. *Place Branding*, **2**, 130-143.

Tikkanen, I. (2007). Maslow's hierarchy and food tourism in Finland: Five cases. *British Food Journal*, **109**, 721-734.

Timothy, D., and Ron, A. (2013). Understanding heritage cuisines and tourism: Identity, image, authenticity, and change. *Journal of Heritage Tourism*, **8** (2-3), 99-104

Travel Industry Association of America and Edge Research (2006). *Profile of Culinary Travelers*, 2006 Edition.

Tresidder, R., and Hirst, C. (2012). *Marketing in Food, Hospitality, Tourism and Events: A Critical Approach*. Oxford: Goodfellow.

Trubek, A. (2009). *The Taste of Place: A Cultural Journey into Terroir. California Studies in Food and Culture.* Berkely and Los Angeles: The University of California Press.

Turner, V. (1969). Communitas: Model and process. In, V. Turner (Ed.), *The Ritual Process: Structure and Anti-Structure*, 131-165. Aldine.

Tussyadiah, I. (2005). A gourmet trip : One direction of domestic tourism In Japan. *Tourism Review International*, **9**, 281-291.

Unruh, D. (1979). Characteristics and types of participation in social worlds. *Symbolic Interaction*, **2**(2), 115-130.

Unruh, D. (1980). The nature of social worlds. *Pacific Sociological Review*, **23**(3), 271-296.

UNWTO (2012). *Global Report on Food Tourism*. Madrid: World Tourism Organization.

Uysal, M., Gahan, L., and Martin, B. (1993). An examination of event motivations: A case study. *Festival Management and Event Tourism*, **1** (1), 5-10.

Vargo, S., and Lusch, R. (2004). Evolving to a new dominant logic for marketing. *Journal of Marketing*, **68** (1), 1-17.

Vujicic, S. (2008). Photographic messages in tourism advertising. Advertisers' planning for the production of as well as potential tourists' interpretation of photographic messages in tourist brochures. University of Gothenburg, Sweden, Doctoral thesis. ISBN/ISSN: 978-91-7246-263-2.

Vujicic, S. Getz, D. and Robinson, R.N.S. (2013), *Food Tourists: Who are they, what do they want, how do you package offers, and reach them?*. Sweden: Göteborg & Co, available at http://www.experiencec.com/Assets/foodies/executive%20foodie%20report.pdf

Watson, P., Morgan, M., & Hemmington, N. (2008). Online communities and the sharing of extraordinary restaurant experiences. *Journal of Foodservice*, **19**(6), 289-302.

Wolf, E. (2006). *Culinary Tourism: The Hidden Harvest*. Dubuque: Kendall/Hunt.

Wolf, E. (Ed.) (2014), *Have Fork Will Travel: A Practical Handbook for Food and Drink Professionals*. Portland OR: World Food Travel Association.

Yeoman, I, (2012). 2050 - *Tomorrow's Tourism*. Bristol: Channel View.

Zaichkowsky, J. (1985). Measuring the involvement construct. *Journal of Consumer Research*, **12**(3), 341-352.

Zittlau, J., and Gorman, C., (2012). Farmers markets as an authentic experience: The case of Dublin. Paper presented at the Dublin Gastronomy Symposium, 2012, School of Culinary Arts & Food Technology, Dublin Institute of Technology (accessed March 3, 2014, at: *arrow.dit.ie/dgs*).

Zumbado-Morales, F. (2010). Agrotourism and agro-ecotourism in Costa Rica. *E-Review of Tourism Research*, **8,** 196-210.

■ Further reading

Beardsworth, A., & Keil, T. (1997). *Sociology on The Menu: An Invitation To The Study of Food And Society*. London: Routledge.

Gatti, S., & Incerti, F. (1998). The Wine Routes as an instrument for the valorisation of typical products and rural areas, typical and traditional products: Rural effects and agro-industrial problems. 52nd Seminar of the European Association of Agricultural Economists, Parma, Italy, June 19-21, 1997, Parma, Italy.

Getz, D., & Robinson, R. (2012). Understanding and researching food tourism. In, M. Romano & M. Natilli (Eds.), *Wine And Food Tourism*, pp.43-86. Pisa: Edizioni ETS.

Grew, R. (2000). *Food in Global History*. Oxford: Westview Press.

Haber, B. (2007). Culinary history vs. food history. In, A. Smith (Ed.), *The Oxford Companion to American food and Drink*, pp. 179–180. Oxford University Press.

Hall, C. M. (2005). Rural wine and food tourism cluster and network development. In, D. Hall, I. Kirkpatrick and M. Mitchell (Eds.), *Rural Tourism and Sustainable Business*, 149-164. Bristol: Channel View.

Lashley, C., Morrison, A., & Randall, S. (2004). My most memorable meal ever! Hospitality as an emotional experience. In, D. Sloan (Ed.), *Culinary Taste*, 165-184. Oxford: Butterworth-Heinemann.

MacLaurin, T. (2004). The importance of food safety in travel planning and destination selection. *Journal of Travel & Tourism Marketing*, **15**(4), 233-257.

Getz, D., Robinson, R.N.S., & Vujicic, S. (2014). Demographic history of food travelers. In, E. Wolf (Ed.), *Have Fork Will Travel: Food Tourism Handbook*, pp. 63-69. Portland Oregon, World Food Travel Association.

Santini, C., Cavicchi, A. & Canavari, M. (2011). The Risk™ strategic game of rural tourism: How sensory analysis can help in achieving a sustainable competitive advantage. In, K. Sidali, A. Spiller, & B. Schulze (Eds)., *Food, Agriculture and Tourism. Linking Local Gastronomy and Rural Tourism: Interdisciplinary Perspectives, pp. 161-179.* Berlin: Springer.

Strong, R. (2003). *Feast: A History of Grand Eating*. London: Pimlico.

Tardi, A. (2007). Spacious food bazaar in Turin plans Manhattan branch. New York Times, October 24, 2007, http://www.nytimes.com/2007/10/24/dining/24eata. html?pagewanted=print&_r=0

Unioncamere (2013). Impresa Turismo 2013, Istituto Nazionale Ricerche Turistiche. Available at: http://www.ontit.it/opencms/opencms/ont/it/documenti/02970.

R

A Appendix

Some of the results of this pioneering study, conducted by researchers based at The University of Queensland's School of Tourism, have been previously published by Robinson and Getz (2013; 2014), Getz and Robinson (2012), and Robinson, Getz, and Vujicic (2014).

Research methods and descriptions of the samples

■ Australia

Results of this pioneering study, conducted by researchers based at The University of Queensland's School of Tourism, have been previously published by Robinson and Getz, Getz and Robinson (see the References). Their aim was to learn more about what it means to be a foodie, and how that leads to various lifestyle and travel choices. A major part of the work was developing and testing an involvement scale that would reveal the relative importance of various dimensions of being a foodie; these dimensions were postulated from a number of interviews with food lovers and professionals as well as from the available literature, including previous work on wine tourists (e.g., Brown and Getz, 2005). As with all research based on purposive samplings, findings cannot be generalised to the whole population of foodies or Queenslanders.

After a pre-test on students, which resulted in some changes, the final questionnaire was administered in an online format, using the Qualtrics® software platform. We targeted networks of foodies and various media including food and wine clubs' mailing lists and newsletters, professional networks, readers of online food-related magazines and blogs. A note was also placed in a weekly newsletter circulated to the university community via email. An incentive of a 2-for-1 deal at a local destination restaurant was negotiated, for all respondents. The survey was open from early May, 2010 and closed at the end of June. Completion time was about 25 minutes, and researchers reasoned that the survey would be stimulating enough to maintain interest. In total 707 responses were received but response rates showed a downward trend and 24% of respondents failed to answer the final question. After data cleaning, a total of 541 valid respondent cases were retained for analysis. Only five respondents were non-nationals, so as expected 99% (n=526) of the sample were Australian. Only two respondents provided a home post/zipcode outside of the state of Queensland.

One concern with the data is the gender imbalance, as 80% of respondents were female. While this kind of response bias is consistent with the greater tendencies of females to respond to surveys, especially as found by Sparkes et al., (2005) with regard to wine and food, it also reflects a general finding of researchers that females are more interested in food tourism than males (Ignatov & Smith, 2006). Our Swedish research achieved a much better gender balance, no doubt in large part to sampling through formal market-research panels.

Fifty-six per cent of respondents were under 40 and the modal age of the sample (31-40 years of age) is consistent with the median for Queensland (36.2) and Australia (36.9) (ABS, 2010). The modal sample salary ($50K-$60K) is consistent with the general population ($45.3K) as reported by the ABS (2010). It appears promoting the study via a university online newsletter may have affected the education level distribution and possibly the employment rates and income. However, this profile also accords with previous research suggesting the affluent and well educated characteristics of potential food tourists (TAMS, 2001; TIAA, 2006).

Table A.1: Demographic profile of the Australian sample. Adapted from Robinson & Getz, 2014, p.696.

Variable	Categories	Frequency (Valid %)
Gender n=532	Male	20
	Female	80
Age n=527	18–30 years	28
	31-40 years	28
	41-50 years	18
	51-60 years	19
	>61 years	7
Income n=497	>$20K	7
	$20-$39K	13
	$40-59K	29
	$60-$79K	27
	$80-$99K	11
	<$100K	13

Sweden

Agricultural and tourism agencies in Sweden funded this consulting study, reflecting that nation's commitment to develop food tourism. The full report of this major research project is available online, free of charge, at: (http://www. experiencec.com/En/Page.asp?PageId=276)

Some of the results have been published in journals. In the References, see articles on foodies and food tourism by T. Andersson, D. Getz, R. Robinson, and S. Vujicic.

The purpose of this project was to identify the different dimensions of being a foodie; what foodies want and need from food and travel experiences; how foodies communicate, and their travel patterns and preferences related to food. The ultimate use of this market intelligence is to attract more high-yield food tourists to Sweden through development of attractive experiences and more targeted marketing and communications. The research focused on four target markets: Norway, U.K., Germany and Italy. Focus groups were conducted in each of the four countries, and a large international online survey was executed. Our survey generated 3137 responses, of which over 2700 were from the four target countries.

Focus groups provided insights that both informed the questionnaire and aided in interpretation of the survey results, especially in terms of differences between males and females.

The basic premise underpinning this research is that love of food does not necessarily lead to food-motivated travel, and so it is necessary to identify the niche segments, called 'foodies', that do travel with food-related experiences as a specific goal. Traditional market research, mostly relied upon by today's tourism/hospitality industries, does not give full understanding of who food tourists are and what they want. Destinations and countries generally work to position themselves as food tourism destinations based on the products they offer, which might be exceptional, but without the benefit of knowing what foodies want and need, their preferences related to food, and their travel patterns, destinations and countries run the risk of missing important niche markets and wasting time and money on misdirected communications.

This project was in many ways innovative. We used involvement theory and pioneering methods to study food lovers and identify the highly-involved foodies who are potential visitors to Sweden. This approach concentrates attention on the segment of society that is especially interested in food, then examines their travel patterns and preferences. We also used photo elicitation to focus on the kinds of experiences, and experience packages, that foodies desire and are willing to pay most for. Finally, various advanced statistical techniques have been used to test relationships among variables and in particular to identify dynamic food-

A

ies, active foodies and passive foodies and the characteristics and preferences of these three segments. Our conclusions provide an unprecedented look at foodies and food tourism, followed by important implications for the development and marketing of food tourism to Sweden.

In order to fully examine this special-interest group, we deliberately excluded sampling the general population. Most people do not have the means to travel for a special interest, or are not food lovers. Both our internationally open online survey and the survey conducted through market research panels specified that respondents are to be food lovers. This self-selection process ensures that we are getting information from the target audience.

Our analysis confirmed that the highly-involved from the panels are very similar (statistically significant) to the highly-involved of the non-panel respondents, and furthermore these two highly-involved groups are very similar to the respondents obtained from 'Other' category (i.e., other than Germany, Norway, Italy or the U.K.).

The entire sample of food lovers was then analyzed using a triangulation of methods to ensure that we fully understand foodies and food-tourists:

- We separately analyzed the top 11% of respondents based on their replies to the involvement scale. They are called the Highly Involved Foodies (HiFs) and are quite different from the remainder of foodies. This scale works very well to determine how involved people are with food and food tourism, but on its own does not reveal the full story. Analysis of this HiFs group reveals that they are also highly travelled.

- Foodies who have already travelled internationally for a food-related experience were also analyzed on their own. This is a larger group, constituting 39% of the total, but we also sorted them out by reference to how frequently they had travelled. The most travelled (i.e. four or more times in the past 12 months) are very similar (statistically significant) to the 11% called HiFs. Therefore, it becomes clear that the HiFs are also dedicated food tourists.

- We employed cluster analysis to generate and profile three segments, in the traditional marketing style. These clusters represent high, medium and low levels of involvement, although we have given them names for added clarity. The top group, called 'dynamic foodies' are naturally a prime target market for Sweden. The relation between HiFs and the three segments is significant (sig.) but not very strong. Out of the amount of HiFs (11%), 36% of the HiFs are also 'dynamic foodies'. This means that 64% of the 'dynamic foodies' are less highly involved than the HiFs.

Through experimentation we learned that clusters work best (that is, they maximise between-group differences) when the basis for segmenting the sample was their attendance at events. This means that event attendance (in addition to travel) is also a primary indicator of being a highly-involved foodie, a fact that is reflected in many ways in our results.

Overall, the three approaches to analyzing the data and singling out the most highly involved food tourists are complementary. Accordingly, we are extremely satisfied that the conclusions reflect a deep understanding of foodies, highly-involved foodies, and food tourists – all related to their potential for becoming food tourists to Sweden.

Our analysis of three segments or clusters, of the highly-involved 11%, and of the foodies who have already travelled for food experiences produces the best possible analysis. The three segments were based on event attendance but the dynamic foodies segment is very similar to the top 11% and both of those segments overlap considerably and significantly with the already-travelled segment.

Figure A-1 illustrates our approach, showing how our selection of food-lovers enabled analysis of the highly involved and the experienced food tourists, and resulted in identification and description of three segments - of which the dynamic foodies are the most important for target marketing.

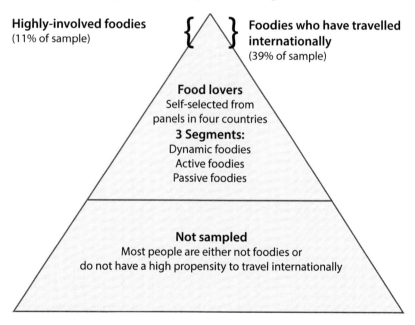

Figure A.1: Sampling and analyzing foodies in the multi-country survey

In total 3137 participated, but most participants were from the four targeted countries, namely Germany, Norway, U.K. and Italy. One other group of countries was identified and called the 'Other' category. This category mostly consists of Australians (46 participants), Swedes (75 respondents), and Americans (60 participants).

Respondents gave us their year of birth, with 1967 being the most frequent.

Norwegians were older on average than other participants. Fifty-four per cent of participants were women, but females outnumbered males more in the German sample (19% more women), followed by Italians (7% more women) and British (7% more women).

Almost half of the participants were married (i.e., 1392 participants or 45.9%), while another 830 (27.4%) were in a relationship; singles consituted 26.8% (n=812). More Germans were single (199; 29%) or in a relationship (190; 27%). A higher proportion of Italians were married (374; 52%). Of those respondents with children living at home, 14% had one child and 9% had two.

More than 50% of the participants had some sort of higher education: 41.2% had studied at a university/college (Bachelor's degree/Master's degree) and another 7.7% had an advanced degree completed (PhD). A fairly large proportion had some relevant work experience: 43% of respondents worked in the past or currently as chefs, or in agriculture, restaurants, catering, tourism or hospitality, and this might be either a cause of involvement with food, or a consequence - that remains a research question. 11% currently worked in restaurants/catering and tourism/hospitality.

Higher education is correlated with higher incomes, and in this sample Norwegians earned the most; almost one third of the Norwegians were high or very high-income people,compared to 24.6% of the 'Other' countries, 8.2% of the Germans, 6.3% of the British, and 4% of the Italians.

Index

I

I